This book examines the performance of Greek tragedy in the classical Athenian theatre. Whilst post-structuralist criticism of Greek tragedy has tended to focus on the literary text, the analysis of stagecraft has been markedly conservative in its methodology. David Wiles corrects that balance, examining the performance of tragedy as a spatial practice specific to Athenian culture, at once religious and political. The reader or practitioner of today must recognize that Athenian conceptions of space were quite unlike those of the modern world. After examining controversies and archaeological data regarding the fifth-century performance space, Wiles turns to the chorus and shows how dance mapped out the space for the purposes of any given play. Through an examination of contemporary material, including vases and temples, as well as the structure of extant theatres, he shows how the space of performance was organized in respect of axes embodying oppositions such as inside and outside, east and west, above and below. The Athenian audience was both outside the performance and embraced as part of it. We as readers are brought closer to understanding the dramatic action and staging of classical Athens.

Tragedy in Athens

TRAGEDY IN ATHENS

☙

Performance space and
theatrical meaning

DAVID WILES

Reader in Drama
Royal Holloway College, University of London

CAMBRIDGE
UNIVERSITY PRESS

PUBLISHED BY PRESS SYNDICATE OF THE UNIVERSITY OF CAMBRIDGE
The Pitt Building, Trumpington Street, Cambridge CB2 1RP, United Kingdom

CAMBRIDGE UNIVERSITY PRESS
The Edinburgh Building, Cambridge CB2 2RU, United Kingdom
40 West 20th Street, New York, NY 10011–4211, USA
10 Stamford Road, Oakleigh, Melbourne 3166, Australia

© Cambridge University Press 1997

First published 1997

Printed in the United Kingdom at the University Press, Cambridge

Typeset in Adobe Garamond 10.5/12.5 pt

*A catalogue record for this book is available from
the British Library*

Library of Congress Cataloguing in Publication data

Wiles, David.
Tragedy in Athens: performance space and theatrical meaning /
David Wiles.
p.   cm.
Includes bibliographical references (p.   ) and index.
ISBN 0 521 46268 1
1. Theater – Greece – Athens – History.   2. Theaters – Greece – Athens –
History.   3. Greek drama (Tragedy) – History and criticism.
I. Title.
PA3201.W55   1997
792′.0938′5–dc20   96-28237   CIP

ISBN 0 521 46268 1 hardback

Contents

Illustrations

Acknowledgements

Many people have given me their help. I am particularly indebted to Lowell Edmunds, Simon Goldhill, Leslie Read, Rush Rehm, Richard Seaford and Rosemary Wright, who have looked at substantial sections of this book in draft form, and given me their comments and advice. Richard Green, Nick Lowe, Fiona Macintosh, Karina Mitens, Christiane Sourvinou-Inwood, and Katerina Zacharia have looked at shorter sections and contributed their comments. For specialized bibliographical advice I am grateful to Robert Parker, Lene Rubinstein, Derek Sugden and Dahlia Zaidel. The British Academy gave me a grant to visit the theatres of Attica. Royal Holloway College funded necessary sabbatical leave. The Ashmolean Library has been an invaluable resource. My students have taught me much. Gayna Wiles contributed the drawings and has seen to my visual education. Oliver Taplin has done much to promote the study of Greek performance, and will, I hope, feel able to forgive me and regard the attention paid to his work in these pages as a compliment.

I have been old-fashioned in my transliteration of Greek names. Here and in my translated play titles I have used the forms that seemed most familiar, at whatever cost to logic. My objective is to defamiliarize space, not language. I have assumed throughout that the Greek spectator was male.

Abbreviations

BCH	*Bulletin de correspondance hellénique*
BICS	*Bulletin of the Institute of Classical Studies*
COAD	Eric Csapo and William J. Slater, *The Context of Ancient Drama* (Ann Arbor, 1995)
DFA	A. W. Pickard-Cambridge, *The Dramatic Festivals of Athens*, revised by John Gould and D. M. Lewis (Oxford, 1968)
GR	Walter Burkert, *Greek Religion*, tr. J. Raffan (Oxford, 1985)
GRBS	*Greek, Roman and Byzantine Studies*
GTA	Oliver Taplin, *Greek Tragedy in Action* (London, 1978)
HGRT	Margarete Bieber, *The History of the Greek and Roman Theater* (Princeton, 1961)
JHS	*Journal of Hellenic Studies*
LIMC	*Lexicon Iconographicum Mythologiae Classicae* (Zurich and Munich, 1981–)
MTAG	Jean-Pierre Vernant and Pierre Vidal-Naquet, *Myth and Tragedy in Ancient Greece*, tr. J. Lloyd (New York, 1990)
NTDWD	John J. Winkler and Froma I. Zeitlin (eds.), *Nothing To Do With Dionysos? Athenian drama in its social context* (Princeton, 1992)
PIE	Nicolaos C. Hourmouziades, *Production and Imagination in Euripides: form and function of the scenic space* (Athens, 1965)
SA	Oliver Taplin, *The Stagecraft of Aeschylus: the dramatic use of entrances and exits in Greek tragedy* (Oxford, 1977)
TDA	A. W. Pickard-Cambridge, *The Theatre of Dionysus in Athens* (Oxford, 1946)

CHAPTER I

∾

The problem of space

Plato's Atlantis purports to be the ideal city-state which existed in the golden age before human beings lost their portion of divinity. Plato conceives his ideal *polis* as a macrocosm of the body, and his conception of the body is dualist: the head, which in the body houses the soul, becomes in the state the home of political power.[1] While the 'body' of the *polis* is conceived as a rectangular grid, divided by canals, power resides in a circular island surrounded by two concentric rings of land. Communication with the outside world is necessarily by sea, and is channelled via this circular 'head'. Water passes through the 'head' to the 'body' just as air passes to the body through the head of the human being. At the centre of the 'head' in Atlantis is a sanctuary, with its standard Greek appurtenances of a temple, a grove and a spring, so 'god' is equivalent to 'soul'. Close to the sanctuary is the palace, for the king is a descendant of the god Poseidon, and there is no cleavage between religion and politics in this utopia. The inner ring-island is primarily defensive, and is occupied by warriors who maintain the power of the regime at the centre, whilst the outer ring-island contains a horse-racing circuit. There is of course no theatre in this state, for theatre, as Plato argued in *The Republic*, offers its public a debased view of the gods. The horses orbit the sanctuary of Poseidon at the centre as the planets orbit the earth, for the sacred circle of this city is not only a macrocosm of the head but a microcosm of the universe. Plato drew inspiration from the cities of the east. Herodotus describes the real city of Ecbatana as surrounded by seven concentric rings of fortification modelled upon the seven planetary spheres.[2]

Plato's Atlantis illustrates the importance of space in Greek religious, political and philosophical thought. The implementation of democracy involved the careful division of Attica into political units so that ten tribes would each

---

[1] Plato, *Critias*. The dialogue (extant only in a fragment) is a sequel to the *Timaeus* in which Plato worked out at length the relationship between the geocentric cosmos and the human head.   [2] Herodotus i.98.

I

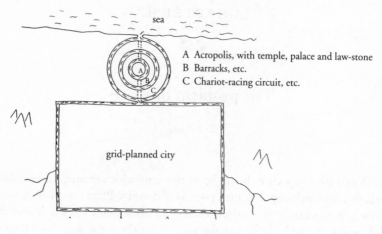

sea

A Acropolis, with temple, palace and law-stone
B Barracks, etc.
C Chariot-racing circuit, etc.

grid-planned city

Figure 1 Atlantis

have an equal weighting of membership from different interest groups. For our purposes Atlantis must be seen not as a utopia but as a heterotopia that defines by its difference the spatial conceptions and practices of classical Athens. Plato's city is sacred not to Athene but to Poseidon, in myth Athene's rival for control of Attica. In Athens we see the same opposition of circle and grid, for the Peiraeus was laid out on a grid pattern in the mid fifth century, in accordance with the geometric logic of equal distribution, to house a swelling urban population behind secure walls, but the sacred centre of the city remained the Acropolis with its ring of fortification surrounding the temple of Athene. In democratic Athens, unlike Atlantis, the seat of political power separated itself from the religious centre and lay elsewhere, in the Agora and the Assembly. This was a schism that Plato sought to rectify, and he makes his point by comparing Atlantis with a golden-age Athens built on a huge, fortified Acropolis that contains both temple and palace. Plato's most radical conceptual innovation was his dualist separation of head and body, and this new schism was to have enormous influence in the Christian era. The soul or breath of life was not located in the head in fifth-century thinking but in the body, and topographically Athens was at the centre of Attica rather than an appendage on the periphery. Atlantis is structured in order to illustrate Plato's new conception of space that is simultaneously dualist and centred.

By way of festive celebration (for 'entertainment' is too secular a term, and thus too modern), Plato offers a chariot race sacred to Poseidon, god of horses, in which we may assume that representatives of the ten tribes descended from the god's ten sons competed. In Athens representatives of the ten tribes competed by dancing a circular dance in honour of Dionysus in a location that was likewise on the margins of the sacred centre. Plato describes how in a kind of game the ten kings of Atlantis chased ten bulls loose in the precinct, sacrificed them at a central stone on which the laws were inscribed and then feasted before finally dispensing justice. There is again a parallel with the Dionysia, when representatives of the ten tribes took bulls to the sanctuary, sacrificed them and organized a feast before the tragedies were performed.[3] Tragedy might by this analogy be seen as a mode of dispensing painful justice to the people, following a symbolic reaffirmation of the god-given structure of the community.

Plato's conception of space as a repository of truth, allowing one to move from the microcosm of the human individual and the macrocosm of the god-given universe to the difficult question of how human beings should live together in society, provides a context for my enquiries in this book. Space was not an objective, scientific given in classical Athens but a subject for speculation, experiment and negotiation. Theatre is pre-eminently a spatial medium, for it can dispense with language on occasion but never with space. Like Atlantis, the theatre must be seen as a 'heterotopia', a term which I borrow from Foucault to refer to a place where 'the real sites, all the other real sites that are found within the culture, are simultaneously represented, contested and inverted'.[4] I do not propose to set up any sharp dichotomy in this book between the theatre and the play for the two are functionally interdependent, just like the Parthenon and the giant statue of Athene Parthenos which it housed. The question must be how events in a heterotopia dedicated to Dionysus represented, contested and inverted the *polis* at large.

Peter Brook's words have become famous: 'I can take any empty space and call it a bare stage. A man walks across this empty space whilst someone else is watching him, and this is all that is needed for an act of theatre to be engaged.'[5] As early as 1922, Gordon Craig pleaded for the theatre to be an 'empty space' in which one could insert a stage design and auditorium appropriate to each performance;[6] but Brook's were inspirational words in the revolutionary year of 1968, suggesting in their context the abolition of the red curtains and foyer rituals of the 'deadly' bourgeois theatre. They provided an ideological underpinning for a generation of black box studio theatres where allegedly anything can happen, any actor–audience relationship can be established. The reality is

---

[3] On festive arrangements, see Pauline Schmitt Pantel, *La Cité au banquet* (Rome, 1992) 125, 131–2.

[4] Michel Foucault, 'Of other spaces', tr. J Miskowiec, *Diacritics* 16 (1986) 22–7.

[5] *The Empty Space* (London, 1968) 9.

[6] Marginalia cited by Denis Bablet in *Le Lieu théatral dans la société moderne* (Paris, 1969) 22.

that these 'neutral' spaces impose their own rigid constraints, and the dream of 1968 that human beings are infinitely adaptable soon faded. Peter Brook was well aware that he could not 'take any empty space' when in 1974 he established his permanent operational headquarters in a faded Victorian theatre in Paris, the Bouffes du Nord. To create theatre to his satisfaction he needed a space crafted with skill and imbued with history.

The idea that there can be an 'empty space' has been discredited. Physics has demonstrated that the empty space of the cosmos is bounded and filled with mysterious particles. Ernst Gombrich, in his seminal work on visual perception, has shown that the artist never starts from *tabula rasa*, a blank canvas, but modifies received schemata. His work develops the recognition of Ernst Kris 'that art is not produced in an empty space, that no artist is independent of predecessors and models'.[7] The mind of the viewer is no empty bucket waiting to receive sensory data, but forms hypotheses and searches for differences that separate one sign from another. Gombrich develops the insight of structuralism that human communication depends upon establishing a system of differences, and sounds or images *in vacuo* have no meaning. Foucault's post-structuralist essay on space pursues the same theme: 'We do not live in a kind of void, inside of which we could place individuals and things . . . we live inside a set of relations'.[8] My theme in this book will be that the Greek theatre was not an empty space. Greek performances were created within and in response to a network of pre-existent spatial relationships.

The idea that Greek drama should be understood in relation to the visual arts as much as the literary arts runs against the grain of the academic tradition. The academic world has been preoccupied rather with the dimension of time than with space: the errors that have crept into the text, prior authorial thinking realized by the text, later critical readings of the text, the relationship of the playwright's thought to grand historical narratives. Archaeology has likewise been obsessed by periodicity, uncovering the different temporal layers of an excavated structure. The space of the theatre and the question of what is said (and done) in that space are relegated to different sub-disciplines within classics. Early in the twentieth century, the 'Cambridge anthropologists' were less diffident about performance, for they were happy to see drama as a 'ritual'. Gilbert Murray was happy both to edit an Oxford Classical text and to translate for professional performance. It was perhaps the rise of 'English Literature' to a position of hegemony within the Arts faculty that made classicists look to their laurels and offer Greek literature as a competing product, not primitive ritual but a sophisticated art touching the highest realms of consciousness.

---

[7] Gombrich, *Art and Illusion* (London, 1977) 25.   [8] 'Of other spaces' 23.

While Arthur Pickard-Cambridge in the 1940s looked at the context of drama – the theatre and festival of Dionysus – other scholars concerned themselves with the quite separate question of content. In the 1950s and 1960s T. B. L. Webster and scholars associated with him (notably A. M. Dale and N. Hourmouziades) pursued energetic research into monuments and textual detail in order to clarify the performance conventions of Greek tragedy, but the question of what the play meant remained, if not a *noli me tangere*, at least little touched by this body of research.

The publication of Oliver Taplin's thesis *The Stagecraft of Aeschylus* in 1973 in many ways opened a new era. Taplin insisted that the playwright wrote for the spectator, and that meaning is to be sought in the visual image. He staked out his ground around the phrase 'visual meaning', restoring the Aristotelian category of *opsis* to a place of more honour than Aristotle himself allowed.[9] His work demonstrated that the analyst of stagecraft had to engage in the academically respectable activity of close reading, and it was a clear inference that editors who failed to examine the text with due attention to the requirements of performance were failing in their duty. At the same time, Taplin had a magic wand to wave with his 'working hypothesis that there was no important action which was not also signalled in the words'.[10] There is no logical basis for this hypothesis, since playwrights did not in the first instance compose their works for a reading public, and, if not actors themselves, they were present in person to advise the actors. Taplin nevertheless attempts a justification: 'If actions are to be significant, which means they must be given concentrated attention, then time and words must be spent on them.'[11] This was manna to philology because it confirmed that the written text represents the complete work of art. Language remains pre-eminent, and time wins out over space. The philologist needs to acquire a new bag of tricks, but can continue in the same trade of scrutinizing words and words alone.

I shall examine at some length Taplin's popularizing sequel *Greek Tragedy in Action* (1978) because in that book many aesthetic and ideological assumptions latent in *The Stagecraft of Aeschylus* become overt. Taplin's work has had enormous influence, and represents what I take to be a normative position within the academic community vis-à-vis Greek tragic performance. There is no *tabula rasa* for academics any more than for painters, and an analysis of Taplin's work will enable me to articulate my own very different point of view.

Taplin's first premiss is the existence of an 'author's immutable meaning'.

---

[9] On *opsis* (spectacle) see Taplin's appendix in *SA* 477–9; Lowell Edmunds argues for a more positive Aristotelian view in 'The blame of Karkinos' *Drama* I (1992) 214–39. I have examined Taplin's work in the light of Simon Goldhill's critique in 'Reading Greek performance' *Greece and Rome* 34 (1987) 136–51.   [10] *SA* 30.   [11] *SA* 31.

There is, he argues, a communicative intention behind the work which the critic has to uncover. Taplin concedes also that the author may not have been fully conscious of this meaning, for the human mind works on many levels. The only way for the critic to gain access to this meaning is thus to enquire:

'Is it there?' If the point is to be accepted, it should (broadly speaking) meet three conditions: it should be *prominent, coherent* and *purposeful*. There is no definitive court of appeal on this (though time and the community of informed opinion form a lower court). Ultimately the interpretation of art is subjective and personal; it is not verifiable.[12]

The argument turns full circle. If interpretation is ultimately subjective, then the question 'Is it there?' has to be reformulated as 'Do I see it?' The reference to majority opinion over the years comprising a kind of lower court of appeal is full of dangers, and Taplin himself plainly attempts to change received opinions. Modern perceptions of Greek tragedy have been shaped by a Renaissance tradition leaning heavily upon Aristotle and Horace. 'Time and the community of informed opinion' may, I would suggest, be a highly misleading guide to the drama of a democratic culture which, in the eyes of most Hellenistic, Roman and Renaissance critics, constituted a highly dangerous political model.

In place of Taplin's absolutist 'Is it there?', I shall attempt to open up a gap in this book between 'Do I see it?' and 'Did they see it?' Although he acknowledges some value in cultural relativism, Taplin's liberal-humanist approach focusses on what humans have in common: 'But to lay exclusive stress on the *differences* is no less of a distortion than to assume unqualified similarity. Difference is a matter of degree and quality. And ultimately it is the almost uncanny similarity or timelessness of the Greeks which demands our attention.'[13] He rejects a 'naive historicist' approach to the culture of the past which attempts an imaginative identification with the original audience. I would prefer to reverse Taplin's formulation and suggest that 'our attention demands of the Greeks an uncanny timelessness'. In arguing for the universality of Greek tragedy, Taplin places himself squarely within the Aristotelian tradition.[14] He repeats the plea of Shylock and urges that we all 'have hopes, fears, feel sorrow and joy – live with bread, feel want, taste grief, need friends'. Tragedy, he asserts 'is essentially the *emotional experience of its audience*'.[15] Pity and fear, it would seem, are the same, whether felt by a fifth-century Athenian or a twentieth-century Englishman.

My own approach to Greek tragedy stems more from Plato than from Aristotle. In *The Laws*, Plato explores the diversity of human responses to

---

[12] *GTA* 6. Taplin's italics.   [13] *GTA* 7–8.   [14] *Poetics* ix.3–1451b.
[15] *GTA* 8, 169. Taplin's italics.

drama. The unjust man finds that injustice looks pleasant, the just man does not, and a double response is possible in the case of the man who has only superficially become just. When human beings differ from each other so much, there can be no question of a universal emotional response. Plato condemns as an insupportable doctrine the majority view – implicitly, the majority view that has emerged during the fourth century – that art should be judged simply on its power to give pleasure.[16] Looking back nostalgically at the fifth century, he identifies an audience that behaved with more restraint, and allowed the panel of judges to be 'teachers', evaluating the kind of pleasure that the audience has received. He constructs an ideal fifth-century spectator who is capable of (1) recognizing what has been shown, (2) evaluating the skill of the representation through an understanding of its technique, and (3) forming a moral evaluation. Plato allows the Dionysiac chorus to remain as an institution in *The Laws* because he understands the spectator as someone capable of rationality, not merely of feeling.[17] His faith in the thinking spectator is supported by the evidence of Aristophanes. In *The Frogs* the poets are judged upon technique, and upon whether their plays will save the city. Technique in *The Frogs* always has a moral dimension. In *Women at the Thesmophoria*, Aristophanes likewise assumes that his audience will be interested in how plays are made. In both plays he parodies Hippolytus' line 'My tongue it was that swore.' The audience was fascinated by this line not because it induced feelings of pity and fear, one may surmise, but because of intellectual outrage. Anecdotes tell of strong audience response to intellectual sentiments about the subjectivity of moral values, the goodness of money, and the merely nominal existence of Zeus.[18] I am not suggesting that the audience was unfeeling, but rather that its emotions could be triggered by ideas, and by the relationship of what it saw inside the theatre to what it knew of the world outside the theatre. The thought/feeling dichotomy is unacceptably reductive. Taplin's audience learns from tragedy 'to understand and cope with' the 'misfortunes of human life'.[19] It was this model of the passive spectator who copes with life rather than changes it that led Brecht and Boal to their influential Marxist critique of 'Aristotelian' theatre.[20]

Taplin's view of tragedy is strictly Aristotelian. It is important to him that tragedy should be a closed system, and Aristotelian closure (the principle that a play should have a clear beginning, middle and end) governs space as well as narrative. The boundary between the world of the audience and the world of the play is seen as hermetic. There is, Taplin writes, 'in my view not one single

---

[16] *Laws* 655–6. [17] *Laws* 659, 669. [18] *DFA* 274–5. [19] *GTA* 171.
[20] Augusto Boal in *Theater of the Oppressed*, tr. C. A. and M.-O. L. McBride (London, 1979), chapter 1, develops Brecht's glancing references to Aristotle into a systematic critique of a 'coercive system of tragedy'.

place in the whole of Greek tragedy where there is direct audience address, or specific reference to the audience or to members of the audience'.[21] The idea that we today and the Athenians then share the same basic human response to the play presupposes a clear subject–object relationship: the spectator as subject gazing at the play as object. If, instead, we see the Athenian audience as an integral part of the event created in the Theatre of Dionysus, being in itself a semantic element, then we shall find it impossible to separate 'the play' from the audience watching that play. We shall cease to construe the audience as co-subject, watching the play as we do, and will have to construe it as part of the event that we are trying to understand. The phenomenon of 'the play itself' becomes impossible to isolate. Taplin's insistence upon an absolute divide between play and audience is a necessary rider to his proposition that behind 'the play' lies an immutable authorial meaning. My own search as critic will not be for an authorial meaning existing somewhere within, behind or prior to the text, but rather for an event set in space and time, and for a process or system of communication.

Taplin shares Aristotle's preference for Sophocles over Euripides – an aesthetic judgement that was not shared by later antiquity. He begins by confessing subjectivity, but rapidly slides into a more authoritative stance:

I will not disguise the fact that I find Euripides the least great of the three great tragedians. His oeuvre is uneven in quality, and several of the tragedies are very uneven internally . . . He is the most explicitly intellectual of the three, and sometimes contrives set-piece conflicts for the sake of the issues themselves rather than integrating those issues in a convincing human setting. These may be brilliant; but judged by the highest standards they are still flawed.[22]

By what canon, we may ask, can one ever define absolute aesthetic standards? Can one ever say, for example, that Greek art is 'better' than Egyptian art? Euripides is apparently faulted because he does not create artistic unity, and does not privilege the emotional vis-à-vis the cognitive. Taplin's criteria are humanist and psychological: everything must be subordinated to and contained by a 'convincing human setting'.

In accordance with his humanist vision, and his sense that Greek tragedy is timeless, Taplin denies any significant place to religion in the making of the dramatic event. Ritual activities connected to the festival of the god are seen as extraneous:

the fact is that these circumstances have left no trace whatsoever on the tragedies themselves, no trace of the Dionysiac occasion, the time of year, the priests, the surround-

---

[21] *GTA* 187 n.5.   [22] *GTA* 28.

ing rituals, nothing . . . I do not see any way in which the Dionysiac occasion invades or affects the entertainment . . . To put it another way, there is nothing intrinsically Dionysiac about Greek tragedy.[23]

Again, we see Taplin setting up a hermetic environment for the play that he will analyse. He is at one with the materialist thinking of Aristotle when he denies any religious element to artistic experience. Plato's understanding of drama in *The Laws* is very different, and his concern is emphatically with festival rather than text:

The gods took pity on the human race, born to toil, and gave it an alternative in the form of religious festivals to serve as a respite from labour. They provided as festive companions the Muses, together with Apollo leader of the Muses, and Dionysus – so that by sharing their feasts with gods men could set straight their way of life.[24]

The Dionysiac chorus is central to Plato's concept of theatre. He is concerned with the way music and dance train the body and thus fashion the soul. In *The Laws* he subverts the conventions of the festival he knew by having the old rather than the young dancing in the Dionysiac chorus. In order to make this possible, the young will be denied wine, the old will be allowed wine. The god of wine and the god of theatre is conceived by Plato as a single entity.[25] Dionysus, festival and chorus are placed at the centre of Plato's analysis, but marginalized by Aristotle. Taplin follows 'time and the community of informed opinion' in opting not for Plato the Athenian but for Aristotle the cultural outsider. Plato's conception of tragedy as in essence a Dionysiac dance may to us seem culturally alien and metaphysical, but that is no reason to discard it in favour of what seems familiar.

The chorus is conspicuous by its absence from Taplin's pages. He explains that 'the chorus will inevitably receive comparatively little attention in this book, since it is not as a rule closely involved in the *action* and plot of the tragedies'.[26] Taplin follows the Aristotelian premiss that a tragedy is an imitation of an action, and that plot (*mythos*) has theoretical primacy. It is the place of choral song, he writes, 'to move into a different world'. The relationship between the world of the plot that is 'tied down in place and time' and this 'different world' is not one that Taplin is concerned to explore, because of a preference for the material over the metaphysical. My own premiss in this book will be that both worlds are coexistent in theatrical space, and each informs the other. Taplin adds one final comment on the chorus: 'If only we knew more of

---

[23] *GTA* 162.
[24] *Laws* 653. I have borrowed some phrases from the translation by T. J. Saunders (Harmondsworth, 1970), but have rejected Saunders' reference to men being 'made whole again'.   [25] *Laws* 666.   [26] *GTA* 13.

their choreography and music, then the tragic chorus might find a larger place; but, as it is, my glass will inevitably focus on the actors.' We return to the problem of 'significant action' which Taplin alleges is always knowable. Here he seems to confess that it might not be. He asserts in broad terms that differences between us and the Greeks are less striking than similarities, but refuses to look at the chorus because he feels that he is not in a position to understand. If he elects to focus on the areas that seem easy for the modern world to understand, then differences will perforce vanish. Taplin's conclusions about Greek tragedy follow inexorably from his premises.

Let us pass from theory to practice and see how Taplin's methodology generates a particular way of analysing stage action. I shall quote, as a representative sample, his analysis of the stage action at the end of *Hippolytus*.

I have already touched on the suggestion that in the last 20 lines of *Hipp* the mortals are made to compare favourably with the petty vindictiveness of the two goddesses. The simple, noble stage actions contribute to the moving quality of this final episode. Hippolytus has probably been lain down on a bier earlier: he calls on his father:

Ah, darkness now descends upon my eyes.

Hold me, my father, and set straight my corpse.

So the two form a close group, with Theseus probably kneeling by his son and embracing him. At this point Hippolytus releases him from all guilt for his death: this is not just a noble gesture, it meant in Attic law that the killer was absolved from all further prosecution and punishment. Theseus tries to comfort Hippolytus, but there is no help for it:

My strength is spent. Yes, father, I am dead.

Quick now cloak my face over.

So Theseus covers his head with a veil (in very different circumstances from other more notorious veilings); and then he stands up. The separation of death is compulsory. Theseus turns to go into the desolated palace, and Hippolytus' companions presumably follow him with the corpse. As he goes, his last line – 'How keenly, Kypris, shall I dwell on your malice' – recaptures the contrast between god and man in the whole preceding tragedy.[27]

The great value of Taplin's book, which I do not wish in any way to underestimate, lies in its insistence that the reader must look at the visual action. Taplin rightly emphasizes that this closing scene of *Hippolytus* is built around a striking stage action when Theseus covers the face of the dying Hippolytus. The problems come when Taplin tries to reach towards the authorial meaning which is supposed to lie behind the stage action.

Taplin's precept that modern and ancient spectators share the same human response to human emotions has to be reconciled with the fact that viewing

---

[27] *GTA* 71–2. I have omitted cross-references and line references included in Taplin's text.

requires cultural knowledge. Taplin states explicitly that the Athenian audience would have interpreted Hippolytus' words of forgiveness in terms of Athenian law; and implicitly, he indicates that the Athenian audience would have found an intertextual meaning in the act of covering, because it had witnessed Euripides' earlier version of the Hippolytus story in which Hippolytus veils himself as an expression of shame. The assumption that Hippolytus is carried into the house stems from Taplin's knowledge of funeral custom. The Greeks interpreted the stage action in the light of a body of experience that we can recover only with difficulty. Given that the Greek audience brought a different body of knowledge to the play, it seems hard to be confident that we and they share identical feelings.

The veiling is seen as the culmination of a scene in which Hippolytus demonstrates nobility vis-à-vis the gods. Taplin thus proffers an overtly humanist moral for the scene and for the play. Theseus' final remark to the statue of Kypris/Aphrodite is construed similarly, for the translation 'malice' has a motivational force lacking in the impersonal *kaka* (bad things) of Kypris that one finds in the Greek. A very different reading is possible when we recall (as Taplin notes in another passage) that the corpse of Phaedra is visible throughout.[28] Phaedra has not been forgiven by Hippolytus or by Theseus, and Theseus' condemnation of Kypris contains no acknowledgement of the fact that Hippolytus offended the goddess by ignoring her. Implicitly, when Theseus condemns Kypris, he also condemns her agent, lying on the ground and most probably unveiled. Taplin sees the nobility of man in relation to god, he does not see the ignobility of man in relation to woman. He keeps the gods at arm's length, psychologically coherent in themselves and safely outside the ambit of the human. As soon as we think of the gods as part of human beings, as soon as Kypris becomes an aspect of Phaedra, then this humanist value system breaks down. Taplin's perception of the scene stems not from 'what is there' but from what his orientation allows him to see.

Taplin's marginalization of the chorus is relevant here because the ever-present chorus must have encouraged the audience to view the action through female and mythopoeic eyes. When the chorus sing of how Phaedra came over the sea from Crete, they do much to bind the identity of Phaedra to the sea-born goddess, Kypris/Aphrodite. The chorus open up a different kind of dramatic space, and establish a different kind of relationship between the human and the divine. On the human level, the presence of twelve or fifteen women within the theatrical space must serve to generalize Phaedra's condition as a

---

[28] See *GTA* 136. On the theatrical importance of Phaedra's corpse, see Nicole Loraux, *Tragic Ways of Killing a Woman*, tr. A. Forster (Cambridge, Mass., 1987) 22.

woman, for these women are fearful that Kypris might come to them as she
came to Phaedra. Taplin's gender-blindness becomes apparent when in his
commentary he sees the exit of Hippolytus' corpse, but makes no mention of
what happens to Phaedra's corpse. The dialogue does not allude to the departure of either corpse. The removal of Phaedra's corpse must be a piece of 'significant action' even though the text fails to provide the information we
require. She may be carried into the house, and so reabsorbed within the
family; she may be carried off by the chorus, and so absorbed into a community of women; she may be carried off in the opposite direction from the
chorus by male attendants, and so be isolated from both family and community; she may be left in a final tableau, as a silent image left to challenge the
audience; the actor may have removed his mask immediately, disrupting the
emotional responses of the audience. We do not know which of these options
was followed, but we do know that in performance 'visual meaning' must in
some such way have been created. Taplin's comfortable notion that we can
deduce all that we need to know does not stand up to scrutiny.

When Taplin refers to the 'last 20 lines' of the play, he excludes from
consideration the final five lines of the chorus, presumably holding them to be
an interpolation.[29] Here the chorus state that this is a shock to all citizens for
'stories of the great are more worthy of grief'. This is not mere sententiousness,
for it points up the difference in condition between the aristocratic Hippolytus
and commoners like the chorus. It also seems to break down the actor/audi-
ence divide, for women cannot properly be regarded as *politai* (citizens). Taplin
strategically refrains from commenting on Theseus' lines after covering the face
and before addressing Kypris: 'Oh famous boundaries of Athens and Pallas,
what a man you have lost. Wretched am I' (1459–60). The incorporation of the
audience could scarcely be more explicit, but the lines cannot be reconciled
with Taplin's hermetic model of art, and so are quietly overlooked. He can only
see what his intellectual schemata allow him to see. The psychological/human-
ist reading suppresses not only the metaphysical dimension, but also the political dimension, and these dimensions need to be reinstated.

At the end of the analysis are we any the wiser about what the central visual
action, the veiling, means? For Taplin, it is a function of a father–son relationship, and he is moved by the nobility of that relationship. But one could
equally see the veiling as a function of the Hippolytus–Phaedra relationship.
Both die entangled in ropes. He is veiled, she is not. He exonerates Theseus,
she does not. He spares Theseus from ritual pollution by having his face

---

[29] The authenticity of the passage is questioned in W. S. Barrett's commentary on the text (Oxford,
1964): note to 1462–6. On Barrett and audience address in this play, see pp. 218–19 below.

covered, she does not. For Charles Segal, the veiling marks the final feminiza-
tion of Hippolytus.[30] Much depends on our assumptions about Greek ritual.
The covering of the head at death was conventional in Greece,[31] but to the
modern spectator may appear unusual and thus laden with psychological significance. The significant stage action, here as so often, turns out to be a ritual
action, placed, as it were, within quotation marks through its reenactment in
the theatre. We think of Greek theatre as essentially familiar, Greek ritual as
essentially foreign. Yet, upon examination, theatre and ritual have a habit of
converging. We may well feel confident that we can understand a father–son
relationship, and far less confident about our ability to understand funerary
customs. Yet to prise apart the essence of a father–son relationship from its
external expression in culturally patterned action is an activity of doubtful
value.

Taplin slides from logical deductions about movement to subjective asser-
tions about meaning in a manner that may not be clear to the casual reader.
Such sliding is inevitable until one confronts the fact that seeing is not a neutral
act. One can never simply see 'what is there'. To see, as Gombrich demonstrates, is to test hypotheses, to interpret on the basis of prior knowledge. I have
examined Taplin's work at length because we need to be clear that his positivist
quest for the visual meaning is saturated in presupposition. His approach to
Greek theatre, he states, is based methodologically upon Granville-Barker's
Prefaces to Shakespeare (1927–47), and he does not engage with any form of
post-war theorization of performance. He does, on the other hand, demonstrate a powerful interest in contemporary theatre practice, and urges that the
director should not seek to reproduce a carbon copy of the original.

[T]he culture of the Athenians and Elizabethans, their familiarity with the conventions
of their drama, and the expectations that familiarity gave them, their common aspirations and concerns in life all passed on with them. What was new is now old, what was
immediate is now distanced. So though we might (in theory) see and hear a performance indistinguishable from that which they saw and heard, our response would
be bound to be different, irreparably different.[32]

As a modern theatre-goer, Taplin seems to open the door here to cultural relativism, to the abolition of the 'we' whose normative emotional response the
critic is supposed to chart. But Taplin never steps through this door, returning
to the mystificatory notion of 'life latent within the work'. (The equivalent

---

[30] 'Theatre, ritual and commemoration in Euripides' *Hippolytus' Ramus* 17 (1988) 52–74 – especially p. 62.

[31] See R. B. Onians, *The Origins of European Thought* (Cambridge, 1951) 133 n.1.

[32] *GTA* 177.

Aristotelian term would be the *psychê* of the work.)[33] The job of the modern director is to make contact with and renew this 'life'. Because the 'life' of the play is essentialized, the material environment in which the play was performed falls away.[34] The conceptual distinction between the inner life of the play and its external realization is a distinction that in this book I shall seek to obliterate.

Taplin, like most others who have concerned themselves with ancient 'stage-craft', evinces no interest in critical theory, which is to say the methodological revolution that has been sweeping through literary studies since the 1960s. Let us review some of the categories that once seemed secure but have now fragmented in the post-modern era. (1) *Meaning.* The concept of an immanent meaning has plunged into a void created by the opening of a gap between signifier and signified. If meaning is created through a process of decoding, then non-hegemonic groups like women, non-Europeans or the socially deprived may decode differently from the traditional arbiters of aesthetic value. (2) *Self.* The concept of an autonomous ego has collapsed, as the self seems to be compounded of a network of acquired discourses. Verbal codes are superimposed upon genetic codes to create the sense of being a 'subject'. (3) *Art.* Art is no longer a self-justifying category but a social construct. The urinal placed in a museum can become a work of art. (4) *Materialism.* Realist art placed the autonomous human subject in relation to an objectively knowable background; but the secure parameters of time and space that governed the Newtonian cosmos have collapsed, and matter can no longer be analysed into its irreducible elements. Marxist materialism has to deal with the problem that material objects like food and clothing are inescapably also signifiers of moral values. In the light of these philosophical challenges, we have to throw out time-honoured Aristotelian premises and look afresh at the phenomenon of performance.

Structuralism has been the driving force in the critical revolution, and within classics its impact upon the study of literature and myth has been enormous, yet its impact upon the study of performance has been minimal. At the heart of the structuralist project is the prioritizing of space over time. In his famous analysis of the Oedipus myth, Lévi-Strauss takes a diachronic narrative and lays out its elements synchronically. The binary oppositions which he identifies are spatial: concerned on the vertical plane with a human's relationship to the earth and on the horizontal plane with monstrous clumsiness of

---

[33] *GTA* 178; *Poetics* vi.14–1450a.

[34] Taplin quotes with approval Granville-Barker's remark: 'We can play the *Agamemnon* in the very theatre for which Aeschylus wrote it, but it cannot mean to us what it meant to its audience.' *GTA* 193 n.9, citing *On Dramatic Method* (1931).

movement.[35] The logic of the method, whatever the merits of the execution in this instance, is to pass from the temporal to the spatial. Charles Segal, Lévi-Strauss' most influential follower in the field of classical drama, analyses Sophocles' plays in spatial terms, without, however, seriously examining the relationship between the verbal medium of literature and the spatial medium of theatre.[36]

The most important work on the structure and semiotics of theatre space has taken place at the Sorbonne, around the figure of Anne Ubersfeld, and I shall examine some of her central propositions in order to suggest how they may be of value for the analysis of Greek drama. In *Lire le théâtre* she looks at the dramatic text in relation to the formula $T + T' = P$, where T' signifies all that is needed to fill the holes left by the text (T) in order to represent the performance (P). The dramatic text has necessarily to be understood as an incomplete document.[37] In her sequel *L'Ecole du spectateur* she turns her attention to the decoding processes of the spectator in the theatre. She commences her analysis with space because all other theatrical signs are located in space.

Ubersfeld distinguishes three modes of space: theatrical (the entire building), scenic (the acting area) and dramatic (the text). The 'theatrical *space*' becomes open to two types of analysis: in its external relation to the surrounding city from which it is demarcated, and in the internal relationship which the building sets up between auditorium and acting area. In respect of the internal structure, Ubersfeld discerns a continuing oscillation between two polarities: the bourgeois proscenium stage ('le théâtre de boulevard') which places the audience on one side, and the platform stage which allows the audience to sit all around. We can usefully pursue these lines of enquiry in relation to Greek theatre.

To begin with the external relations of the place: the Theatre of Dionysus in Athens can be seen in relationship to a congruent hillside auditorium nearby, the Pnyx, where political decisions are made. The theatrical space is physically linked to an earlier performance area in the Agora by a route lined with theatrical monuments, and it stands next to an exotic building with a roof shaped like a tent. All these relationships need to be examined if we are to grasp what the 'theatrical' space may have signified in the late fifth century. Whether the temple of Dionysus is internal or external to the 'theatrical space' is an ambiguity that needs to be investigated.

In the internal relationship of acting area to auditorium, we can discern a historical shift upon the introduction of the *skênê* or façade. Initially there was

---

[35] 'The structural study of myth' *Journal of American Folklore* 78 (1955) 428–44.

[36] *Tragedy and Civilization* (Cambridge, Mass., 1981).

[37] *Lire le théâtre* (Paris, 1982) 23.

no stage wall, and the audience gathered around a dancing space which did not in any way purport to mirror reality. Such a performance would be termed by Ubersfeld as *ludus* (festive enactment) rather than *mimesis* (imitation of reality) within an acting space which approximates to her 'platform' model.[38] The *skênê* created a hidden off-stage area and the consequent illusion that the visible action extended where the audience could not see it. In the fourth century, with the relegation of the actors to a shallow high stage, the performance moves decisively towards the proscenium model. Spectators no longer have other spectators within their gaze as they focus upon the *skênê*, and the fictive world of the play is separated from the world of the audience by the barrier of the *orchêstra*. The stage action can now purport to mirror social reality, as in the plays of Menander. For the intervening period, incorporating the last six decades of the fifth century, we are left with the task of determining how the theatrical space should be described in relation to the polarities of 'proscenium' and 'platform'. It will be critical to determine whether or not there was any kind of raised stage in the fifth century.

'Scenic space' is easily distinguishable from 'theatrical space' in modern theatre, for it is the sphere of the designer. Ubersfeld discerns a steady move-ment in contemporary theatre towards the ideal of the 'empty space' – a space freed from signs of 'reality' to become overtly a field of signs articulated by the imagination. When we turn to Greek tragedy, however, it is hard to make any useful distinction between 'theatrical space' and 'scenic space' since the acting area is merely a function of the building. There is no evidence that scene paint-ing was used by Sophocles in *Philoctetes* to create a desert island any more than it was used by Shakespeare in *The Tempest*. I shall investigate, however, the extent to which altars and other icons served as signifiers of place. Ubersfeld also identifies a 'dramatic space' which is 'the entire imaginary space which is constructed on the basis of the text, is evoked by it, and may or may not be portrayed on stage'. The modern designer working on *Philoctetes*, for example, might select barren rocks, or an expanse of sea, or a squalid dwelling as the single metonymic element to be depicted, and eliminate the rest, making very clear the division between scenic and dramatic space.

An essay by Michael Issacharoff attempts to erect a firm distinction, within the category of dramatic space, between a 'mimetic space' that is shown and a 'diegetic space' that is described. The reader of the text has the task of deter-mining whether or not the language is indexical, pointing to something that

---

[38] *L'Ecole du spectateur* (Paris, 1981) 52ff. Ubersfeld's analysis of space is developed further in Georges Banu and Anne Ubersfeld, *L'Espace théâtral* (Paris, 1992). A summary of her method-ology can be found in A. Helbo, J. D. Johansen, P. Pavis and A. Ubersfeld, *Approaching Theatre* (Bloomington, 1991) 152–64.

is seen by the spectator.[39] This is a step that Ubersfeld wisely avoids, recognizing the difficulties of placing a frame around the visual signifying field. It is interesting, however, to see why Issacharoff's distinction is so problematic. Let us consider two readings of an Aeschylean chorus. Lattimore's rendering creates a space that is plainly narrated or 'diegetic':

> The father prayed, called to his men to lift her
> with strength of hand swept in her robes aloft
> and prone above the altar, as you might lift
> a goat for sacrifice, with guards
> against the lips' sweet edge, to check
> the curse cried on the house of Atreus . . .
> by force of bit and speech drowned in strength.[40]

Fagles, on the other hand, translates less for semantic accuracy than for rhythm and movement:

> Her father called his henchmen on,
>   on with a prayer,
>   'Hoist her over the altar
> like a yearling, give it all your strength!
> She's fainting – lift her,
>   sweep her robes around her,
> but slip this strap in her gentle curving lips . . .
>   here, gag her hard, a sound will curse the house' –
> and the bridle chokes her voice . . .[41]

Fagles attempts to reawaken the sound and choreography used by the performers to reenact the sacrifice of Iphigeneia which, supposedly, took place ten years previously. If the passage is understood as a reenactment, in cinematic terms a kind of flashback, then Argos in some sense becomes Aulis for this short section of the play.[42] The aged masks of the chorus and the past tense of the verb are formal reminders that the action is supposed to be set in Argos, but the movement of the actors creates a setting in Aulis. The clear mimetic/diegetic (scenic/dramatic) distinction breaks down. The spectator *simultaneously* constructs an imagined Argos and an imagined Aulis. The same uncertainty arises when we consider narrative speeches in Greek tragedy. When

---

[39] 'Space and reference in drama' *Poetics Today* 2 (1981) 211–24.

[40] *Agamemnon* 231–8 in *Oresteia*, tr. Richmond Lattimore (Chicago, 1953).

[41] *The Oresteia*, tr. Robert Fagles (Harmondsworth, 1977).

[42] Kernodle envisages this in 'Symbolic action in the Greek choral odes?' *Classical Journal* 53 (1957/8) 1–6. B. M. W. Knox describes how in Andrei Serban's production the enactment of this passage clarified Clytaemnestra's motives – *Word and Action* (Baltimore, 1979) 74–5.

Sophocles' Oedipus describes how he killed a stranger at the place where three roads meet, his gestures may well recreate in some way the blow which he gave to the man above him in the chariot. The Messenger may likewise recreate Oedipus' physical movement of stabbing his eyes. In modern theatre, the actor's face provides the audience with a secure point of reference, and the narrator is understood to be a psychologically coherent figure, reacting in the here and now to an experience in the past. When both Oedipus and Messenger are masked, the performance within the performance can easily elide to become, simply, the performance, just as the rhapsode reciting Homer becomes Achilles or becomes Priam.

It becomes hard to isolate a 'dramatic' or 'diegetic' space that is not simultaneously part of the 'scenic' or 'mimetic' space. Ubersfeld's theatrical/scenic/dramatic schema is appropriate to the modern theatre, where the spectator may be reassured by the compartmentalization of 'where I sit', 'what I see' and 'what I imagine'. In respect of the ancient theatre her typology of space starts to break down, for there are few visual signifiers to prevent the scenic space of a desert island eliding into the theatrical space where Dionysus is worshipped. The phenomenon of the chorus is crucial here. When we consider that the chorus are simultaneously actors and onlookers within the scenic space, and fellow-citizens within the theatrical space, that the masks of the chorus signify simultaneously that the dancers are Greek sailors (or whatever their fictive role is) and that they are worshippers of Dionysus in an Athenian festival, then we have to lay aside any straightforward theatrical/scenic/dramatic segmentation.

Saussure argued that human beings only make sense of language through identifying binary oppositions, and Lévi-Strauss applied the same reasoning to the language of myth. Jurii Lotman, in his seminal structuralist work on literature, argues that the artist 'models' the universe, a metaphor which he prefers to reflection because it does not raise the issue of illusion.

The language of spatial relations turns out to be one of the basic means for comprehending reality. The concepts 'high–low', 'right–left', 'near–far', 'open–closed', 'demarcated–not demarcated', and 'discrete–continuous' prove to be the material for constructing cultural models with completely non-spatial content and come to mean 'valuable–not valuable', 'good–bad', 'one's own–another's', 'accessible–inaccessible', 'mortal–immortal' and so on. The most general social, religious, political, and ethical models of the world . . . are invariably invested with spatial characteristics, sometimes in the form of oppositions such as 'heaven vs. earth' or 'earth vs. the nether regions' (a vertical tri-partite structure organized along the vertical axis) and sometimes in a form that involves ethically marked oppositions such as 'right–left' . . . Historical and ethnical linguistic models of space become the bases of organization for the construction of a 'picture of the world' – an integral spatial model inherent in a given type of culture.[43]

Ubersfeld applies Lotman's insights to the pre-eminently spatial medium of the theatre, and seeks out oppositions which structure the performance. The important coordinates which she examines are horizontal/vertical, depth/surface, open/closed, empty/filled, inside/outside, circular/rectangular, and centred/uncentred.[44] She does not mention left/right which was of considerable importance in medieval and in eighteenth- and nineteenth-century theatre practice, but is of relatively small importance in the 'empty space' of twentieth century performance, and has no meaning in modern theatre-in-the-round. She also does not mention light/shadow which is important not only in the age of gas and electric lighting but also in forms like medieval theatre which exploited the light of the sun. Although Ubersfeld's list is incomplete, the quest for binary opposition seems to me to be of enormous value because it allows us to see how a given culture (in our case Athens) used art (in our case tragic performance) in order to create a model of the universe, a universe invested with ethical, political and religious values. It rescues us from the reality/illusion dichotomy which casts so much confusion upon most attempts to analyse theatrical meaning.

Structuralism and post-structuralism, whilst making spatial analyses of verbal constructs, tend nevertheless to regard language as the ultimate paradigm. Barthes ascended the Eiffel Tower in order to look at a view which gave him Paris 'to *read* and not only to perceive'.[45] The performance analyst likewise commonly looks at the performance as a kind of 'text'. The viewer is placed in the detached and cerebral position of decoder, and is not part of the signifying field that lies before his or her eyes. From a Marxist materialist standpoint, Henri Lefebvre in 1974 made a fierce critique of this aspect of post-structuralism, which he saw as an extension of a Judaeo-Christian tradition privileging mind at the expense of body. He accepts the notion that each culture has a spatial code but insists that that code can only be understood in relation to a particular 'spatial practice', and that the decoder must be placed bodily within a set of power relations. His project is in a sense to reconcile Marxism with post-structuralism. The mode of production is a spatial practice,

---

[43] *The Structure of the Artistic Text* tr. G. Lenhoff and R. Vroon (Michigan Slavic Contributions, Ann Arbor, 1977) 216. Lotman's work on the theatre is limited by his focus on realist drama. See his 'Semiotica della scena', tr. S. Salvestroni *Strumenti critici* 15 (1981) 1–29.

[44] *L'Ecole du spectateur* 91ff.

[45] Roland Barthes, 'The Eiffel Tower' in *Barthes: selected writings* ed. S. Sontag (London, 1983) 236–50 – p. 242 (Barthes' italics).

and meaning is constructed in space, so the classic Marxist base/superstructure dichotomy dissolves.[46]

For Lefebvre, the space of any given culture is best understood in terms of a larger triad – space as it is visible, conceived and experientially lived:

> spatial practice: what members of a society actually do, how they have learned to live and work in space, following practices that ensure social cohesion.
>
> representations of space: a society conceptualizes or scientifically analyses space, often through use of words.
>
> representational spaces: members of a society experience space through complex symbolism as the imagination attempts to appropriate space and gain power over it.[47]

Theatre poses a particular problem for Lefebvre because the actor is materially present, engaged in a social practice, but is also a sign, part of a representational space. The theatrical space created by the architect is necessarily conceptual, a 'representation of space'.[48]

Space for Lefebvre is not simply a given, nor is it filled or encoded by society: rather, it is 'produced' by a society. Tracing the history of space, which is by definition 'social space', he discerns a movement from the 'absolute space' of early antiquity to the 'abstract space' of the present. In 'absolute space' part of the natural world is defined as being sacred and imbued with a divine presence, but that sacredness stems simply from how the natural world is. The rejection of Euclidean perspective in around 1910 marked a major shift in the history of space, and symptoms of the ensuing 'abstract space' of late capitalism are Klee and the Bauhaus movement. Lefebvre condemns the conception of a *tabula rasa* (Brook's 'empty space'), which he describes as a space from which signs of the social have been obliterated, a space which through its homogeneity conceals the apparatuses of knowledge and power, and leaves the viewer in the position of one who gazes uninvolved.[49]

Lefebvre's totalizing conception of a society's spatial practice may be exemplified by his treatment of Greek and Roman buildings. In Rome the architecture is massive and has a downward force, which implies the power of Roman law, power that lies in the ownership of land, and the power of relig-

---

[46] For this problem in Marxist aesthetics, see Raymond Williams, 'Base and superstructure in Marxist cultural theory' in his *Problems in Materialism and Culture* (London, 1980) 31–49.

[47] Henri Lefebvre, *The Production of Space*, tr. D. Nicholson-Smith (Oxford, 1991) 33.

[48] *The Production of Space* 188.

[49] *The Production of Space* 285–6. Lefebvre's historical schema is usefully clarified in Derek Gregory, *Geographical Imaginations* (Oxford, 1994) 368ff.

ion to exorcise the underworld. In Athens the architecture is light implying the triumph of *logos*, and the ability of human beings to separate themselves from the underworld. Roman architecture is based on the controlling gate and on the façade, a marble facing over walls of conglomerate. In classical Greece public architecture knows no false façade and columns are preferred to walls because in contrast to Rome there should not seem to be any hidden or remote source of power. The temple can be walked around and seen in its completeness. There is an integrity of materials because there is no conceptual separation of the good from the beautiful. This is not to idealize Greece because, for example, women are excluded from the political order. The Greek hearth set down into the earth is the sphere of the female. Greek citizens could think in the terms they did because they continued to work their fields while inhabiting the city. The *polis* with its multiple monuments and use of the landscape is seen as 'at once means and end, at once knowledge and action, at once natural and political'.[50]

Lefebvre offers a valuable check upon Ubersfeld's structuralist approach through his insistence on the materiality and historicity of space. For him the spectator is no detached observer but is physically present and engaged in a spatial practice as a member of Greek society. I shall be concerned in this book to establish the extent to which the fifth-century performance space remains in the category of 'absolute space' and is not, like Hellenistic theatres, the product of conceptualization by mathematicians and architects. This is necessarily a question of history. Lefebvre writes of the Greek *polis* that its 'absolute space cannot be understood in terms of a collection of sites and signs; to view it thus is to misapprehend it in the most fundamental way. Rather, it is indeed a space, at once indistinguishably mental and social, which *comprehends* the entire existence of the group concerned . . . The thing signified, political in nature, resides in the religious signifier.'[51] The rites of Dionysus were not something that the citizen could sit back and decode; the Theatre of Dionysus was part of what made him what he was: an Athenian.

Perhaps the most significant shift in recent criticism has been the recognition that tragedy belongs under the heading *political institution* as much as it does under the heading *art*. The work of Vernant and Vidal-Naquet in France has been complemented by that of Goldhill in England, Meier in Germany and Zeitlin in the USA.[52] This reclassification is plainly related to the other

---

[50] *The Production of Space* 249; for the argument 244–50.   [51] *The Production of Space* 240.
[52] See especially *MTAG*; Christian Meier, *The Political Art of Greek Tragedy*; and essays by Simon Goldhill and Froma Zeitlin collected in *NTDWD*. Goldhill's *Reading Greek Tragedy* (Cambridge, 1986) is concerned more with the discourses of the *polis* than with dramatic performance.

great paradigm shift from *dramatic literature* to *dramatic performance*, for the notion of performance helps to root the play in the Athenian specifics of time and place. At the same time the categories of *politics* and *religion* have started to coalesce. The work of Vernant and Vidal-Naquet has again been crucial, and more recently Richard Seaford has demonstrated in great detail how the Dionysia must be seen as a political institution.[53] Lefebvre's notion of 'spatial practice' is a helpful means of engaging with these new paradigms, and Lefebvre has himself learned much from Vernant's analysis of space which we shall examine in chapter 3. An example of the kind of critical stance which I shall seek to adopt is Loraux's study of Athenian ideology in relation to the Acropolis and the Kerameikos (the cemetery).[54] This is a classic piece of structuralism in setting up a spatial opposition between the highest and the lowest spaces of Athens, between centred and decentred spaces. At the same time, however, it is an exploration of fifth-century spatial practices, of how people processed and how they buried their dead; and it is also a study of what she terms 'representational space' – the tombstones of the Kerameikos and the statuary of the Acropolis. This is the kind of critical synthesis that I shall try to effect in relation to the representational space and spatial practices of tragic performance.

[53] *Reciprocity and Ritual* (Oxford, 1994) especially chapter 7.
[54] Nicole Loraux, *The Children of Athena*, tr. C. Levine (Princeton, 1993) 42–6.

CHAPTER 2

~~

The Theatre of Dionysus

Most, if not all, extant Greek tragedies were written for the Theatre of Dionysus Eleuthereus in Athens.[1] Alas, archaeological evidence for the shape of that theatre in the mid fifth century is confined, effectively, to a tiny arc of half a dozen stones, for the rest has vanished in the course of a sequence of rebuildings. Archaeologists dispute whether the auditorium was round or trapezoidal, whether the playing area was circular or rectangular (and if circular, how large a circle), and whether or not there was a stage. Rather than confront the arguments directly, we shall begin by examining a number of other early theatrical spaces where there was no subsequent metropolitan development, and the evidence remains relatively intact. A study of comparable spaces, in the context of how they were used, will help us to understand how the Athenians would have conceived a space for theatrical performance. We shall look for evidence not of spaces but of spatial practices.

Our starting point must be the deme theatres of Attica. The demes were organized as the city in microcosm,[2] and in many we hear of 'theatres', together with performances of tragedies, comedies and dithyrambs. Across Attica there was an organizational infrastructure that we can only glimpse. Although most of the evidence for dramatic performance is from the fourth century, it is reasonable to infer that the tradition is older. A fifth-century decree from Ikarion refers explicitly to a system of *chorêgia* and to a full tragic chorus.[3] The 'rural Dionysia' seems the obvious place for apprentice dramatists and actors to learn their craft. We know of fourteen demes that had

---

[1] It remains possible though that some were performed in the sanctuary of Dionysus Lenaeus. The scanty evidence is reviewed in Niall Slater, 'The Lenaean Theatre' *Zeitschrift für Papyrologie und Epigraphik* 66 (1986) 255–64. For the location, see Noel Robertson, *Festivals and Legends: the formation of Greek cities in the light of public ritual* (Toronto, 1992) 12. Euripides' *Andromache*, according to the scholiast on line 445, was not produced in Athens.

[2] The standard study is David Whitehead, *The Demes of Attica 510–250 BC* (Princeton, 1986).

[3] *COAD* 126. On deme performance, see Whitehead, *Demes* 215–20; P. E. Arias, *Il teatro greco fuori di Atene* (Florence, 1934) 20–34; *DFA* 45–51, 361; *COAD* 124–32. The only certain fifth-century records relate to Ikarion and Peiraeus.

theatres, but only four survive to be examined (if we exclude the late theatre at Peiraeus). In two of these the space cited in inscriptions as the 'theatre' is little more than a level area adjacent to a slope convenient for spectators. At Rhamnous we know that comedies were performed, and at Ikarion tragedies. In both these demes, a group of ornate stone thrones identifies the playing space as theatrical. The deme, like the city, honoured a man who served it by crowning him and bestowing *prohedria*, the right to sit on one of these thrones at a dramatic performance.[4]

The isolated fortress town of Rhamnous, the northernmost deme of Attica, has its 'theatre' beneath the gateway to the citadel, where the slope has been terraced to create a flat rectangle.[5] Some spectators would have watched from the fortress walls. The obvious theatricality of the setting lies not in the playing space itself but in the processional route that leads to it. The sacred way passes from the great local monument, the temple of Nemesis, down past a long sequence of tombs, and up through the outer walls of the acropolis, before skirting the gymnasium to reach the eastern side of the playing area (the audience's left) below the gates of the citadel. The five ceremonial thrones are placed not centrally vis-à-vis the playing area but to the east (audience's left) side where the honorands can greet the procession as it comes up the hill. Also greeting the procession, on the left of the thrones but on the same plinth, stood a statue, which to judge from the inscription on the thrones belonged to the hero or semi-divine patron of the deme: 'Dedicated to Dionysus by the priest of the Founder-Hero . . . crowned by the council and deme members and soldiers'. The inscription hints at how this 'theatre' beneath the fortress gates had the function of drawing together the indigenous population and the temporary garrison. To the right of the thrones, defining the front line of the auditorium, are some stone tablets (*stêlai*). Men who served their deme, by for example funding a dramatic chorus, could be rewarded by having their names inscribed on such a tablet.[6] The tablets can be seen as vicarious spectators, occupying the

---

[4] Whitehead, *Demes* 123–4. For Athens, the standard study is M. Maas, *Die Proedrie des Dionysostheaters in Athen* (Munich, 1972).

[5] See J. Pouilloux, *La Forteresse de Rhamnonte* (Paris, 1954) 72–8; V. Petrakos, *Rhamnous* (Athens, 1991) 48–51. For surveys of the deme theatres, see also Arias, *Teatro greco fuori di Atene*; O. A. W. Dilke, 'The Greek Theatre Cavea' *Annual of the British School at Athens* 43 (1948) 125–43; R. Martin, *Recherches sur l'agora grecque* (Paris, 1951) 248–55; J. Travlos, *Bildlexicon zur Topographie des antiken Attika* (Tübingen, 1988). A. E. Stanley, 'Early theatre structures in ancient Greece' (Ph.D. thesis, Berkeley, 1970) is of secondary importance, but occasionally offers points of clarification. Excavations at Rhamnous continue.

[6] As at Aixone in 313/12: see Whitehead, *Demes* 235–6; *COAD* 128. For the complexities of the community at Rhamnous, see Robin Osborne's analysis in *The Greek City from Homer to Alexander* ed. O. Murray and S. Price (Oxford, 1990) 277–85.

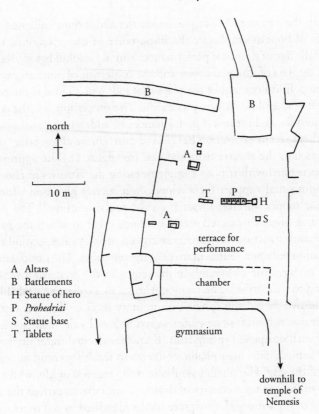

north

↑

10 m

A Altars
B Battlements
H Statue of hero
P *Prohedriai*
S Statue base
T Tablets

terrace for performance

chamber

gymnasium

downhill to temple of Nemesis

Figure 2 Rhamnous (after Petrakos and Travlos)

honorific front row alongside the enthroned honorands of the moment. A building of some kind served as backdrop to the playing area, but we do not know its nature, and it may have been part of the gymnasium. There is no sign of seating, and the audience probably sat on the hillside.

The remains at Rhamnous illuminate our understanding of Athens in three ways. First is the link between theatre and *agora*. The Greek *agora* was in the first instance a political meeting place and cult centre, and only in the second instance a mercantile centre. A series of shrines and public inscriptions mark out the area as a centre for the community, and one inscription found in the 'theatre' specifically refers to the site as the '*agora*'.[7] This is consistent with the tradition that theatrical performance in Athens began in the Agora and was

[7] Frank Kolb, *Agora und Theater* (Berlin, 1981) 2–3 on the *agora* in general, 66–72 on Rhamnous, and n.29 for the inscription. See also R. E. Wycherley, *How the Greeks Built their Cities* (London, 1962) 51ff. on the broad relationship of theatres and *agoras*, and 163 on Rhamnous.

moved to the Theatre of Dionysus when the auditorium collapsed.[8] Second, the seats of honour emphasize the importance of the ceremonial that commenced the day of dramatic performance. Simon Goldhill has stressed how, in Athens, displays of imperial power and the conferring of honours gave emphasis to the political content of the plays that followed.[9] Third is the position of the 'theatre' as end-point of a procession. The procession was the core of the rural Dionysia, and theatrical performances an addendum.[10]

In Athens recent excavation has cleared much more of the Street of Tripods that leads into the theatre from the east (see figure 8). The approach to the theatre was lined with tripods commemorating the victories of choruses, and one monumental support for a tripod, four metres high and adorned with Dionysiac motifs, survives intact from the fourth century.[11] The procession which came down this sacred way was a huge event in which the *polis* put its identity and structure comprehensively on display. Responsibility for its organization fell upon representatives of the ten tribes. The 1,000 dancers who were to perform the dithyramb in the sequel to the procession were divided according to their tribes. The council who sat as a collective probably walked as a collective, as did the ephebes on military service. Women were present, and their role as bearers of new life was symbolized by the maiden who walked in front with unripened spring fruit. Even the criminal fraternity was put on display. Subject states sent phallic emblems so that they could be represented as part of the city. The phallus symbolized the renewal of life, whilst a sacrificial ox symbolized the necessity of death. While citizens carried the wine that belonged to the wine-god, foreign residents identified by red robes carried the water and empty mixing-basins, symbolizing their inferior status in the social mix of Athens. The other sacrificial oxen needed to feed the participants were probably incorporated in the procession. The *chorêgoi* in rich robes and crowns must have been accompanied by their choruses, perhaps dressed in the phallic uniform of the satyr. The statue of Dionysus had been escorted to the theatre by the ephebes on a previous night, and probably came out of the sanctuary to meet the procession.[12] Tragedies, under the eyes of the god, were the culmina-

[8] For sources, see *TDA* 11–15.   [9] 'The Great Dionysia and civic ideology' *NTDWD* 97–129.
[10] Whitehead, *Demes* 213.
[11] Robin Barber, *Blue Guide: Athens and environs* (London, 1992) 52–3. On the monuments see the reports by Manolis Korres in *Archaiologikon Deltion* 35 (1980) 'Chronika' 9–20, and *ibid.* 37 (1982) 15–18, and by A. Choremi-Spetsieri in *The Archaeology of Athens and Attica under the Democracy* ed. W. D. E. Coulson *et al.* 25–30.
[12] See *DFA* 61–3; *COAD* 110–15; S. G. Cole, 'Procession and celebration at the Dionysia' in *Theater and Society in the Classical World* ed. R. Scodel (Ann Arbor, 1993) 25–38; C. Sourvinou-Inwood, 'Something to do with Athens: tragedy and ritual' in *Ritual, Finance, Politics* ed. R. Osborne and S. Hornblower (Oxford, 1994) 269–90.

tion of a process of communal self-display and self-definition. The dithyramb, which combined the processional mode with the narrative mode, was the point of transition when procession gave way to tragedy and participants became spectators.

In the mountain village of Ikarion the excavations are less extensive than at Rhamnous, and offer little sense of the processional route. What is striking here is the close relationship between a temple, an altar and a playing area. As at Rhamnous, the front line of the audience is marked by a group of thrones on the left and a row of tablets on the right. (Here as elsewhere in this book, all descriptions will be from the point of view of the audience.) In relation to this front line of the audience, the wall or colonnade which marks the back of the playing area is neither parallel nor central. The thrones are, however, more or less centred in relation to supports (now vanished) in the middle of this wall that could once have supported a podium or statue.[13] The wall/colonnade is central vis-à-vis the auditorium only if the priest facing east to sacrifice at the great altar is taken to be part of the audience, acting as representative of the god hidden inside the temple. The statue inside the temple has a view which extends across the great altar into the playing area.[14] The wall at the rear of the acting area is perhaps angled in order to point the gaze of the arriving procession towards the altar and statue above. There is inevitably more sense of awe if one comes up the hill to confront a sacred place.[15]

The temple overlooking the theatre belonged to Pythian Apollo, and at its centre evidently housed an *omphalos* or 'navel-stone'.[16] Adjacent, and set back from Apollo's temple, are traces of another temple that perhaps belonged to Dionysus. The village had close associations with Dionysus, who was supposed to have introduced the vine here, and a monumental sixth-century statue of the god has been recovered.[17] A sixth-century inscription found by the altar commemorates gifts to the two gods, Dionysus and Pythian Apollo, and one is reminded of the practice at Delphi where the worship of Dionysus supplanted that of Apollo during the winter months, the time of the rural

---

[13] See C. D. Buck, 'Discoveries in the Attic deme of Ikaria 1888' *Papers of the American School of Classical Studies at Athens* 5 (1892), and William R. Biers and Thomas D. Boyd 'Ikarion in Attica: 1888–1981' *Hesperia* 51 (1982) 1–18. Although the excavations are now in poor condition, Biers and Boyd identify spaced flat stones that might have supported columns in the present remains of the stage wall.

[14] Biers and Boyd 4. The original excavators gave an asymmetrical position to the doorway, but Biers and Boyd have doubts.

[15] Vitruvius IV.ix notes that temples should be planned so that the sacrificiant gazes up at the statue in the temple.

[16] Biers and Boyd 4. They note that an *omphalos* is apparently found in all sanctuaries of Apollo.

[17] Whitehead, *Demes* 215.

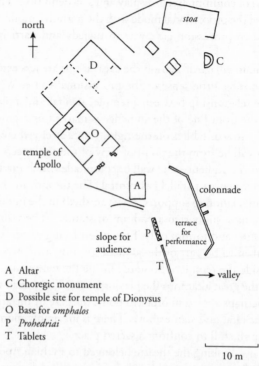

north

stoa

D

C

temple of
Apollo

O

A

colonnade

slope for
audience

P

terrace
for
performance

T

valley

A Altar
C Choregic monument
D Possible site for temple of Dionysus
O Base for *omphalos*
P *Prohedriai*
T Tablets

10 m

Figure 3 Ikarion (after Buck and Travlos)

Dionysia.[18] The playing space at Ikarion is unambiguously theocentric. Travlos' attempt to provide the deme, on the basis of a single retaining wall next to the altar, with a symmetrical trapezoidal auditorium, is an attempt to salvage rationalist values of order, balance and reason in respect of a playing space that seems antipathetic to such values.[19] We see on the ground at Ikarion what we see in Athens on vase paintings: that the audience shared in the world of the god, for there was no split between the human and the divine.[20] The space is laid out in relation to fixed points that are immovable, however inconvenient, because they are sacred. A symmetrical auditorium is commonly

---

[18] For the inscription, see *Hesperia* 17 (1948) 142; for Delphi, see L. R. Farnell, *The Cults of the Greek States* (Oxford, 1896–1909) v.106.

[19] Travlos, *Bildlexicon* 88 fig. 98. Travlos' reconstruction is followed in Richard and Helen Leacroft, *Theatre and Playhouse* (London, 1984) 5. An arc of stones behind the retaining wall suggests that the original boundary of the auditorium may have been different.

[20] See J. R. Green 'Theatrical motifs in non-theatrical contexts of the later fifth and fourth centuries' in *Stage Directions: essays in honour of E. W. Handley* ed. A. Griffiths (*BICS* supplement 66, London, 1995) 93–121, p. 109.

designed to give aesthetic pleasure and optimum reception to a human group, but the clear assumption behind the spatial practice of the Ikarians is that their god is the pre-eminent spectator, and humans take second place. The acting space is cramped, and the convenience of actors and dancers has scarcely been considered. Thespis, legendary founder of drama, came from Ikarion, and here in this village of the wine-god comedy was supposed to have been invented,[21] so it seems likely that the archaic qualities of the space were deliberately fostered in the fourth century as a sign of tradition.

The deme of Euonymon stood not far north of the present Athens airport, and its theatre was constructed in the mid fourth century.[22] Six thrones stand on the left (east) side of a more-or-less rectangular playing space – a disposition that echoes Rhamnous and Ikarion. A front row of marble seats forms a sharp right angle around the thrones, but on the right-hand side the angle of the seating is rounded off. Although the playing space is quadrilateral, the auditorium is constructed in a rough curve around it, and the stones have been laid out to accommodate straight planks used for seats. The thrones are positioned in order to secure a view through the east *eisodos* (side-entry), where blocks embedded in the wall suggest that this was some kind of sanctuary. The eastern *eisodos* is wider than the western, confirming that this side was used for processional entries. Monuments stood on either flank of the auditorium – perhaps the two statues of Dionysus found on the site.

The deme stood on a shallow slope, and the *orchêstra* had to be sunk into the earth, with a resultant problem of flooding. There are traces of 21 rows of seats, and leg-room is very constricted, so we might envisage at least 2,000 spectators in what was one of Athens' largest demes.[23] Two gangways on the north side of the auditorium and a central doorway in the *skênê* offer a gesture towards the ideal of symmetry. A stone foundation 2 metres forward of the stage wall supported a colonnade, and slots at either end could have been designed for tablets or for removable scenic panels.[24] The rake of the auditorium is such that

---

[21] According to the Parian Marble: *COAD* 120; also Athenaeus 40a–b. For the context, see M. Detienne, *Dionysus at Large* ed. A. Goldhammer (Cambridge, Mass., 1989) 29–30.

[22] The site was excavated in the late 1970s, but only a minimal account has been published, and the auditorium is now disintegrating, so I write primarily from my own observations in 1995. The basic report is Olga Tzachou-Alexandre 'Anaskaphê theatrou stous Trachones Attikês' *Praktika* (1980) 64–7. There are two useful photographs in Leslie du S. Read 'Social space in ancient theatres' *New Theatre Quarterly* 43 (1993) 316–28.

[23] The rows are confirmed in *BCH* 101 (1977) 531. As an index of size, Euonymon sent 10 representatives to the Council as against Rhamnous 8, Thorikos 5/6, Ikarion 4/5 – Whitehead, *Demes* 369–73.

[24] Columns are mentioned in the *BCH* report, and L. du S. Read confirms to me their existence. Removable panels would have served the same purpose as *periaktoi* – see David Wiles, *The Masks of Menander* (Cambridge, 1991) 41–3.

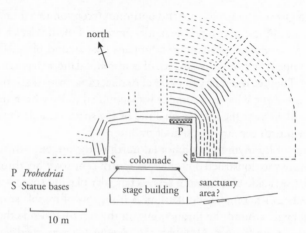

north

P *Prohedriai*
S Statue bases

colonnade

P

S   S

stage building   sanctuary
                          area?

10 m

Figure 4 Euonymon

Plate 1 Euonymon

sightlines on the *orchêstra* are poor from the back seats, and the columns and massive *skênê* walls must have supported some sort of stage used for speeches and for performances that did not involve choral dancing.

The deme theatre at Thorikos is on a comparable scale, and its importance is incalculable because it is the sole Greek theatre to have survived in substance from the fifth century. A fourth-century extension has not obscured the layout of the original structure. The first theatre was substantial, with a capacity of 2–3,000, and doubtless owes its existence to wealth from the nearby silver mines at Laurium. The terraced playing area was used by the community in the late sixth century, and stands high above an ancient cemetery that was still in use in the fifth century. On the left side of the theatre, the rock has been cut away and a long row of seats has been carved into the rock and enclosed by a chamber. The chamber must have been a gathering-place for the chorus, but could have had other ceremonial purposes too. The most striking features of the fifth-century theatre are the temple of Dionysus on the right-hand side, and the altar on the left. The irregular shape of the auditorium seems to be determined by the fixed or pre-existent positions of temple, altar and chamber. Although the temple and altar are considered to be fifth-century like the auditorium, we must recognize that architecturally these sacred elements have primacy, and the auditorium is arranged in order to accommodate cult activity. We do not have to follow the original excavators who lamented the 'want of means or want of taste under which the remote rural deme of Thoricus laboured'.[25] Our task must be to understand rather than dismiss the spatial practices of fifth-century Attica. The Thorikians were plainly not concerned in the first instance to create a harmonious architectural composition, but were adapting a sacred space that lay above the bodies of their ancestors. We may guess that Dionysus was worshipped here not only as god of the theatre but also (as at Athens in the Anthesteria) as a god associated with the spirits of the dead.

In essence the acting space is a road that has been widened to create a plaza. Above the first auditorium, an imposing fifth-century building added grandeur to the scene. Thrones are not in evidence, but seat numbering above the centre front row suggests that the seats of privilege were here. Three slabs of white marble in the centre of the straight front row encourage the same inference. Processional entries must have been made, as elsewhere, from the left, east, side. Coming up the road that ascends from the harbour, perhaps

25 Walter Miller in *Papers of the American School of Classical Studies at Athens* 4 (1885/6) 32. The standard archaeological reports are: T. Hackens, *Thorikos* Vol.III (Brussels, 1965) 75–96; H. F. Mussche, *Thorikos* (Brussels, 1974); H. F. Mussche *et al.* (eds.), *Thorikos and the Laurion in Archaic and Classical Times* (Ghent, 1975). For the back-dating of the cemetery and its significance for the site, see H. F. Mussche, 'Das Theater von Thorikos – einige Betrachtungen' *Sacris Erudiri* 31 (1989/90) 309–14 and 'Thorikos during the last years of the sixth century' in *The Archaeology of Athens and Attica* ed. W. D. E. Coulson *et al.* (Oxford, 1994) 211–15. Note a forthcoming analysis of the theatre in *Miscellanea Graeca* 9. The fourth-century rectilinear theatre at Lato, with its altar on the left and chamber on the right, has been considered an architectural analogue: *BCH* 95 (1971) 515ff.

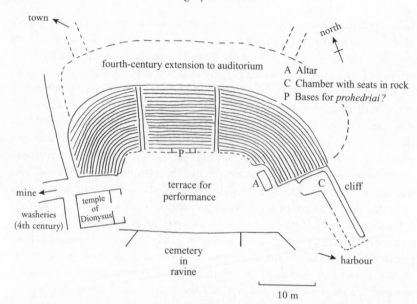

town

fourth-century extension to auditorium

north

A Altar
C Chamber with seats in rock
P Bases for *prohedriai*?

mine

washeries
(4th century)

temple
of
Dionysus

terrace for
performance

A   C   cliff

cemetery
in
ravine

harbour

10 m

Figure 5 Thorikos (after Travlos)

Plate 2 Thorikos

commemorating the landing of Dionysus,[26] the procession would have passed the rock-hewn chamber and been viewed from afar by the god in his temple and by honorands in the centre. The gangways may be off-centre in order to leave clearance for the sacrificial victims around the altar while the people mounted to their seats in the auditorium. The right, west, *eisodos* which leads more directly to the town would not have been used for a ceremonial entry. That road passes through a narrow gap beside the temple and immediately encounters dwellings, washeries for ore and mine workings. These, although later than the theatre, would not have been allowed to degrade a sacred route.

The playing area is located between the temple and the altar. The statue of the god inside the temple is thus the honorific spectator, and the play must seem to be given for his benefit as much as for the audience. The place of the temple both here and at Ikarion is reminiscent of Athens, where the temple of Dionysus would have been a striking feature in the audience's right visual field. The difference is that in Athens the temple lay beneath the playing area, and for performances the statue was moved to the centre of the auditorium in order to view the play performed in the god's honour. The statue of the Founding Hero at Rhamnous was a principal spectator in much the same way. The altar in Athens is as we shall see aligned with the god in the auditorium rather than the god in the temple. The enclosed chamber on the left at Thorikos may be functionally equivalent to the huge enclosed Odeon in Athens.

There was no space for a stage building at Thorikos, and only a temporary façade could have been erected. The curvature of the sides of the auditorium creates a good acoustic, but the huge width of the playing area, some thirty metres, creates significant problems of visual focus. With the gangways being off-centre there is no discernible centre point. If two actors play a scene together, and try to fill the available space, then they will move apart to the point where the spectator cannot contain both within his or her field of vision. It is this lack of focus that makes Thorikos an untenable model for the fifth-century theatre in Athens. Although we have several records of dramatic performances at Thorikos, the playing-space seems naturally suited to choral and processional forms of presentation. We have a detailed description, for example, of the Spartan Hyacinthia, where the whole community gathered in the 'theatre' before the temple of Apollo in order to watch the arrival of the procession at the place of sacrifice, accompanied by horsemen, and maidens on chariots. Boys played on the lyre and choruses of boys danced paeans.[27] This is the kind of communal spectacle that the theatre at Thorikos would ideally suit. To place theatrical performance in context, we must recall that the rural

[26] Mussche in *Archaeology of Athens* 214, citing Eratosthenes.
[27] Athenaeus 139e; discussed in Angelo Brelich, *Paides e parthenoi* (Rome, 1969) I.141–8.

Dionysia was one in a programme of sixty annual sacrifices at Thorikos, and the altar must have been the major deme altar for there is no evidence of a separate *agora*. Assemblies of the deme as a political unit must have been held here. The rectangular *orchêstra* at Euonymon, surrounded by an encircling auditorium and apparently created at a time when circular *orchêstras* were the norm, needs to be contextualized in the same way. Theatrical performance was but one purpose, amongst many, of the gathering point at the centre of the deme.

The functions of these 'theatres' in the demes are effectively divided amongst three spaces in fifth-century Athens: the Theatre of Dionysus, the Agora and the Pnyx. Theatrical activity in the Agora is associated with the north-west corner, close to the altar of the twelve gods, where dances during the Dionysiac procession can be construed as a memorial of the ancient location of dramatic performances. The nature of the performance space is unclear, and Kolb's attempts to argue for an orchestral circle are unconvincing.[28] Archaeological evidence is far better in respect of the Pnyx, the meeting-place of the Assembly.

Three phases have been securely identified. The first Pnyx was simply a straight-walled terrace on the hillside, prompting the excavators to make comparisons with Thorikos and Ikarion.[29] The speaker would have had some kind of podium, and the audience would have spread out to his left and right. There is no evidence of any architectural boundary line around the auditorium, and a ritual marking out of the space behind those who had gathered would seem to have sufficed.[30] There may have been some wooden seats at the front for the presiding tribe, but most of the audience would have sat on the hillside. A major change took place at the end of the fifth century, when much earth was hastily moved to reverse the orientation, so that the audience faced into the hillside. Plutarch's attribution of the change to the 30 tyrants at the end of the Peloponnesian War is consistent with the archaeological evidence.[31] There are several possible explanations for the change. The first is shelter from the winter winds. The second is acoustical, an enclosed bowl being created. More interesting is the political explanation, for entry into the bowl could be controlled. The tyrants placed their trust in a select 3,000, and this group

---

[28] As Sourvinou-Inwood plausibly argues in 'Something to do with Athens'. See Kolb, *Agora und Theater* 39–51.

[29] K. Kourouniotes and H. A. Thompson, 'The Pnyx in Athens' *Hesperia* 1 (1932) 90–217 – p. 107. Thompson's latest reflections on chronology are found in 'The Pnyx in Models' in *Studies in Attic Epigraphy, History and Topography presented to E. Vanderpool* (*Hesperia* supplement 19, Princeton, 1982) 133–47.

[30] See M. H. Hansen, *The Athenian Ecclesia II* (Copenhagen, 1989) 145–53.

[31] Plutarch, *Themistocles* 19 explains that the tyrants did not want the speaker to stand facing seawards, since the navy was the root of democracy. This sounds like a rhetorical point culled from a speech, but hints nevertheless at the symbolic importance of orientation.

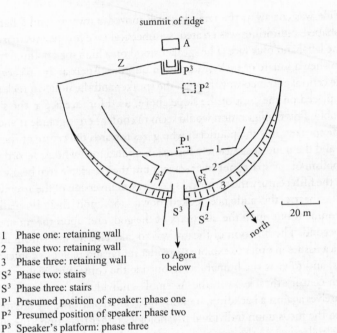

summit of ridge

A

Z

P³

P²

P¹

1

2

S²

S³

S³

S²

north

20 m

to Agora
below

1   Phase one: retaining wall
2   Phase two: retaining wall
3   Phase three: retaining wall
S²   Phase two: stairs
S³   Phase three: stairs
P¹   Presumed position of speaker: phase one
P²   Presumed position of speaker: phase two
P³   Speaker's platform: phase three
A   Altar
Z   Sanctuary of Zeus

Figure 6 The Pnyx (after Kourouniotes and Thompson)

would have needed a place in which to meet. Controlled entry was crucial both for an oligarchy that needed to vet the status of all who voted, and later for the restored democracy which remunerated those who attended debates.[32] The arc of the new retaining wall created a formation similar to that of the theatre. The performative implications of the change are fascinating. In the fifth century the people of Athens looked down on their politicians, and saw as a backdrop the *Agora* spread out beneath. Symbolically, the politician was in a subordinate position vis-à-vis the populace, and the focus of debate was not the individual politician but the needs of the city that lay constantly in view. In the fourth century, all changed: the politician was on a level with the people, and against the backdrop of rock the people could focus upon his personality.

In the mid fourth century the Pnyx attained its present form.[33] More of the

---

[32] This is the explanation favoured in Hansen, *Ecclesia* 143–7.

[33] This is the commonly accepted date, though some have favoured a date in the reign of Hadrian. For the current view see M. H. Hansen and T. Fischer-Hansen, 'Monumental political architecture in archaic and classical Greek *poleis*' in *From Political Architecture to Stephanus Byzantius: sources for the Greek polis* ed. D. Whitehead (Stuttgart, 1994) 23–90, p. 61 n.138.

hill-side was cut away, the retaining wall moved outwards, and a harmonious fan-shaped auditorium was created, symmetrical save for the sanctuary of Zeus on the left-hand rock face. The speaker stood on a high rock podium in front of a semi-hewn square of rock of uncertain purpose. An axial line passes from the single central entrance-way through the speaker and the unhewn rock to a huge altar placed on the crest of the slope above, used for sacrifice at the start of an assembly. This configuration would seem to confer heroic grandeur and sanctity on the speaker. It is the politician who gazes towards the centre of the community, and the populace must rely for vision upon a man who is, according to the symbolism of the space, not their servant but their leader, a step below the gods.

In the fifth century the theatrical space was an inversion of the assembly space. In the theatre the audience looked down not upon their immediate civic environment but upon the sanctuary of the god, and upon the mountains and sky beyond. The function of theatre was to take citizens away from immediate political issues in order to explore the wider moral and religious context of those issues, and to view the human being outside the context of civilization. In the fourth-century theatre, as in the Assembly, individual actors began to present themselves against a backdrop, standing on a raised platform. By this means they placed the focus upon individual psychologies rather than upon the supremacy of the collective. As the spatial distinction of Assembly and Theatre dissolved, the theatre came increasingly to be used for public assemblies.[34] The distinction between theatre and politics vanished completely in 294 BC when Demetrius the Macedonian walked across the stage like a tragic actor, and cowed the Athenians into submission by his paratheatrical display of authority.[35] For a few years the festival of Dionysus was to become the festival of Demetrius.[36]

The deme theatres provide misleading evidence for the Theatre of Dionysus in Athens insofar as they are both small and multi-functional. We must turn to surviving fourth-century theatres built on a comparable scale to the Athenian Theatre of Dionysus where the fourth-century plan is not obscured by later redevelopment.

The theatre at Megalopolis is securely dated to the 360s when the small city-states of Arcadia confederated and formed themselves into a new model city strong enough to withstand the power of Sparta.[37] The Arcadians constructed for themselves the largest theatre in Greece. The *raison d'être* of the new city

---

[34] See W. A. McDonald, *The Political Meeting Places of the Greeks* (Baltimore, 1943) 56–61.

[35] Plutarch, *Demetrius* 34, cited in Oddone Longo, 'Teatri e *theatra*: spazi teatrali e luoghi politici nella città greca' *Dioniso* 58 (1988) 7–33.

[36] See W. S. Ferguson, 'Demetrius Poliorcetes and the Hellenic league' *Hesperia* 17 (1948) 131ff.

[37] The excavations and political background are well documented in E. A. Gardner, W. Loring, G. C. Richards and W. J. Woodhouse, *Excavations at Megalopolis 1890–91* (London, 1892). On the founding, see most recently Simon Hornblower 'When was Megalopolis founded?' *Annual of the British School at Athens* 85 (1990) 71–7.

was political, and the theatre is on the face of it a political rather than a religious space, forming a single architectural unit with a covered rectangular assembly hall. The theatre held over 20,000, the assembly hall some 6,000 seated, the same complement as the open-air Pnyx in Athens. That this was a dual-purpose arena is certified by the fact that the left, west, *eisodos* is occupied by a scene dock. When used for non-theatrical purposes, the backdrop which greeted the audience was the grand front porch of the assembly hall; but for theatrical performance, a wooden façade the length of the porch could be moved into place in front of the porch, the lowest steps of the porch being removable. The width of the scene dock suggests that it stored a complete stage building.[38] Certainly a heavy rear screen must have run along the single line of stones flush with the porch, and onto this a lightweight painted frontage could have been secured. If we concluded that only a frontage and stage were slid into position, then it would follow that, for lack of space, the theatre made no use of such scenic devices as the crane and the *eccyclêma*. It is much better to conclude that a complete building was moved out of the vast dock. The lines of a later stone *proscaenium* now mark out the position which the removable wooden stage building must once have occupied.

We should not make too much of a dichotomy between the enduring world of politics (symbolized by stone) and the transient world of theatre (symbolized by the wood of the stage building). For dithyrambs requiring a full circle for dancing, and for musical recitations, the stage building would have remained in storage. To gather in one place and watch theatre was inherently a political act in fourth-century Arcadia.[39] The seats of honour are intact, and were dedicated by a prominent politician of the 360s. Six of the nine wedges of the auditorium were allocated to named tribes, and we have later evidence from Athens and Syracuse that seating there too was on this tribal basis. It seems unlikely, however, that the fifth-century audience in Athens was arranged quite so neatly.[40] Nevertheless, the organizers of the procession in

---

[38] E. Fiechter in *Das Theater in Megalopolis* (Stuttgart, 1931) conceives a wheeled waggon rolling out on a railway. See the useful critique in Caroline Buckler, 'The myth of the movable *skenai*' *American Journal of Archaeology* 90 (1986) 431–6.

[39] Kolb, *Agora und Theater* emphasizes the dual role of ancient theatres. His views are echoed in Longo, 'Teatri e *theatra*' *Dioniso* 58 (1988) 7–33. However, Hansen and Fischer-Hansen, 'Monumental political architecture' 51–3 take issue with Kolb and argue that the theatrical purpose was always primary.

[40] *DFA* 269–71; L. Polacco and C. Anti, *Il teatro antico di Siracusa* (Rimini, 1981) 45. The wedges in Athens are of radically uneven capacity, so the tribal allocations can scarcely have covered all the citizen body. Hansen and Fischer-Hansen, 'Monumental political architecture' 53 note the important evidence from Samos that markers were set up in the theatre auditorium to divide the audience into its component chiliads when the theatre was used for an assembly. Hansen and Fischer-Hansen 49, 57, also record that the Syracusan theatre was a normal place of public assembly, and that the rectilinear assembly place at Argos seems to have dividing marks.

Plate 3 Megalopolis

Athens came from the ten tribes, so did the ten judges, and the ten generals who poured libations, and festival money was distributed on a tribal basis. Some fourth-century tickets have tribal names.[41] We may infer that the dithyrambic dancers would have watched each other perform and so would have seated themselves in blocks. To some extent the audience in the Athenian theatre must have put itself on display as a political entity. At Megalopolis the perfect circular form of the auditorium overtly symbolizes the unity of the disparate peoples who had surrendered their homes and local identities in order to become part of the 'Great City'. Within this man-made theatre, the residual symbol of the natural world and a divine presence was an ever-running spring. The sacred route that linked the shrine of Dionysus outside the theatre to his spring within it was marked out as a race-track.[42]

With the theatre in the Macedonian capital city of Aigai, we move into a very different political environment. The theatre is linked architecturally not to a parliament building but to a royal palace,[43] and it probably belongs to Philip II's building programme in the 450s.[44] The Macedonian kings had long been patrons of the arts, and here Euripides is said to have produced his final

---

[41] *DFA* 58, 95, 97; Lucian, *Timon* 49 cited in *COAD* 294; *DFA* 271.   [42] Pausanias viii.32.1–3.

[43] The theatre is documented by Manolis Andronicos in *Vergina*, tr. L. Turner (Athens, 1987) 46–9, and 'Anaskaphê Veryinas: to theatro' *Praktika* (1983) 46–50.

[44] For Philip's attempts to contract Greeks to build temples, etc., see N. G. L. Hammond, *Philip of Macedon* (London, 1994) 55–6. Andronicos points to architectural parallels with Megalopolis.

plays. His fellow tragedian Agathon likewise retreated to Macedon.[45] Here too
Aristotle helped to inculcate in the young Alexander a love of Greek tragedy.
Philip used theatre as a powerful symbol of his Greek identity. On the eve of
a Panhellenic invasion of Persia, before a huge gathering of Greeks at a theatrical performance, he was assassinated. Diodorus tells us how a procession
made its way from the palace in order that Philip could enter the theatre at
sunrise.[46] He would have entered from the east, the side on which the ground
rises towards the palace, thus framed by and linking himself to the rising sun.[47]
Accompanying him were magnificent statues of the twelve Olympians, and a
thirteenth of Philip himself, who claimed descent from Zeus. The intention,
no doubt, was to place the statue of Philip on the central wedge of the auditorium, where in Athens the statue of Dionysus stood, and in later years a statue
of Hadrian.[48] Religion and politics yet again prove themselves indisseverable.
There are no thrones or inscriptions for Macedon is a monarchy, and no place
for common mortals to be honoured in perpetuity.

In the centre of the circle a rectangular stone survives, and plaster smooth-
ing over the roughness of two sides testifies that this stone was not freshly
carved as a geometric marker but was incorporated as a pre-existing sacred
object. To this extent, the architectural conception remains sacred rather than
political. A permanent proscenium wall intersects the perfect circle of the
orchêstra, and as at Megalopolis must have replaced an earlier wooden stage
building.[49] The most unusual aspect of the theatre is the fact that it has no
stone seats behind the front row. This may simply have been a matter of convenience in timber-rich Macedon, but it may equally be the case that the
Macedonian monarch, like the nobles of republican Rome, preferred a temporary auditorium to a stone theatre that would be both a symbol of democracy and a potential meeting-place for a democratic assembly.[50]

Later than these two theatres, built in 330–320,[51] is the theatre of Epidauros,

---

[45] COAD 15.   [46] Diodorus xvi.92–4.

[47] Compare Vitruvius IV.v.I: an instruction that images should be placed east of an altar so that
they may seem to rise up and gaze at supplicants or sacrificiants.

[48] DFA 60; TDA 142, 263.

[49] Read, 'Social space' 328 is confident that these foundations are later. The remains intrude upon
the east eisodos, and must belong to a phase when all emphasis was on the stage.

[50] See E. Frézouls, 'La Construction du theatrum lapideum et son contexte politique' in Théâtre
et spectacles dans l'antiquité: actes du colloque de Strasbourg, 5–7 nov. 1981 (Strasbourg, 1983)
193–214.

[51] The date is securely attested by building records: Annual of the British School at Athens 61 (1966)
297. The standard account is A. von Gerkan and W. Müller-Wiener, Das Theater von Epidauros
(Stuttgart, 1961). These archaeologists believe the upper half of the theatre to be a later addition.
However Lutz Käppel in 'Das Theater von Epidauros' Jahrbuch des Deutschen Archäologischen
Institut 104 (1989) 83–106 dissents, seeing the overall geometric design as integral.

admired by Pausanias for its beauty and 'harmony',[52] and visited by countless modern tourists who take from it their basic understanding of what classical theatre was like. The theatre of Epidauros is located within the sanctuary of Asclepius, and in several important ways is quite different from the urban theatre of Megalopolis and the court theatre of Macedon. The theatre does not stand in any architectural relationship to sacred buildings but is a structure entirely complete unto itself. A symbol of this completeness is the pair of arches which join the auditorium to the stage building and create a fully enclosed space. Another is the stone curb which, apparently for the first time in Greek theatre architecture, is marked out in a complete circle around the floor of the orchêstra. The proportions are calculated in cubits, a unit of measurement that relates not to gods but to an idealized human form.[53] The rake of the auditorium follows the 'golden section' and the horizontal lay-out is planned on the pentagram in accordance with a Pythagorean conception of the ideal.[54] The lower auditorium is divided into twelve wedges and the number twelve has an obvious cosmic symbolism. Cosmology and acoustics were closely related, the Pythagorean assumption being that the planets stood in a mutual relationship of perfect musical harmony.[55] The theatre of Epidauros is the architectural expression of an age that saw the flowering of Greek mathematics, and the growing influence of the Pythagorean and Platonic idea that number is the key to the divine. Because there are twelve wedges of seats, there is no central wedge. The central wedge in Athens served not only for the statue and priest of the god, but also for the Council of 500,[56] and at Aigai it would have seated the king and his thirteenth statue. At Epidauros there is no locus of political power.

Epidauros did much to inspire the design of the Olivier Theatre in London's National Theatre complex. Peter Hall (artistic director of the National Theatre) visited Epidauros with the architect of the Olivier and observed the space with the eye of a practitioner. He was shown how the symmetry was never 100 per cent perfect, because the human body is never quite symmetrical and the ancient architect wanted the theatre to feel human rather than a product of mere geometry. He regretted the modern use of stage lighting, observing how the theatre seemed part of the landscape, growing out of the hillside, in accordance with the idea that the natural world was inhabited by

[52] Pausanias ii.27.5.
[53] COAD 83. For the basis of ancient architecture in the human form, see Vitruvius III.i.
[54] See the detailed analysis in Käppel, 'Das Theater von Epidauros'.
[55] See Vitruvius I.i.16, v.vi.1.
[56] DFA 269. Most Hellenistic theatres have central wedges, though Corinth and Argos are notable exceptions.

gods. He concluded from his visit that the theatre remained what it always was, a 'place of healing'.[57] As Hall instinctively recognized, the harmonious proportions of the theatre are related to the Asclepian premiss that the elements of a sick body are in a state of disharmony, and that a cure of the spirit is necessary for a cure of the body.[58] We can interpret the theatre as the architectural embodiment of the principle of 'catharsis' outlined in the *Poetics*, the principle that tragedy exists not to articulate and clarify conflict but to purge and purify the emotions of the audience.[59]

Epidauros is often considered to be the first theatre to possess not only a circular curb but also a stone stage. The stage could become a permanent structure here, I would suggest, precisely because it lay outside the circle. For the performance of classical drama, the new arrangement throws up certain problems. If performance is to be in the orchestral area, upon which the lines of the auditorium seem to converge, then the actor entering through the *eisodos* has to negotiate a powerful circumference line that has no obvious theatrical purpose. The organization of entries and exits, as Taplin has shown,[60] is a key to the performance of Greek tragedy, and the stone circle adjacent to the *eisodos* marks an onstage/offstage boundary that seems at best an irrelevance. It is possible that by the time the theatre was built the performance of new plays had been transferred to the roof of the stage building, which now constituted a high stage, and created an absolute physical separation between actor and chorus.[61] This is scarcely a satisfying explanation, however, since at Epidauros the circle isolates the stage and makes it seem visually weak (although remaining excellent acoustically).[62] Sightlines from the side wedges onto the stage are atrocious, as Leslie Read's photo demonstrates.[63] Although the sides of the auditorium open outwards slightly away from the circumference of a single

---

57 Peter Hall, *Peter Hall's Diaries* ed. J. Goodwin (London, 1983) 165; *Making an Exhibition of Myself* (London, 1993) 311–12. The scarcely discernible irregularities to which Hall refers must be the slightly steeper rake of the upper half of the auditorium, and the opening out of the semicircle to form a horseshoe.

58 See T. Papadakis, *Epidaure: le sanctuaire d'Asclépios* (Athens, 1978). Käppel sees the architecture as symbol of Hygeia, goddess of health.

59 For bibliography on catharsis, see Brian Vickers, *Towards Greek Tragedy* (London, 1973) 609–15. Note also Taplin's apologia for the Aristotelian position in *GTA* 167–70. Note that Aristotle's principal discussion of catharsis is in the *Politics* in relation to music.

60 *SA passim.*

61 See Wiles, *The Masks of Menander* 36ff. For the roof/stage transition, see also R. F. Townsend, 'The fourth-century skene of the Theatre of Dionysos at Athens' *Hesperia* 55 (1986) 421–38.

62 The *orchêstra* floor serves as a reflector. See François Canac *L'Acoustique des théâtres antiques: ses enseignements* (Paris, 1967); Lothar Cremer, 'Different distributions of the audience' in *Auditorium Acoustics* ed. R. Mackenzie (Barking, 1975) 145–59.

63 Read, 'Social space' 322 reinforces the point with a second photograph from higher up.

Plate 4 Epidauros

circle, and to the rear of the diameter line a stone bar links the circular curb to the seating shifting the apparent point of balance backwards, the stage always seems to lie outside the natural focus of the audience. It was not the stage that gave Hall the feeling of an authentic classical experience, and when he took his *Oresteia* to be performed at Epidauros in 1982 he would not have dreamed of locating his actors there.[64]

It is possible that a wooden stage was set up in front of the stone stage, bringing the actors further forward. A better explanation, perhaps, is that the architect did not have tragedy and comedy in mind as his first priority. Hellenistic theatres were used by now for other entertainments. The Greeks whom Alexander summoned to Susa in 324 BC included conjurors, a reciter of Homer, pipers and players of the *kithara*, singers to those instruments, choruses that danced to the pipes, a harpist, a trio of tragic actors and a trio of comic actors. The tragedian from Argos or the comedian from Rhodes who later visited Epidauros probably performed extracts to music rather than complete plays in accordance with the 'anthological' tendencies of Hellenistic culture.[65] We

---

[64] For the *orchêstra* as focus here, see for example J. Michael Walton, *Greek Theatre Practice* (Westport, 1980) 81. Hall's production used a shallow stage before the *skênê* for certain static effects such as the *eccyclêma* but the main action took place in the orchestral area.

[65] *COAD* 237, with evidence from later Hellenistic festivals in *COAD* 190–6. Käppel cites inscriptional references to performances, and also notes the importance of hymns in the cult. On

might do best to explain the distinctive qualities of Epidauros in relation to the cult of Asclepius. The god was associated less with drama than with the paean, the most famous of which was written by Sophocles. The extant fragment refers to the accompaniment of flutes, and was presumably performed by a chorus dancing in a circle.[66] The architect, I would suggest, was more concerned with 'thymelic' contests – music and dance contests presented in the *orchêstra* – than with 'scenic' contests – dramas presented on stage.[67] The privileging of music and dance would be consistent with a Platonist ideology delighting in geometry and mistrustful of theatrical mimesis. A distinctive cultic usage would account for the fact that the theatre was never modified by the Romans.

The cult of Asclepius is not without some bearing on fifth-century drama in Athens, for the shrine of Asclepius was built next to the Theatre of Dionysus in the 420s. The cults of Asclepius and Dionysus were not only spatially but also temporally contiguous, for the feast and procession of Asclepius coincided with the *proagon*, the preliminary festive day of the Dionysia.[68] Sophocles is said to have become a priest of Asclepius,[69] and his last two plays are plainly concerned with the idea of healing. These plays may be signs of a broader historical move away from the agonistic or dialectical idea of drama towards the holistic, cathartic ideal embodied by Epidauros. Vitruvius, when laying out a theatre, chose to give equal cultic significance to Apollo and Dionysus.[70] Nietzsche's famous dichotomy of the Apolline and the Dionysiac offers a useful way of formulating the change that took place in the Greek conception of theatre. Asclepius was the son of Apollo, and his theatre at Epidauros exemplifies the Apolline ideal: a space embodying order, and acoustically perfect for the paean, Apollo's lyre and Homeric recitation.[71] The deme theatres of Attica are the embodiment of Dionysiac disorder, respecting the irrational at the expense of aesthetic harmony. Somewhere between these polarities we might

anthologizing, see Bruno Gentili, *Theatrical Performances in the Ancient World* (Amsterdam, 1979) 21–31.

[66] E. J. and L. Edelstein, *Asclepius* (Baltimore, 1945) 1.325–6 (text) and II.199ff. (commentary). For the paean as a choral mode, with bibliography, see Ian Rutherford, 'The tragic paean' *Arion* 3 (1995) 112–35; for the circular form, see Claude Calame, *Les Choeurs de jeunes filles en Grèce archaïque* (Rome, 1977) 1.147–52.   [67] For the term 'thymelic' see *TDA* 168.

[68] *DFA* 64.

[69] The biographical sources are the anonymous *Life of Sophocles* II and *Etymologicum Magnum* under 'Dexion'; Marinus, *Vita Procli* 29 adds that the sanctuary of Asclepius in Athens was famous because of Sophocles.   [70] Vitruvius I.vii.I.

[71] In Plato, *Ion* 530a, the rhapsodist announces that he has come from Epidauros, where he won a contest in Homeric recitation. This was of course prior to the building of the theatre. For a discussion of Nietzsche's *Die Geburt der Tragödie*, see Marvin Carlson, *Theories of the Theatre* (Ithaca, 1984) 260–3.

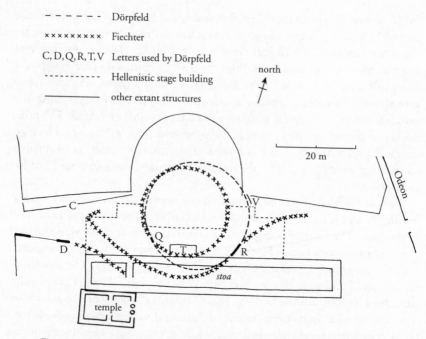

Figure 7 The pre-Periclean *orchêstra*: the reconstructions of Dörpfeld and Fiechter

expect to locate the theatre of Aeschylus, Sophocles and Euripides. I have
stressed the innovative and unusual nature of Epidauros because it has dominated popular conceptions of fifth-century theatre. Standard introductions to
Greek theatre commonly offer a plan or photograph as the guide to how things
were in Athens.[72] The Apolline model is seductive, and we must be cautious of
it.

The key evidence for the early theatre in Athens is a rough arc of stones excavated by Wilhelm Dörpfeld in the 1880s (referred to by him as **R**).[73] Dörpfeld
linked this arc with a smaller line of stones (**Q**) too small to identify a curve,[74]
and a shallow cutting made in the bed-rock probably to assist drainage (**V**), in
order to project a circular boundary for a primitive acting/dancing area with a
diameter somewhere between 24 and 27 metres. The diameter is comparable

[72] E.g. *GTA* plates 1 and 2; Erika Simon, *The Ancient Theatre*, tr. C. E. Vafopolou-Richardson
(London, 1982) fig. 1; Walton, *Greek Theatre Practice* 81; John Gould in *The Cambridge History
of Classical Literature* ed. P. E. Easterling and B. M. W. Knox (Cambridge, 1985) 267 – fig. 1
and pl.IVa; *COAD* pl.15b; R. Sowerby, *The Greeks* (London, 1995) 80.

[73] See W. Dörpfeld and E. Reisch, *Das griechische Theater* (Athens, 1896).

[74] One stone has vanished subsequent to the early excavations: John Scott Scullion, 'The
Athenian Stage and Scene-setting in early tragedy' (Ph.D. thesis, Harvard, 1990) 28–30.

with theatres like Megalopolis (30 metres) and Aigai (28¼ metres). Seen by the visitor today, the arc of stones makes a striking contrast to the rectilinear lines of all the later walling around it, and Dörpfeld's conclusions would seem an obvious inference: **R** should belong to a wall which supported a circular dancing area half cut into the hill-side and half extending from it.

Unfortunately, Dörpfeld's conclusions did not commend themselves to his successor at the excavations, Ernst Fiechter.[75] Fiechter seems to have been a man obsessed with geometrical perfection and determined to make Athens conform to the ideal of Epidauros. Scholars of Dörpfeld's generation were steeped in a romanticism which found its academic fruition in the work of the Cambridge anthropologists. For them primitivism was nothing to be ashamed of, and, though unexpected, Dörpfeld's primitive stone circle was for a time acceptable. There was a very different attitude to order in the Germany of the 1930s, and Fiechter's Apolline view of the Greek theatre stems from a view of Athens as the acme of European civilization. Theatre fell into the self-justifying category of 'art', and social context was of no interest to him. Nor was archaeological context. In order to realize his vision of the theatre, Fiechter introduced a new smaller circle centred on the axes of the later auditorium and *eisodoi*, and at a tangent to a later stage wall. His reconstruction is entirely a projection backwards from later remains, and effectively takes no stock of Dörpfeld's finds. The arc of stones, because one end seems to flatten slightly, was identified as part of an S-shaped retaining wall. Why the Athenians did not prefer a sturdier and aesthetically tidier straight wall as at Thorikos was not explained. The other smaller group of stones on Dörpfeld's circumference formed a tangent with the new circle, but this was dismissed by Fiechter as mere coincidence since these stones could have had no structural function buried deep in the midst of the presumed terrace.

Fiechter's vision has had an extraordinary hold upon subsequent scholarship because of the way it salvages a balanced, orderly and hermetic environment for the Greek tragedians. Two important followers in essentials were Arthur Pickard-Cambridge (in his still standard monograph on the theatre published in 1946) and John Travlos. Travlos' contribution was to accept the arc as an arc and convert the S-shaped terrace wall back to a neat outer semi-circle, framing a postulated inner circle inspired by Fiechter and by Epidauros. Having eliminated asymmetry from the retaining wall, Travlos took a further step in order to remove all remaining asymmetry from Fiechter's model. He shifted the axis

---

[75] See E. Fiechter, *Das Dionysos-Theater in Athen* (4 volumes, Stuttgart, 1935–50). Fiechter's revision of Dörpfeld was attacked by William Dinsmoor, 'The Athenian theater of the fifth century' in *Studies Presented to David Moore Robinson* ed. G. E. Mylonas (Saint Louis, 1951) 309–30. Scullion follows Dinsmoor in essentials.

of the early theatre westwards, in order to align his semi-circular auditorium with an older retaining wall that on the west side once shored up the flank above the *eisodos* (Dörpfeld's wall **C**). This helped to release the theatre from any troublesome relationship with the nearby Odeon.[76] Later writers of popular introductions have felt free to follow these authorities.[77]

A more recent and currently fashionable challenge to Dörpfeld comes from those who reject an orchestral circle entirely, and reconstruct a quadrilateral theatre. The reference point for these scholars is not Epidauros but Thorikos, though always a sanitized, Apolline version of Thorikos. The argument began when Carlo Anti in 1947 identified a series of rectangular playing-spaces in sixth-century Crete, and pointed to similarities with Thorikos.[78] Margarete Bieber helped to popularize his work, favouring a polygonal auditorium in the second edition of her *History of the Greek and Roman Theater.*[79] An essay published by the American archaeologist Elizabeth Gebhard in 1974 did most to tip the scales of scholarly opinion in favour of a rectilinear theatre.[80] In 1990 Anti's pupil Luigi Polacco published a monograph on the Theatre of Dionysus, reconstructing a trapezoidal auditorium and rectangular playing area complete with stage. The 'rectangular' thesis will have to be discussed at some length because its implications for performance are fundamental, and I shall focus on Gebhard's influential essay.

In support of the idea that quadrilateral theatres were an early norm, Gebhard examines the Attic deme theatres at Ikarion and Thorikos with which we are now familiar, and straight-sided auditoria at Argos and Syracuse. The seating at Argos and Syracuse is unquestionably early, probably mid fifth-century, but whether these auditoria were used primarily or at all for purposes of theatre remains unknown. Gebhard implies that we can trace an evolutionary development from rectangular to circular theatres, but the evidence cannot

---

[76] John Travlos, *Pictorial Dictionary of Ancient Athens* (New York, 1971) 540 fig. 667.

[77] E.g. *GTA* fig. 1; Graham Ley, *A Short Introduction to the Ancient Greek Theatre* (Chicago, 1991) fig. 2. The circle with *skênê* behind it is taken for granted in J. Michael Walton, *The Greek Sense of Theatre* (London, 1984) and Peter D. Arnott, *Public and Performance in the Greek Theatre* (London, 1989).

[78] C. Anti, *Teatri greci arcaici da Minosse a Pericle* (Padua, 1947); Luigi Polacco, *Il teatro di Dioniso Eleutereo ad Atene* (Rome, 1990).   [79] *HGRT* especially figs. 221, 238 and 281.

[80] 'The form of the orchestra in the early Greek theatre' *Hesperia* 43 (1974) 428–440. Recent converts to agnosticism in the matter of orchestral shape include J. R. Green in 'On seeing and depicting the theatre in classical Athens' *GRBS* 32 (1991) 15–50, p.19; Rush Rehm, *Greek Tragic Theatre* (London, 1992) 33; and Oliver Taplin, 'Greek theatre' in *The Oxford Illustrated History of Theatre* ed. J. Russell Brown (Oxford, 1995) 13–48. There is a useful survey of the debate in Clifford Ashby, 'The case for the rectangular/trapezoidal orchestra' *Theatre Research International* 13 (1988) 1–20.

sustain a simple evolutionary model. An interesting case study is Morgantina, where an asymmetrical trapezoidal auditorium with a large altar on the left (east) side seems to be of later date than the adjacent Dionysiac theatre planned in the normal way around a circle.[81] The theatre at Euonymon in Attica was laid out around a rectangle some half-century after many theatres elsewhere had been planned around a circle, and there is no evidence that the stonework at Rhamnous and Ikarion is any earlier. At Argos and Syracuse rectilinear auditoria lie alongside later circle-based theatres, suggesting that the two types of 'theatre' had differentiated functions. In the Athenian *Agora*, four rows of steps below the Theseion were clearly laid out as a kind of auditorium in the fifth century, and the first Pnyx had a straight terrace wall, and here in Athens we can be confident that neither space was designed for theatre. The steps were probably seats for a law court.[82] None of Gebhard's examples of an evolutionary development from rectangle to circle proves convincing. Her own doctoral research centred on the theatre at Isthmia, which she offers as a prime instance. The only evidence, however, is a trapezoidal drainage ditch, which she takes as the line of an early auditorium.[83] A straight-sided drain removes torrential rainwater more quickly than a curved drain, and can scarcely justify the reconstruction of a straight-sided auditorium. We find just such a drainage line carved into the semi-circular stone auditorium at Syracuse. Polacco and Anti argue that this irregular trapezium marked the line of the original audience seating, but it is impossible to conceive why the builders of this theatre would not have obliterated an ugly scar ripping through their perfect circular lines. Far more plausible is the explanation that the Romans cut the channel when they flooded the theatre for water sports.[84] Gebhard draws on a tendentious analysis by Anti and Polacco of the seating in the shrine of Amphiaraus in Attica. A straightish row of stones that seemed to Arias to be a retaining wall holding back the hillside is regarded as the vestige of an auditorium commanding the

---

[81] For documentation, see Karina Mitens, *Teatri greci e teatri ispirati all'architectura greca in Sicilia e nell'Italia meridionale c. 350–50 a.C.* (Rome, 1988) 105–8.

[82] Hansen and Fischer-Hansen 'Monumental political architecture' (n.33 above) 77, citing A. Boeghold.   [83] E. R. Gebhard, *The Theater at Isthmia* (Chicago, 1973) 15.

[84] The argument for a trapezoidal auditorium on the site of the circular theatre is developed at length in Luigi Polacco and Carlo Anti, *Il teatro antico di Siracusa* (Rimini, 1981). For difficulties see J. R. Green in *Lustrum* 31 (1989) 22; also J. C. Moretti, 'Les débuts de l'architecture théâtrale en Sicile et en Italie méridionale' *Topoi* 3 (1993) 72–100, pp. 83–6. Water sports is the explanation offered in R. J. A. Wilson, *Sicily Under the Roman Empire* (Warminster, 1990) 63. Mitens, *Teatri greci* 117 also rejects the trapezoidal thesis and follows the chronology of L. Bernabò-Brea; likewise C. Courtois, *Le Bâtiment de scène des théâtres d'Italie et de Sicile* (Louvain, 1989) 29.

distant altar of the god.[85] In respect of Tegea, her inferences have been proved false by subsequent excavation.[86]

It is an important premiss for Gebhard that the form of the *orchêstra* does not differ from the form defined by the seating.[87] This is clearly unsustainable. At Euonymon (not excavated at the time Gebhard wrote) we have seen how the seating slabs and planks are curved around a rectangle.[88] Rectangular bases were used in the early circular theatre at Corinth.[89] The discovery of straight-sided seating blocks (up to 1.75 metres long) in the Theatre of Dionysus at Athens dating from the fifth century cannot therefore be used as evidence for the shape of the *orchêstra*.[90] They tell us only what we knew already, that the audience sat on planks. The blocks that have been discovered could easily have surrounded a circular playing area.

In order to dismiss Dörpfeld, Gebhard does no more than place blind faith in Fiechter. She dismisses as irrelevant the stones that Fiechter dismissed. She applies a straight ruler to two stones towards the end of arc **R** in order to concur with Fiechter (against Travlos) that the arc flattens out.[91] Having pointed out the imperfections of the arc in its present condition, she removes it from further consideration, offering no thoughts about why such a line of stones might be there, beyond the proposition that it defined the edge of the early seating area – which suggests an auditorium of an unprecedented shape.

The underlying flaw in the reasoning of Gebhard and her school is a failure

---

[85] Compare the discussion in C. Anti and L. Polacco *Nuove ricerche sui teatri greci arcaici* (Padua, 1969) with Arias, *Teatro greco fuori di Atene* 66. See also *TDA* 204–5. The same issue arises in respect of Chaeronea, also documented by Anti and Polacco.

[86] Read, 'Social space' 328 n.13.   [87] Gebhard, 'Form of the orchestra' 440.

[88] E. Pöhlmann, another leading proponent of the rectangle, obliterates these features and sharpens the curve in his schematic and tendentious diagram of the theatre: 'Bühne und Handlung im Aias des Sophokles' *Antike und Abendland* 32 (1986) 20–31 fig. 4. Note that at Thorikos only the front row is actually straight. W. W. Wurster cites the example of Metapontion in southern Italy, where the pre-classical assembly-place (over which the theatre was subsequently built) was a perfect oval amphitheatre surrounding a rectangular playing/speaking area. 'Die Architektur des griechischen Theaters' *Antike Welt* 24 (1993) 20–42, p. 40.

[89] R. Stillwell, *Corinth: the theatre* (Princeton, 1952) 22. For similar seating in the 'round' theatre at Morgantina, see Mitens *Teatri greci* 106; also Moretti 80.

[90] The case is argued at length in E. Pöhlmann, 'Die Proedrie des Dionysostheaters im 5. Jahrhundert und das Bühnenspiel der Klassik' *Museum Helveticum* 38 (1981) 129–46. He draws on M. Maass, *Die Prohedrie des Dionysostheaters in Athen* (Munich, 1972). Wurster, 'Architektur' 24–5 follows Dinsmoor in identifying the blocks as the base for planks, not thrones.

[91] N. G. L. Hammond, defending Dörpfeld, points out that the stones have deteriorated and their packing has been lost since the nineteenth-century excavations, and that Dörpfeld's drawings must therefore be trusted. 'More on conditions of production to the death of Aeschylus' *GRBS* 29 (1988) 5–33.

to distinguish multi-purpose spaces designed for religious and political gatherings from the Theatre of Dionysus, which was designed for the express purpose of honouring the god at his festival. The rationale for the existence of the Theatre of Dionysus was precisely its difference from the *Agora* and from the Pnyx. It is possible, as Travlos believes, that a circular *orchêstra* above the precinct of Dionysus was in the first instance built for dancing, and that only subsequently was drama transferred from the *Agora* to the dancing space.[92] The principal dance at the festival of Dionysus was the dithyramb, and this was consistently known in antiquity as the 'circular chorus'.[93] Modern scholars tend to be interested in the dithyramb only because of Aristotle's statement that tragedy stemmed from it.[94] In the classical period, however, although the dithyramb only occupied the first of the 5 days of performance, we must remember that this first day accounted for almost three-quarters of choregic expenditure on the festival, and involved 1,000 citizen performers. Surviving monumental tripods commemorate victory in the dithyramb, not drama.[95] If the dithyramb was the primary event of the Dionysia, it would seem to demand a circular space. A photograph taken in 1899/1900 depicts Austrian classicists dancing in a circle around the edge of the *orchêstra* at Epidauros to greet the new century, and 25 people seem to occupy half the circle. It is hard to see that a circular dance involving choreographed movement could be performed by 50 in a significantly smaller space.[96]

One further piece of documentary evidence needs to be accounted for. In 415 BC a man alleged that he saw 300 conspirators emerging from the Odeon, where they had presumably been skulking to avoid being noticed. The men under the light of a full moon allegedly went into the *orchêstra* of the theatre where they 'stood in a circle in groups of fifteen or twenty'.[97] It is scarcely conceivable that a group of this size could have stood in a circle in a rectangular playing space. It is conceivable in a (very large) rectangle that 50 people should link hands and dance in circular formation, but it is quite another thing to suppose that clusters of people would arrange themselves in a perceptible circle unless the space dictated that arrangement. To accommodate

---

[92] Travlos, *Dictionary* 537. I cannot accept the Periclean date which Travlos attaches to such a move.   [93] *DFA* 361.

[94] *Poetics* iv.12–1449a. W. R. Connor sees Aristotle's statement as evidence that the dithyramb was the earliest constituent of the festival as established by Cleisthenes: 'City Dionysia and Athenian democracy' *Classica et Mediaevalia* 40 (1989) 7–32.

[95] The budget of a victorious *chorêgos* is set out by Lysias: *COAD* 147; *DFA* 87. We do not know how far the figures are distorted by the cost of the monument celebrating victory. For other references to expenditure, see *DFA* 88. On numbers, see *DFA* 75. On tripods see Pierre Amandry, 'Trépieds d'Athènes: 1. Dionysies' *BCH* 100 (1976) 15–93.

[96] Wurster 'Architektur' 38 fig. 44.   [97] Andocides, *On the Mysteries* 38.

these numbers, a circle of Dörpfeld's proposed size would seem to be indicated.

Defenders of the rectangle have also failed to explain how and why at the end of the fifth century theatres planned around a circle emerged across Greece. Fourth-century architecture, apart from some exceptional and famous *tholoi* and para-theatrical council-chambers, remained consistently rectilinear. Athens was the home of the most famous Greek dramatists and eventually became home to the first guild of actors.[98] It is a reasonable historical inference that theatre architects outside Athens adopted the circle because of its success in Athens where tragedy and comedy originated. We have otherwise no explanation of the source of the distinctive form.

The alternative to a circular theatre, as proposed in Polacco's monograph for example, is scarcely satisfactory. The trapezoidal auditorium envisaged by Polacco would have involved a formidably difficult task of earth-moving in defiance of the lie of the land, and without the use of stone blocks the resulting structure would not have stood up to the weather. Sightlines and more importantly acoustics would be inferior to those offered by a more-or-less circular auditorium, considerations which become more pressing in proportion to the scale of the theatre. There is an applied common sense behind Vitruvius' statement that sound travels in circles like the ripples set up by a pebble thrown into a pond, and that interruptions to the circle disturb the flow of sound.[99] Anti sketched a primitive theatre with only ten rows, but when Polacco starts to envisage a theatre with thirty to forty rows, the practicalities of the rectangle become acute.[100] The regular trapezium is a historical chimaera inspired by an irregular drainage channel at Syracuse.[101] Polacco's overall aesthetic project is to create a Greek theatre that is pictorial and perspectival rather than sculptural and three-dimensional. In a reconstruction of Aeschylus' *Suppliants*, he sets the shrine within a frame of projecting flats (functioning like a modern proscenium arch), and has the emblems of the gods painted on the *skênê* wall.[102] The images in this play should be sculptures, for the dramatic action of the play turns upon the threat of the chorus to hang themselves from these gods (465), but Polacco ignores this simple dramatic requirement in his obsessive determination to create a two-dimensional theatre. Pöhlmann's

---

[98] *DFA* 282.   [99] Vitruvius v.iii.6.

[100] Anti, *Teatri arcaici* pl.2, reproduced as *HGRT* fig. 229; Polacco, *Teatro di Dioniso* 147.

[101] Polacco analysed the irregularity of the shape subsequent to publishing his main work on Syracuse: see 'Le assimmetrie del teatro antico di Siracusa' *Numismatica e antichità classica* 13 (1984) 85–93.

[102] L. Polacco, '*Le Supplici*, come le reppresentavano Eschilo' *Numismatica e antichità classica* 14 (1985) 65–90; cf. his 'Il teatro greco come arte della visione: scenografia e prospettiva' *Dioniso* 19 (1989) 137–71.

reconstruction of the *Ajax* is scarcely less pictorial, with painted representations of the woods on the left and the tent on the right. An *eccyclêma* is placed on each side, and no use is made of the focal central area.[103] The scene change is envisaged in realist terms, and Pöhlmann seems happy for the camera in his mind's eye to pan across from one studio set to another.

The theatres which the 'rectangle' theorists construct are, as J. R. Green has noted, strikingly 'intimate',[104] yet what differentiates the Theatre of Dionysus from the deme theatres and from every modern theatre must be its scale. Plato speaks of a fifth-century audience of 30,000, implying a gathering of the entire male citizen population.[105] No demographic or organizational changes give us cause to postulate a quantum leap in the scale of the fourth-century auditorium. There can be no doubt that the size of the Greek theatre is hard for the modern mind to register. Peter Brook, for example, will not contemplate a theatre with an audience of more than 1,000, nor a distance between actor and spectator of more than 15 metres.[106] Iain Mackintosh, designer of successful intimate theatres like the Cottesloe and Tricycle in London, idealizes the Elizabethan theatre and is forced to argue that the present scale of Epidauros and the Theatre of Dionysus misleads because 'great theatre is rarely originated in large houses'. He adds the qualification, however, that the early Greek auditorium would have been much more densely packed than the Hellenistic stone auditorium,[107] and the seating at Euonymon helps to confirm this proposition. Even if the fourth-century *diazôma*, the lateral gangway that followed the line of an ancient road, marked the top of the formal fifth-century auditorium, the theatre was still on a gigantic scale in modern terms. The actors were lit by the sun from behind and were thus to a large extent in silhouette. In order to make visual sense of such a performance space, we have to think in terms, for example, of a cricket match, where the relative positions and relationships of two distant protagonists and a distant chorus sustain the narrative interest. And we have to think of the acoustic requirement that there should be no spillage, no reverberation and maximum proximity.

The 'rectangular' hypothesis should be laid to rest without further ceremony. The facts are extremely clear. On the one hand, there is no evidence that the auditorium in the Athenian Theatre of Dionysus was ever rectilinear, and

---

[103] 'Bühne und Handlung'.   [104] 'Depicting the theatre' (n.80 above) 19.

[105] *Symposium* 175e, discussed in *DFA* 263, *TDA* 141.

[106] According to Jean-Guy Lecat (technical director and venue finder for Peter Brook): address at a symposium on the Place of Performance at the Institute of Contemporary Arts (ICA), London, 7 May 1994 – ICA audio tapes archive no.1031. The statement does not take account of Brook's *Orghast*, an experiment in mythic theatre in an Iranian quarry.

[107] *Architecture, Actor and Audience* (London, 1993) 159.

on the other, Dörpfeld offers the only acceptable explanation for the ancient arc of stones and for the sudden emergence of circular theatres across the Greek world. For a large-scale performance, no extant rectilinear auditorium offers a viable alternative to the circular model. There is thus no reason to surrender the traditional idea of a democratic Athenian community gathered in a circle in order to contemplate itself in relation to the fictive world of the play. In Aristophanes the spectators view the action in relation to the real Cleon, Socrates or Cleophon whom they know to be seated in the auditorium. Tragedy likewise, though less explicitly, invites the audience to compare their contemporary social order with that of the myth. In the frontal, confrontational space envisaged by Anti, Gebhard, Pöhlmann, Polacco and their school, the world of the play is laid out before the spectators like a mirror image, the audience are watchers of an event rather than participants in an event, and the proposed mode of viewing is individualist. Vernant rightly argues that 'tragedy is born when myth starts to be considered from the point of view of a citizen'.[108] In order to see from the point of view of a citizen, it follows that the spectator needs to be able to see his fellow citizens. In the deme theatres, where collective self-awareness was not a problem because the scale was intimate, rectilinear playing spaces were not sealed confrontational stages, but were surrounded by an encircling auditorium and opened into the thoroughfares of the deme.

The rectangular controversy has been useful in calling attention to the diversity of fifth-century practice, and in demonstrating that Epidauros can no longer be admitted as the perennial ideal. The determination of Fiechter and Travlos to place a perfect circle in front of the stage building is a pure act of faith. There is a far simpler hypothesis, namely that (1) a large circle was set up for the dithyramb and the earliest forms of tragedy, and that subsequently (2) a wooden *skênê* was set up not at a tangent to the circle but intersecting the circle.[109] When Taplin proffers evidence that the adoption of the *skênê* took place just before the *Oresteia*, there is no warrant for his rider that at this point a new smaller circle would have to be marked out in front of the *skênê*.[110] It is easier to imagine a dramatist setting up a screen across the *orchêstra* experimentally for one tetralogy than to imagine him unilaterally redesigning the whole acting area. A screen set across the *orchêstra* need not have been in place on the first day of the festival, when a circle was needed for dithyrambic

---

[108] *MTAG* 33. The wording is attributed to Walter Nestle.

[109] This is scarcely a new hypothesis. See for example Allen's sketch of 1920 reproduced in *HGRT* fig. 232 and in A. N. Modona, *Gli edifici teatrali greci e romani* (Florence, 1961) 22 fig. 19; so more recently N. G. L. Hammond, 'The conditions of dramatic production to the death of Aeschylus' *GRBS* 13 (1972) 387–450.   [110] *SA* 457.

dancing, and when people in the lower seats would have preferred an unobstructed view of the sacrifices taking place in the sanctuary below.[111]

It is an advantage of this developmental hypothesis that we do not have to envisage a high stage suddenly changing the focus of the theatre in the fourth century. The adoption of the Hellenistic 'high stage' would have been a simple transition if the roof of a stage building inside the focal circle came to be used as a platform by actors. The actors would simply have taken over in a more rationalist age a space formerly allocated to gods.[112] The theatre of Megalopolis, with its wooden stage building moved into place to intersect the circle, can be placed neatly in the line of such an Athenian tradition. If Megalopolis lay not beneath a power station but in olive groves a bus ride from Athens, and had been restored as fully as the later theatre of Epidauros, then modern popular assumptions about the Athenian theatre might be very different. Aigai follows the layout of Megalopolis, and Epidauros is the new departure.

As Rush Rehm observes, 'the early theatre was conceived more as a space than as a building'.[113] The question we have now to ask is the intractable one: when did the 'space' at the foot of a hollowed hillside in front of a temple of Dionysus acquire architectural form? The concept of the 'Periclean rebuilding' was an integral part of Fiechter's world view. Fiechter wanted his Theatre of Dionysus to be a second Parthenon, a monument in stone commensurate with the literary monuments bequeathed to posterity by the great tragedians, and he envisaged a huge two-storey frontage, with a stage framed by solid side wings (*paraskênia*) towering over the circle of the *orchêstra*.[114] Polacco in his 1990 monograph fights a rearguard action to preserve this vision, appealing to the wise common sense of earlier scholarship: 'No-one can fail to see that prior to the *stoa* there is nothing here that could be said to constitute a theatre, unless it be an "organic theatre", in the very place where there developed . . . the most glorious, original and imaginative drama there has ever been'.[115] The idea of an 'organic' theatre adapted from the found environment is not one that Polacco can stomach. Yet there is not a scrap of archaeological evidence for rebuilding either in Pericles' day or at any time in the fifth century. Pottery finds have caused the second temple of Dionysus to be dated to the fourth century.[116] The building material of all foundations apart from the first temple, Dörpfeld's arc

---

[111] The portable aspect of early stages is stressed by E. Billig in 'Die Bühne mit austauschbaren Kulissen' *Opuscula Atheniensa* 13 (1980) 35–83.

[112] See on the evolution R. F. Townsend, 'The fourth-century skene of the Theater of Dionysos at Athens' *Hesperia* 55 (1986) 421–38.   [113] *Greek Tragic Theatre* 33.

[114] Fiechter, *Dionysos-Theater* Vol.III, pls.29–38.   [115] Polacco, *Teatro di Dioniso* 166.

[116] Travlos, *Dictionary* 537; P. G. Kalligas, *Archaiologikon Deltion* 18 (1963) 'Chronika' 12–18. The publication is cursory, and some doubts must inevitably remain.

and the related fragments is conglomerate stone, and this is typical of mid fourth-century building.[117] These foundations could be an early example of conglomerate at the end of the fifth century, but building in the Periclean period seems now to be out of the question.

The only structures which are certainly dated earlier than the fourth century are the temple, the fragments of the *orchêstra* and the Odeon. The temple is generally assumed to be of sixth-century date, before the start of the democratic period, and to have been in place when the city festival of Dionysus was established. It housed the wooden statue of Dionysus that came from Eleutherae, and was the focus of ceremonial. Connor believes that the statue came to Athens when Eleutherae seceded from Thebes to Athens, apparently early in the fifth century, and suggests that the temple may in fact be of early fifth-century date.[118] Although no traces have survived, we should expect that an altar stood before the doorway.[119]

In addition to the three traces of a circular *orchêstra*, Dörpfeld found the remains of a wall in the area of the west *eisodos* (wall D). This could have supported a retaining wall if the early auditorium extended its embrace much closer to the temple than was later the case. On the east side lay the Odeon associated with Pericles and probably built in the 440s – a date which does not exclude the possibility that an earlier structure stood on the same site. First thought square and then rectangular, the precise shape of the Odeon is currently unknown.[120] If the Odeon was planned in some kind of functional relationship to Dörpfeld's *orchêstra*, then we have to postulate a highly asymmetrical auditorium. This would scarcely be surprising in view of the deme theatres. It would be far more surprising if the Odeon were planned without regard for the adjacent theatre.

The Odeon was one of the architectural wonders of Athens. The front colonnaded terrace stood some eight and a half metres above ground level, and was an ideal place for viewing the procession as it entered the sanctuary. The obvious analogue is the assembly-hall at Megalopolis, the only other comparable covered hall being at Eleusis.[121] The Odeon was used on the preparatory

---

[117] Dinsmoor, 'Athenian theater' 317–18; R. E. Wycherley, *The Stones of Athens* (Princeton, 1978) 210–11, 273.

[118] Connor, 'City Dionysia' (n.94 above) – for the normal view, see *DFA* 57–8.

[119] Altars normally stood before the east entrance of a temple, slightly over one temple's width distant. See C. G. Yavis, *Greek Altars: origins and typology* (Saint Louis, 1949) 56, 116.

[120] The square columns of the front colonnade were excavated in 1970, indicating a rectangle. By 1980, a huge monument of about 11x7½ metres had been uncovered, overlapping the supposed south-west corner of the rectangle. See the report by M. Korres in *Archaiologikon Deltion* 35 (1980) 'Chronika' 16.

[121] See A. L. H. Robkin 'The Odeion of Perikles: some observations on its history, form and

day of the festival of Dionysus, when the poet with his chorus and actors gave an account of his forthcoming plays, and Vitruvius adds that the place was a refuge from the rain.[122] We may guess that it had many other necessary functions during the festival: as a gathering place for the choruses, and a place to store the tribute and the armour of the dead that had to be presented in the theatre.[123] The unique pyramidal roof seems to have been intended to suggest a Persian tent, in commemoration of Greek victory against Xerxes.[124] The Persian architectural symbolism is interesting because it helps to define the spatial context of performance. On the one side stood the temple of the god, on the other the monument to a Greek triumph. The Odeon can be interpreted as a sign of the exotic barbarian other, and thus was an appropriate gathering point for citizen dancers intent on assuming an identity alien to their own.

If we look at a plan of the theatre complex in its Hellenistic state, before the addition of a Roman stage, we can form a clearer idea of the Odeon/theatre relationship (see figure 8). The *orchêstra* has shifted a few metres westward from the site identified by Dörpfeld. The fundamental change is that the theatral area and the god's sanctuary have become two separate spaces with separate entries. The theatral area has become an enclosed environment, for archways form a bridge between the auditorium and the stage building.[125] Wings (*paraskênia*) on the stage building put a frame around the action, and a wooden stage probably ran between them.[126] The dancing circle and the stage are divided, but the stage is not excluded from the focus of the theatre in the same way as at Epidauros.[127] With the division of theatre from sanctuary, art and religion are relegated to separate spheres. Each space also has its own god, for the sanctuary is now commanded by a new, larger temple, and a person entering the sanctuary immediately confronts the gold and ivory statue within it.

functions' (Ph.D. thesis, University of Washington, 1976) 92. Although Vitruvius speaks of Themistocles as the designer, Robkin accepts a Periclean dating of *c.* 446/5. P. G. Kalligas questions the identity of extant remains, but on inadequate grounds: *The Archaeology of Athens and Attica* (n.11 above) 25–30.   [122] *DFA* 67–8; Vitruvius v.ix.1.

[123] *COAD* 117–18.

[124] Robkin 51. The Persian symbolism is attested in Plutarch, *Pericles* 13.9; Vitruvius v.ix.1; Pausanias i.20.1.

[125] Their site has only recently been uncovered: Korres 11–12 and pl.9. Korres dates them to the 'classical period'.

[126] Townsend, 'Fourth-century skene' reconstructs a colonnade. Dörpfeld also assumed that there was a wooden *proscaenium* between the wings – *TDA* 156–7. How far the lower level was still used by actors is an open question. The stage building was probably modelled on structures like the Stoa of Zeus in the *Agora*.

[127] Wurster 'Architektur' 28 notes that there are two different centre points, one defined by the line of the drainage channel, the other by the line of the auditorium. A circle projected from the first excludes the (presumed) stage, a circle projected from the second overlaps it.

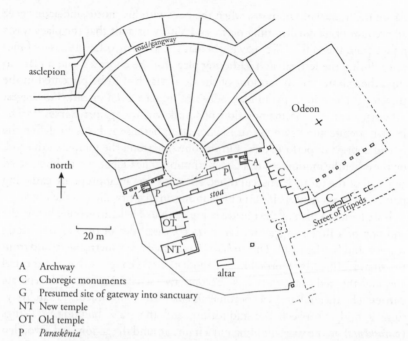

A   Archway
C   Choregic monuments
G   Presumed site of gateway into sanctuary
NT New temple
OT Old temple
P   *Paraskênia*

Figure 8 The Hellenistic Theatre of Dionysus (after Korres)

The new statue is an immobile work of art, an artistic image of the god designed to be looked at by a passive viewer, whereas the older statue was an ancient piece of wood that in some measure partook of divinity, and whose purpose was not to be gazed at (for it would have been clothed) but to partic-ipate in a festival.[128] The new statue symbolizes the new understanding of theatre, that the space is a monument, and that the performance is to be looked at rather than participated in.

The processional route runs round the Odeon and into the theatre through the east *eisodos*. There must also have been direct access into the east *eisodos* from the Odeon. The *eisodos* is aligned upon the mid-point of the Odeon wall, and thus upon the striking pinnacle above. The south terrace of the Odeon stood high above the ground, and there is no archaeological evidence of a huge flight of steps;[129] there is, on the other hand, a gap between the choregic monu-ments at the head of the *eisodos*, and it seems an inescapable conclusion that there was once an entrance to the Odeon here. It is by this route that we should

---

[128] See J.-P. Vernant, 'From the presentification of the invisible to the imitation of appearance' in *Collected Essays* ed. F. Zeitlin (Princeton, 1991) 151–63.   [129] Korres 18.

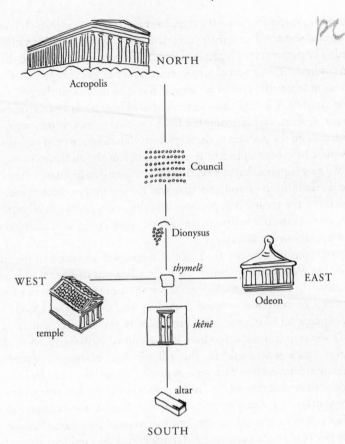

Figure 9 Axes of the performance space

imagine the putative conspirators of 415 BC to have slipped from the Odeon into the theatre. It seems a reasonable corollary that the line of the auditorium and *eisodos* on the east side was deliberately laid out in order to be in alignment with the centre doorway of the Odeon.

Whilst the Odeon commands the east–west axis, the north–south axis has a very different force. The line which runs through the centre of the auditorium where the priest and statue were located, through the centre of the *orchêstra* and through the central doorway points to the great sacrificial altar some forty metres beyond.[130] This axis line explains why the altar occupies an apparently

---

130 Conglomerate foundations, 11.4×3.3 metres. Dörpfeld first thought this a choregic monument. Kalligas (n.116 above) 15 surmises that the altar is Hellenistic, but offers no evidence. For the presence of the statue see *DFA* 60 n.5.

unorthodox position vis-à-vis the temples. Here on the altar many bulls would
have been slaughtered and their innards roasted whilst the dithyrambs were
danced. The performance is physically located between the god and the sacrifice in his honour, in a spatial alignment that we might compare to Thorikos
and Ikarion where the god in his temple had a vista of both the performance
and the sacrifice. We might also be reminded of how the last phase of the Pnyx
was built, with an axis line running from the entry through the centre of the
auditorium and the podium to the altar above. The alignment of god, door and
altar would have been apparent to the majority of the audience in the upper
seats. We may suppose that at an earlier phase in the development of the theatre
the axial relationship of god and altar was more strongly emphasized. In the
first phase of the theatre it is possible that the auditorium was aligned on an
altar in front of the old temple. A removable *skênê* would have afforded a clear
view of activity in the sanctuary.

The relationship between the space of tragic performance and the space of
sacrifice has great symbolic importance. Sacrifice was in a sense another dramatic mode. In Burkert's words, it acted out the 'human aversion to killing and
the feelings of guilt and remorse caused by the shedding of blood'.[131] The
Greek conception of tragedy is closely linked to the idea of sacrifice, and the
Oresteia seems in this respect to have had a seminal influence on how the performance space was used. In the trilogy Agamemnon, Cassandra and
Clytaemnestra are each in turn seen as sacrificial victims, and enter the single
skênê door to be slaughtered.[132] The later dramatists worked many variants on
the convention. In *Antigone* and *Women of Trachis*, for example, the protagonists go off to one side to die, but the woman who embodies the reproductive power of the house is revealed in the end as the sacrificial victim behind
the *skênê* door. Euripides' Pentheus does not die within the house but his
remains are taken inside at the end; Phaethon likewise is carried into the *skênê*,
where his smouldering corpse is mistaken for a sacrifice.[133] The convention of
off-stage death relates to the fact that the playing area is purified,[134] whilst the
blood sacrifice takes place below and beyond the playing area. The gaze of the

---

[131] 'Greek tragedy and sacrificial ritual' *GRBS* 7 (1966) 87–122, p. 106. On the relationship
between sacrifice and the symbolic representation of murder, see also J.-P.Vernant, 'A general
theory of sacrifice' in *Collected Essays* 290–302; and Detienne's introduction to M. Detienne
and J.-P. Vernant, *La Cuisine du sacrifice* (Paris, 1979).

[132] On the *Oresteia*, see Froma Zeitlin, 'The myth of the corrupted sacrifice' *Transactions of the
American Philological Association* 96 (1965) 463–508; Richard Seaford, *Reciprocity and Ritual*
(Oxford, 1994) 369–71. For the convention of the single door, see *SA* 438–40.

[133] Euripides, *Phaethon* 261–5. The text and translation are to be found in Euripides *Selected
Fragmentary plays* Vol.1, ed. C. Collard, M.J. Cropp & R.H. Lee (Warminster, 1995).

[134] *DFA* 67.

cult statue in the theatre passed through the *skênê* door to the area where the real sacrifice took place, and here therefore was the most powerful place for the fictive sacrifice of the tragedy to be sited. Cassandra compares the *skênê* doors to the gates of Hades, approaches the altar meekly like a sacrificial ox, and reels back from the smell of death.[135] Such images are rooted in physical actuality, for the death behind the *skênê* was real, the victim had to acquiesce in death to spare the guilt of his killer, and the smell of the dead animals must have lingered during the days of tragic performance.

We have a relatively clear picture of the Hellenistic theatre, for the most part completed by Lycurgus in the late 330s. Our great difficulty surrounds the interim phase. The principal evidence for that intervening phase is the old retaining wall (Dörpfeld's wall C) that runs south of the existing retaining wall on the west side.[136] This wall seems incompatible with projecting side wings because the *eisodos* would have been almost blocked. It is generally assumed, therefore, that when the *orchêstra* was shifted westward, the first permanent building was the *stoa*. Abutting the *stoa* is a wall with post-holes that must have supported a wooden stage building. Given the orientation of the east *eisodos* upon the Odeon, it would be unwise to assume with Travlos and Dinsmoor that there was once a precisely symmetrical retaining wall on the east side, blocking access to the Odeon. The *orchêstra* must have been shifted west and north in order to create a more steeply raked auditorium, and more space between the Odeon and the performance area. The new arrangement would have created a relatively greater sense of equipoise between left and right, although a perfectly symmetrical auditorium as at Megalopolis and Epidauros remained unattainable because of the way the Odeon cut into its east flank.

The *stoa* was a long colonnaded walkway commanding a view of the sanctuary, and its building was clearly decisive in dividing the theatre from the sanctuary. No longer could a wooden *skênê* be removed to turn the two spaces into one. One obvious motive for enclosing the theatral area is the simple one of regulating access, as in the second Pnyx. Later sources tell us that in the period before the stone theatre was built people tried to claim seats during the night, and there was anarchy as people fought for the best seats. The introduction of payment and ticketing prevented this problem, and our sources associate the change with Pericles.[137] We do not need to adduce that the *stoa* was

---

[135] *Agamemnon* 1290–1312.

[136] H. Lauter-Bufe and H. Lauter attempt to demonstrate that this was too flimsy to be a retaining wall in '"aA": ein Beitrag zur Baugeschichte des athenischen Dionysostheaters' in *Bathron* ed. H. Büsing and F. Hiller (Saarbrücken, 1988) 287–99, but they offer no convincing alternative.

[137] *DFA* 266–7; *COAD* 293–5. The source is probably Philochorus in the early third century.

Periclean on this evidence, but should note merely that enclosure was a factor. The theatre changed progressively from an 'absolute' theocentric space oriented upon the temple and altar towards the model of Megalopolis, symbol of a perfectly planned society. The practicalities of crowd control and the aesthetics of balance both relate to a political concern with order.

The old theory that the main theatre structure was part of a Periclean building programme was attractive because it demarcated the rough-hewn plays of Aeschylus from the surviving plays of Sophocles and Euripides which seem to exemplify more order and polish. It remains an attractive hypothesis that Pericles was responsible for shifting the *orchêstra* to create a more balanced auditorium, at the same time as he introduced the 'theoric fund' to ensure a more orderly and equitable allocation of seating. Recognizing that the conglomerate stone could not have been used so early, Dinsmoor and Newiger both argued that the *stoa* and retaining walls of the auditorium must belong to the late fifth century, and that the intermission in the Peloponnesian War in 421–415 is the logical moment.[138] The evidence that Newiger cites to support a fifth-century date is not impressive. The stone seat-bases could belong to any architectural phase. The only substantial evidence is Pausanias' statement that the statue of Dionysus in the new temple was by a sculptor whom we know to have flourished in the later fifth century.[139] If both Pausanias and the archaeologists are correct, we have to account for the fact that the second temple belongs to the Lycurgan period of building. One explanation could be that the new statue was initially intended for the chamber on the west side of the *stoa*, abutting the old temple. A major reason for building the *stoa* must have been to house the ever-growing collection of masks which actors dedicated to the god, and the statue could have looked out over this Dionysiac display,[140] standing there to be greeted by the actors as they left the theatre crossing the large stone threshold (T). With the building of a stone structure in front of the *stoa* and increasing use of an upper level, the statue would have been cut off from direct commerce with the performance, and a new location for it in the centre of the sanctuary would have been appropriate.

Pausanias apart, there seem no other positive grounds for ascribing a fifth-century date to the *stoa* and support walls of the auditorium. The fifth-century

[138] Dinsmoor, 'Athenian theater'; H.-J. Newiger, 'Zur Spielstätte des attischen Dramas im 5 Jahrhundert v. Chr.' *Wiener Studien* 89 (n.s. 10) (1976) 80–92.

[139] Pausanias i.20.2. Scullion, 'Athenian stage' 16 notes that Pausanias erred in another ascription of work to this artist.

[140] See J. R. Green, *Theatre in Ancient Greek Society* (London, 1994) 81, 85–6. The theatre at Pergamon a century later offers something of an analogue, for the temple of Dionysus stands on the right of the stage building, aligned with it and facing it. The *stoa* must have contained the paintings which Pausanias saw depicting myths concerning Dionysus.

Athenians concentrated their energies upon building temples, and were content with rudimentary political meeting-places until the fourth century.[141] If the *stoa* was built in the later fifth century, then it was probably built because the god needed a *stoa* rather than because the audience needed an impressive new façade. It was the shake-up of Athenian life at the end of the Peloponnesian War that prompted the reversing and enclosing of the Pnyx, and the political gathering-place of the people did not acquire monumental form before the prosperous middle years of the century. In tragedy the major reconceptualizing of the festival was the early fourth-century practice of reviving old tragedies,[142] when the plays of Sophocles and Aeschylus ceased to be transient events and became monuments to a past glory. The texts of the three tragedians were put in an archive and had to be performed as they were written, bronze statues of the three were erected in the theatre, and old comedy was added to the programme of revivals. Full records of victories in fifth-century theatrical competitions were researched by Aristotle, and inscribed on a public monument.[143] When Lycurgus built the auditorium in stone in around the 330s, he took another step to preserve the glorious culture of the past in perpetuity. In Hölscher's words, the fourth-century 'cityscape was mythologized for a second time' as Athens 'was consciously shaped into a monument of its own culture'.[144]

We are no longer impelled in the late twentieth century to demand of our historical sources a correlation between fine buildings and fine texts or performances. As Britain's National Theatre was being cast in concrete, the director Michael Elliott gave a celebrated lecture on the folly of 'building for posterity'.[145] Grotowski has lent respectability to the idea of a 'poor theatre'.[146] Peter Brook has dedicated much of his career to a search for unorthodox playing spaces that will serve particular performances, and has always found old dilapidated theatres more successful than new ones.[147] Theatre designer Iain Mackintosh in 1993 pleads for 'an empty space, but an inspiring empty space that can be filled with images',[148] an important revision of the 1960s ideal

---

[141] Hansen and Fischer-Hansen, 'Monumental political architecture' (n. 33 above) 85. Oddone Longo argues for a monumental *skênê* in 'La scena della città: strutture architettonici e spazi politici' in *Il teatro greco* ed. C. Molinari (Bologna, 1994) 221–36, while Hansen and Fischer-Hansen 51–2 argue for a transient structure. [142] *DFA* 72, 99–100.

[143] *TDA* 137–8; *DFA* 99, 101–4. The statues are presumably those seen by Pausanias: i.21.1–3.

[144] Tonio Hölscher, 'The city of Athens: space, symbol, structure' in *City States in Classical Antiquity and Medieval Italy* ed K. Raaflaub and J. Emlen (Stuttgart, 1991) 355–90, p. 377.

[145] Reprinted in *Making Space for the Theatre* ed. R. Mulryne and M. Shewring (Stratford-upon-Avon, 1995) 16–20. [146] J. Grotowski, *Towards a Poor Theatre* (London, 1969).

[147] See, for example, Neil Wallace, 'Peter Brook, theatre space and the tramway' in *Making Space for the Theatre* 61–3; Mackintosh, *Architecture, Actor and Audience* 83–4, 140–1.

[148] *Architecture, Actor and Audience* 86.

that any space will serve. From within a pluralist theatrical culture, which celebrates flexibility but recognizes the specific qualities of found and inherited spaces, we can assess the relative implications of different spatial arrangements without presuming a single ideal. We can view sceptically the attempts of Fiechter and his successors to foist a monumental theatre on the fifth-century tragedians rather than a flexible environment lending itself to creative innovation. My own assumption, closer to Brook than to Fiechter, is that Greek theatre was the richer for its lack of a finished architectural frame.

It is of course frustrating for the theatre historian that there is no fifth-century monument to which we can confidently turn in order to visualize fifth-century performances in Athens. What I have attempted to uncover is the evidence for a fifth-century spatial practice, and a direction of historical change. What we can do in respect of the fifth century is identify certain important axes marked by auditorium and *orchêstra* centre, god and altar, Odeon and temple. I shall argue in this book that Greek tragedy was a spatial construct, organized in relation to spatial oppositions that were rich in association for the Greek audience. The texts presuppose performance in a space that was not neutral or 'empty' but semantically laden. The theatrical space was not a mere context for the play; rather, the play lent meaning to the space.

CHAPTER 3

❧

Focus on the centre point

The notion that the actors performed (principally) on a stage whilst the chorus performed (principally) in the *orchêstra* is another important twentieth-century chimaera. Although alien to Dörpfeld's view of the Greek theatre, this idea was integral to Fiechter's vision of performance before a grand façade. Pickard-Cambridge was alive to the issue at stake:

A stage implies that it is no longer the chorus, with its ritual solemnity and its prophetic function, as embodying the spirit and soul of the poets' teaching, that is the main interest of the audience, but the actors and their histrionic skill. This transference of interest from religion to technique happened in Athens, or began to happen . . . in the fourth century.[1]

Pickard-Cambridge's sentiments are in line with Plato's view that tragedy is essentially a form of choral dance. Aristotle, taking the opposite view, argued that the chorus should function as a character within the drama, and also states that the central character is not exceptional but just better than average.[2] We should note the corollary that, being homogeneous, both chorus and protagonists ought to share the same acting space. Pickard-Cambridge stressed the hieratic aspect of tragic performance and we need also to consider the democratic aspect. Accounts of Reinhardt's production of *Oedipus* – from the days when Dörpfeld still held sway in Germany – illustrate the primary implication of using a stage: a mass of Thebans at the foot of a stage emphasized the larger-than-life stature of Oedipus the tragic hero. Being a twentieth-century democrat Reinhardt brought his fallen hero down from the stage to the *orchêstra* and in a *coup de théâtre* had him break through the chorus and merge with the audience at the end.[3] Reinhardt recognized that the stage signified hierarchy, and the level *orchêstra* was a moral leveller.

---

[1] *TDA* 71.   [2] *Poetics* xviii.7–1456a; xiii.3–1453a.
[3] J. L. Styan, *Max Reinhardt* (Cambridge, 1982) 78–85; Richard Beacham in *Living Greek Theatre* ed. J. M. Walton (Westport, 1987) 305–12. In the finale Hofmannsthal's adaptation deviated from the Sophoclean text.

Pickard-Cambridge saw a student production in Oxford which convinced him that the chorus and actors did not need to be spatially separated for the sake of mere clarity, and he disposed brusquely of the nonsense that in a play like *Eumenides* chorus and actor as equal parties in a law suit could occupy different spaces. His visual imagination, however, being conditioned in the early 1940s by perspectival art, proscenium theatre and of course Fiechter's vision of the Athenian theatre, necessarily led him to think in terms of foreground and background, and to place the focus on the rear of the acting area. A stepped altar outside and behind the orchestral circle was proposed for Aeschylus' *Suppliants* and *The Libation Bearers*. A raised area in front of the *skênê* was proposed for *Philoctetes* and *Oedipus at Colonus*.[4] This vision encouraged subsequent critics to cling to the idea that a low stage at the rear might partially separate actors from chorus. The most influential proponents of this view were T. B. L. Webster and Peter Arnott. Webster argued that a stage would have the 'advantage of marking actors off from chorus while not hindering communication',[5] but the nature of this 'advantage' is not made clear. Peter Arnott distinguishes a sacrificial altar in the middle of the *orchêstra* from a theatrical altar on top of his four-foot stage that is commonly the focus of performance.[6] The only scrap of archaeological evidence marshalled by Webster and Arnott is a unique fifth-century vase representing a single actor dancing on a trestle stage before two spectators, and there is nothing to link this vase with the city Dionysia.[7] Webster's students Dearden and Hourmouziades continued to argue the cause. Hourmouziades was keen to see the Euripidean chorus as an institution in decline, and thus was happy to see it spatially marginalized. He justifies a low fifth-century stage in evolutionary terms as a phase that anticipates the high Hellenistic stage.[8] Taplin, another critic happy to marginalize the chorus, dismissed the whole question of the stage in 1977 as 'not a very important issue'.[9] If the stage is conceived as a separate acting area, then the issue must be important, though the issue becomes much less critical if the 'stage' is little more than a flight of steps lending an illusion of mass to the *skênê*.

A variant on Pickard-Cambridge's view proffered by N. G. L. Hammond became fashionable in the late 1970s. Hammond proposed that in the

---

[4] *TDA* 70–1.   [5] *Greek Theatre Production* (London, 1956) 7.

[6] *Greek Scenic Conventions in the Fifth Century BC* (Oxford, 1962) 53. Arnott no longer argues explicitly for a stage in *Public and Performance in the Greek Theatre* (London, 1989).

[7] Compare *Greek Scenic Conventions* 16–17 with Pickard-Cambridge's rejection of the evidence at *TDA* 74. E. Billig in 'Die Bühne mit austauschbaren Kulissen' *Opuscula Atheniensia* 13 (1980) 35–83 proffers the same vase, but brings no new evidence to bear.

[8] *PIE*. C. W. Dearden in *The Stage of Aristophanes* (London, 1976) follows his master more blindly.   [9] *SA* 441–2. In *GTA* 183 n.3 he 'doubts' the existence of a stage.

Athenian theatre there remained a lump of living rock adjacent to the left *eisodos*, and that this was used for a variety of dramatic purposes. This postulate rests on no serious archaeological evidence, and stems from a literalistic reading of selected portions of dramatic text. It does not attend to the most basic questions of dramatic focus. Hammond assumes, for example, that the audience's focus throughout the *Prometheus* will be on a spot outside the great orchestral circle.[10] Di Benedetto justifiably finds Hammond's hypothesis 'bizarre'.[11]

Recent attention paid to Thorikos helps to undermine the postulate of a stage, for in this fifth-century theatre there is plainly no space for both stage and *orchêstra*.[12] The space at Ikarion is even more confined. John Gould argues for a stage on acoustical grounds, believing that the rear of the stage acts as a reflector, but experiments at Epidauros no longer support that argument.[13] It does not seem a promising hypothesis that the actors suffered a sudden loss of vocal power when they ventured away from the security of the *skênê*. The advocates of a stage all nullify the aspect of Greek drama that has most attracted democratically minded modern directors such as Stein, Mnouchkine, Hall and Koun: namely, the complex and shifting relationship between actor and chorus. The relationship between the individual and the collective was the

[10] N. G. L. Hammond, 'The conditions of dramatic production to the death of Aeschylus' *GRBS* 13 (1972) 387–450. Taplin approves the 'rock' for Aeschylean plays prior to the *Oresteia* in *SA* 448–9; likewise A. H. Sommerstein, *Aeschylus: Eumenides* (Cambridge, 1989) 32; M. L. West 'The Prometheus trilogy' *JHS* 99 (1979) 130–48. Hammond develops his theory in 'More on conditions of production to the death of Aeschylus' *GRBS* 29 (1988) 5–33, arguing that the rock serves as a concealing wing in *Ajax*. A similar rock was advocated by S. Melchinger in *Das Theater der Tragödie* (Munich, 1974) 90–1. On the archaeology see John Scott Scullion, 'The Athenian stage and scene-setting in early tragedy' (Ph.D. thesis, Harvard, 1990) 67–70. When Dörpfeld describes a channel 1 metre wide cut into the living rock, Hammond infers that all the surrounding rock was cut away, but there is no reason for such an inference. Melchinger's version of the rock, sited closer to the *skênê*, is theatrically preferable, but archaeologically impossible since the area to which he refers has been filled in above the bedrock.

[11] V. di Benedetto, 'Spazio e messa in scena nelle tragedie di Eschilo' *Dioniso* 59 (1989) 65–101, p. 75.

[12] E. Pöhlmann, 'Die Proedrie des Dionysostheaters im 5. Jahrhundert und das Bühnenspiel der Klassik' *Museum Helveticum* 38 (1981) 129–46, p. 146, sees this as a corollary of the 'rectangle' theory. Polacco, however, retains a stage.

[13] P. E. Easterling and B. M. W. Knox (eds.), *Cambridge History of Classical Literature: Greek literature* (Cambridge, 1985) 269. Gould, *ibid.* 267 also describes the *orchêstra* as 'focus'. He presumably relies upon B. Hunningher, *Acoustics and Acting in the Theatre of Dionysus Eleuthereus* (Amsterdam, 1956) 13–14, and François Canac, *L'Acoustique des théâtres antiques: ses enseignements* (Paris, 1967). Canac does not test for sound from the centre. Vitruvius v.v.7 refers to Roman theatres, not Greek. R. S. Shankland cites a Greek director to confirm 'at Epidaurus the acoustics are nearly unimpaired when the temporary stage house is absent': 'Acoustics of Greek theatres' *Physics Today* (Oct. 1973) 30–5, p. 32.

fundamental problem of the democratic *polis*, and tragedy served to articulate that problem.

The separation of actors on stage from chorus below in the *orchêstra* belongs to the Hellenistic era, when democracy had become institutionalized, and the theatre was concerned with individuating human beings, whose existence had become sharply separable from that of the *polis* and of divinities.[14] The fore-ground/background model is deeply engrained in the twentieth-century mind because the modern world has been preoccupied by the relationship between the individual and his or her environment. We have to release ourselves from a dualist vision of space –

stage	:	*orchêstra*
individual	:	society
self	:	body
logos	:	dance
reality	:	myth
theatre	:	sanctuary

– and search for a monadic fifth-century conception, which assumed that these opposites were reconcilable. In this chapter I shall argue that Athenian spatial practice was organized not upon notions of depth but upon the relationship between the centre of the circle and its periphery. In tragedy the focus was not the hypothetical stage but the centre point of the *orchêstra*. The spatial dynamic of Greek tragedy takes the form of binary oppositions that converge or collide at the centre.

Visitors to Epidauros seem to experience a magnetic force that draws them to the *thymelê*, the cylindrical stone at the centre of the *orchêstra*, where they sense they have some kind of command of the auditorium. The guides use this marking stone in order to impress their clients with the acoustics of the theatre, dropping coins or tearing sheets of paper above the stone. At Delphi the centre of the circle is not marked, but the slabs are worn at the centre point where generations of visitors have felt impelled to place themselves. Tourists sense instinctively that these theatres have a focus. Professional actors develop a more subtle intuitive sense of where, in any given building, they have the greatest strength because the gaze and ears of the audience seem best focussed upon them. For the theatre architect, to create a sense of focus is the supreme consideration. The difficulty of using Thorikos as a model for the Theatre of Dionysus is that it does not provide any point of focus for a single actor, though it lends itself well enough to choral dancing.

In many ways the structuralist argument that I develop in this book stands

[14] See David Wiles, *The Masks of Menander* (Cambridge, 1991) 36ff.

independently of the argument that the theatre was circular, but I have insisted upon the point because focus is the *sine qua non* of a satisfactory performance space. Actors will struggle in vain to communicate if the space does not foster a concentration of attention, and in a huge open-air context only an encircling auditorium can create a sufficiently powerful sense of converging eye-lines. That, at least, is my understanding. For the analysis of 'focus', we have to turn to theatre practitioners, for the problem lies outside the normal discourses of classical scholarship. Clive Barker, for example, explains in some detail how 'all spaces have their focal points and positions of strength and weakness relative to this point'.[15] He explains how directors 'increase and decrease tension in a play by working into or away from "points of interest" on a stage'. In his own practice he establishes the focal point by asking actors to move about the stage and sense where they feel strong and physically expansive. The focus in a nine-teenth-century proscenium theatre is 'usually found centre-stage about eight-een inches upstage of the curtain cut or setting line', and fan-shaped seating is essential to create this phenomenon. The actor wanting to be strong on a pro-scenium stage needs to be aware of 'lines of force' orientated upon the focal point, and face accordingly. A circular auditorium linked to a proscenium stage creates a shallow area of strength where the projected circle defined by the walls of the auditorium overlaps the stage – ideal for variety where the focus is on one or two performers establishing close contact with the audience. On the Elizabethan thrust stage, although Barker maintains that the focus is upstage centre, experimentation with the reconstructed Globe in Southwark has begun to reveal that the focal position is in fact downstage centre, at the centre of the architectural circle.[16]

Barker notes that in 360° theatre-in-the-round the focus is the centre point, though he adds that 'in productions this must be one of the least used points on the stage. It creates such an intensity of concentrated attention on any actor standing there that the audience tires if he stays there for long'. Greek theatre did not have an audience on all sides, and a better comparison might be the circular stage of the Olivier Theatre which was in some measure inspired by Epidauros. Theatre designers have not found the quasi-Greek conception entirely a happy one. One comments that the stage lacks focus unless filled with furniture or 'emptied save for one or two actors positioned dead centre'. Another comments that many actors like it because of the feeling of intimacy

[15] Clive Barker, *Theatre Games* (London, 1977) 143–53.
[16] Most participants at a conference in 1995 believed that the acting focus of the Globe should be downstage: *The Globe: the newsletter of the International Globe Centre* (Summer 1995) 7. After a season of workshops on the new stage, Andrew Gurr confidently maintains that the dominant position is at the centre of the circle – lecture, Reading University, 17 Nov. 1995.

which they get when standing in the middle, but that unfortunately these actors play only to the centre of the auditorium. Another argues that a rectangular stage is better than a circular one because: 'Actors will tell you that if you are not at the point of command in a circle, that is dead centre, the actor can feel dynamically weak.'[17] The problems of the Olivier stem from the way a Greek *orchêstra* is set in the corner of an enclosed square room, but the importance of the centre is clear. Greek actors familiar with Epidauros have reported in similar terms that 'the favored positions for performers in the *orchêstra* are near its center (focus) or somewhat behind and at either side of the center'.[18]

The intense acoustical experience of standing at the centre of the theatre at Epidauros is evoked by a Greek playwright in mystic terms as he describes his sense of being imprisoned within a cylinder: 'when you stand in the middle of the threshing floor which according to the ritual represents human fate – your voice surrounds you, as if you are enclosed in a bottle. You speak, and it is as if you have your mouth next to your ear.'[19] Vitruvius' statement that sound proceeds outwards and upwards from a centre point derives from Hellenistic scholarship that must have been inspired by the phenomenon of speech coming from the centre of the theatrical circle.[20] Our most vivid piece of evidence from the Greek world is to be found in Plutarch's account of why Corinth joined the Achaean League. When the populace had gathered in the theatre, the general who had just liberated the city from Macedon descended from the stage and took up his position in the centre of the *orchêstra*. A conqueror could have used the stage in order to hold the audience in his field of vision, and to feel empowered by physical elevation, as Demetrius did when he 'liberated' Athens and appeared on stage like a tragic actor, but the general in this instance chose to present himself as a vulnerable human being, leaning on his spear in a display of complete physical exhaustion. After standing silently to lengthy applause, he successfully persuaded the Corinthians to join the League. The speaker's strategy was to play the democrat rather than the dictator, and to assume the optimum position not to look but to be looked at.[21]

---

[17] Iain Mackintosh, *Architecture, Actor and Audience* (London, 1993) 90; Declan Donnellan and Nick Ormerod, 'Directing, designing and theatre space' in *Making Space for Theatre* ed. R. Mulryne and M. Shewring (Stratford-upon-Avon, 1995) 104–6; William Dudley, 'Designing for spaces' in *ibid.* 97–9.

[18] Members of the Athens Theatre School cited by Shankland in 'Acoustics of Greek theatres' 32.

[19] V. Ziogas cited by A. Bakopoulou-Halls in *Living Greek Theatre* ed. J. M. Walton (Westport, 1987) 262. Shankland explains that the reverberation experienced at the centre would be much harsher if the theatre formed a regular semi-circle.

[20] Vitruvius v.v.5–7. Vitruvius cites 'veteres architecti'. On harmony, his source is Aristoxenus, a pupil of Aristotle.   [21] Plutarch, *Aratus* 23.1–4; *Demetrius* 34.

Plutarch also tells us of a tyrant who was put on trial for his life before the assembly in the theatre in Syracuse. Unable to speak for heckling, the tyrant hurled his cloak into the middle of the auditorium and ran to beat his head against a stone step.[22] It is clear therefore that this speech to the assembly was made from the *orchêstra* and not from the stage. The centre seems the natural position for a democratic orator to assume. The radial lines of the Pnyx converge upon the speaker's platform or just in front. In the extraordinary covered assembly-hall at Megalopolis the speaker's position is central, but somewhat towards the rear, so that he has most of the audience on three sides, but some who are perhaps in office remain behind him. The position is equivalent to that which he would assume in a conventional covered council chamber or in the theatre: the audience embraces him and looks down upon him.[23]

A valuable modern experiment with the spatial arrangements of Epidauros has been conducted at Newcastle, New South Wales. Michael Ewans allowed the *orchêstra* to be used for all the performers in his production of the *Oresteia,* and discovered that 'the further the actor was away from the centre in any direction, the less commanding he became – with the one exception that there was . . . a focus of considerable theatrical power along a line drawn from the centre of the *skênê* doors to the *thymelê* base'.[24] This is precisely in line with Barker's analysis of the proscenium stage. For Barker, the actor standing upstage and facing forwards is strong only when standing on the centre line.[25] More significantly, Ewans' findings in respect of visual focus correlate with the logic of acoustics. Shankland explains:

It is evident from the theatre geometry that the paths of sound travelling from actor to audience are more effective when the actor is near the center or the rear of the orchestra or on the stage (logeion) than when the performer is located near the front or at the extreme side of the orchestra where the sound must propagate over much of the audience at nearly grazing incidence with a resulting high attenuation.[26]

---

[22] Plutarch, *Timoleon* 34. The date is 339 BC Timoleon himself speaks from a carriage which must also have been in the *orchêstra*: *Timoleon* 38.

[23] For sightlines in the assembly-hall, see the plan reproduced in *HGRT* fig. 276. For council chambers see M. H. Hansen and Fischer-Hansen, 'Monumental political architecture in archaic and classical Greek *poleis*' in *From Political Architecture to Stephanus Byzantias: sources for the Greek polis* ed. D. Whitehead (Stuttgart, 1994) 23–90. Hansen and Fischer-Hansen 54–6, 65–71, document a few assembly places in the west of the Greek world that were fully in the round.

[24] Graham Ley and Michael Ewans, 'The orchestra as acting area in Greek tragedy' *Ramus* 14 (1985) 75–84.   [25] *Theatre Games* 148.

[26] 'Acoustics of Greek theatres' 32. Lothar Cremer terms this phenomenon the Békésy effect in 'Different distributions of the audience' in *Auditorium Acoustics* ed. R. Mackenzie (Barking, 1975) 145–59, p. 148.

In other words, the sound is absorbed and muffled if the actor stands within the circle too close to the foot of the auditorium. Visual and acoustical focus are intimately related.

Pickard-Cambridge insisted that the central point of the *orchêstra* could not be a dramatic focus:

> It is hardly necessary to repeat that the altar at which suppliants in various plays made their entreaties is totally distinct from the ritual altar of Dionysus which belonged to the festival, not to the play, and was in the centre of the orchestra; though naturally this may have formed a central point round which the chorus stood or moved in its dances.[27]

His assumption turns upon Christian ideas of sanctity, and ignores the ancient tradition whereby the first actor differentiated himself from the chorus by standing on the sacrificial table in the fields.[28] Rush Rehm, on the other hand, one of the few classical scholars who is also a theatre practitioner, has no doubt that 'the midpoint of the orchestra (however it was shaped) provided the strongest acting area, and we find evidence in the tragedies themselves that the fifth-century playwrights recognized this fact'.[29] Rehm rejects the view that there was any permanent altar at the centre of the *orchêstra*, and it is to the difficult question of the theatrical altar that we must now turn.

The only useful statement from antiquity is Pollux's definition of the *thymelê* as 'either a rostrum or an altar', suggesting that although it was sacred orators or actors could mount it.[30] It would thus resemble in functional terms the 'herald's stone' in the Agora, which could be mounted for the making of proclamations, but had sacrificial victims laid upon it when the archons swore their oaths.[31] Archaeology is more revealing, and indicates that there were four different categories of theatrical altar.

(1) Portable altars, of the kind that we see depicted in vase paintings of comedy. I shall examine these in chapter 9.

(2) Small sacrificial altars at the foot of the auditorium, in the centre, in front of the sacred site which in Athens was reserved for the god Dionysus, and in the imperial period for the deified Hadrian. Such altars are found at Priene, at Cefalu on the island of Kos and at Pergamon, both in the large theatre of Dionysus and in the small theatre in the shrine of Asclepius. In the large theatre

---

[27] *TDA* 131–2.   [28] Pollux iv.123.

[29] *Greek Tragic Theatre* (London, 1992) 36. Rehm sets out his argument at length in 'The staging of suppliant plays' *GRBS* 29 (1988) 263–308.

[30] 'eite bêma ti ousa eite bômos': Pollux iv.123.

[31] See T. L. Shear Jr. 'Isonomous t'Athênas epoiêsatên: the Agora and democracy' in *The Archaeology of Athens and Attica under the Democracy* ed. W. D. E. Coulson *et al.* (Oxford, 1994) 225–48, pp. 242–5.

complex at Pergamon we also find the main sacrificial altar standing between the temple of Dionysus and the *skênê* building.[32]

(3) Sacrificial altars, large enough for the sacrifice of a bull. At Thorikos and Ikarion, we have seen that the deme altar stands on the margins of the acting area, and the god commands a view of both altar and *orchêstra*. At Rhamnous there are sacrificial altars on the right of the performance area and towards the right of the auditorium area. We have noted that at Megalopolis the altar was linked to the theatre by a race-track. At Athens we have seen that the great altar lay in the sanctuary beneath the theatre, in alignment with the *skênê* door. The axial relationship could be likened to that in the shrine of Cybele at Samothrace, where the centre line is orientated upon the front of the 'altar courtyard' surrounding an ancient sacred rock.[33] It was convenient to have the messy and malodorous business of sacrifice kept at a small distance from the place of performance. The business of tragedy was symbolic killing, not real killing. If we exclude cultic auditoria built around altars that stand in their orthodox positions before temples,[34] then we are left with only one possible instance where animal sacrifice may have taken place within the acting area. At Isthmia in the sanctuary of Poseidon there are traces of an altar in front and to the right of the *skênê* door, out of alignment with the rest of the theatre,[35] and we must presume that if this was an altar it pre-dates the theatre.

(4) The *thymelê*. Semantically, the word *thymelê* seems to be associated with the idea of a hearth rather than with a raised altar, and there are no grounds for regarding the *thymelê* at the centre of the *orchêstra* as the base for a raised altar.[36] The archaeological evidence is confined to three Greek examples.[37] At Epidauros a small cylindrical stone (0.7m diameter) is hollowed on the top in

[32] A. von Gerkan *Das Theater von Priene* (Munich, 1921) 26; *Historia* 5 (1931) 623 and 625 fig. 15 (noting also that in P. E. Arias, *Il teatro greco fuori di Atene* (Florence, 1934) 126 fig. 83 the Cefalu altar has been moved to the centre of the *orchêstra*); W. Radt, *Pergamon* (Cologne, 1988) 290; O. Deubner, *Das Asklepeion von Pergamon* (Berlin, 1938) figs. 41–2. There is also an altar base very slightly off-centre in the theatral assembly place at Panionion: Hansen and Fischer-Hansen, 'Monumental political architecture' 68–9. Though these examples are from the east of the Aegean, stone 'J' at Sikyon also looks like an altar base: see the square stone slightly off-centre in *American Journal of Archaeology* 9 (1905) pl.VIII.

[33] Illustrated in *BCH* 80 (1956) 139.

[34] E.g. the sanctuary of Artemis at Sparta illustrated in the *Annual of the British School at Athens* 13 (1906/7) 66, or the Kabirion at Thebes, illustrated by L. Polacco in 'Rites des saisons et drames sacrés chez les grecs' *Cahiers du GITA* 3 (1987) 9–22, p. 15.

[35] E. R. Gebhard, *The Theater at Isthmia* (Chicago, 1973) 13.

[36] A. S. F. Gow, 'On the meaning of the word *thymelê*' *JHS* 32 (1912) 213–38.

[37] Clifford Ashby in 'Where was the altar?' *Theatre Survey* 32 (1991) 3–21 refers to *thymelai* at Argos and Eretria, but has evidently been misled by photographs. I am grateful to him for responding to my enquiry.

a way that suggests a repository for offerings rather than a slot to receive a column.[38] At Aigai a rectangular stone (0.4m × 0.7m) is described by the excavator as an altar base, but the size seems too small, and the tiny hole in the top may rather serve as a precise marker of the centre. The excavator also concluded from the way one rough side was made regular by plastering that the stone must have been ancient and vested with sanctity.[39] Finally, in the huge third-century theatre at Dodona a square stone (0.6m × 0.6m) stands in the centre.[40] The only other relevant example is Eretria, where access from an underground tunnel was effected at the centre point, and we may assume that this exit was normally covered by a prominent structure.[41] These examples seem enough to confirm the general principle that at the focal centre point was a marking stone prominent enough to define the sacredness of the centre but not large enough to interfere with the dramatic action. The stone was sacred, but not so sacred that it could not be moved when the *orchêstra* was repositioned.[42] Such a *thymelê* would have served as the focus for ritual activity: for the circular dance of the dithyramb with the piper at the centre, the pouring of libations, and the purification of the theatre by *periestiarchoi* – 'men who go around the hearth'.[43] At Athens a circular depression in the paved floor looks as if it was designed to support an altar in the Roman period, and probably commemorates the tradition of marking the centre.[44] Claude Calame has ventured the suggestion that the lump of unhewn rock in the famous Pronomos vase, located in the composition to counterbalance the choregic monument, represents the Athenian *thymelê*.[45] The rock is knee-high, roughly cylindrical, and is not protected by taboos for a chorus-man casually rests his foot on it. Calame's theory is attractive because it is hard to see what else the rock could signify in its context.

In very many spheres of Athenian democratic activity we see spatial relationships organized in terms of a fixed centre and a more-or-less circular periphery. Very many plays, as I shall seek to demonstrate, are organized around the

---

[38] A. von Gerkan and W. Müller-Wiener, *Das Theater von Epidauros* (Stuttgart, 1961) 7–8.

[39] Manolis Andronicos in *Vergina* tr. L. Turner (Athens, 1987) 46–9, and *Praktika* (1983) 47 and fig. 2.   [40] *Archaiologikon Deltion* 16 (1960) 20, 26, and pls.4, 6.

[41] See Carleton L. Brownson 'The theatre at Eretria' *American Journal of Archaeology* 7 (1891) 266–80. Slots remain for a square slab or trap-door. The opening is not square to the auditorium so was probably not in itself an architectural feature.

[42] As Rehm notes in 'Staging of suppliant plays' 267. On the fixed location of sacrificial altars, see C. G. Yavis, *Greek Altars: origins and typology* (Saint Louis, 1949) 56; *GR* 87–8. The 'herald's stone' in the Agora seems to have been moved on account of redevelopment.

[43] *DFA* 67.   [44] *TDA* 258.

[45] *The Craft of Poetic Speech in Ancient Greece*, tr. J. Orion (Ithaca, 1995) 133. For the vase see *DFA* 186–7 and fig. 49.

focal point of an altar or tomb, a focus encouraged by the layout of the theatrical space. My first task will be to contextualize the centripetal space of tragedy and demonstrate why the relationship of centre and periphery has such importance in Athens at large.

The cosmos was taken to be geocentric, meaning that the planets rotated about a central earth, and the human race was at the centre of the cosmos. An important shift in geocentric thinking took place in the late fifth century. While the earliest cosmological thinkers considered that the flat earth was in some way rooted or fixed into whatever lay beneath, some fifth-century thinkers such as Parmenides began to conceive of a spherical earth held in equipoise because it was equidistant from the margins of the cosmos.[46] Aristotle accepted the theory of a spherical earth, but refused to relinquish the old principle of absolute parameters, insisting that top and bottom, right and left, front and back still had absolute rather than relative meaning.[47] In Lefebvre's terms, Aristotle did not want to relinquish completely the idea of 'absolute space'. In later chapters I shall examine the extent to which the parameters of above/below, left/right and front/behind retained an absolute rather than relative meaning for fifth-century spectators on the slope of the Athenian Acropolis.

The earliest sixth-century maps of the earth seem to have represented the earth as circular, surrounded by Ocean in the form of an encircling river.[48] Democritus early in the fourth century challenged the circular conception, and argued for a rectangular version of the known inhabited earth, his views reflecting the dominant east–west axis of the Mediterranean. Whether arguing for a circle or a rectangle, ancient cartographers seem to have thought in terms of axes. On the earliest circular maps, it is likely that the axes intersected at Delphi, though some Ionian versions certainly located the centre further to the east. The axial conception allowed the four cardinal points to be associated with four winds and with four races: Indians to the east, Ethiopians to the

---

[46] J.-P. Vernant in *Mythe et pensée chez les grecs* (Paris, 1990) 206 discerns in Anaximander the idea of a spherical cosmos. I follow Furley and Wright in assuming that Anaximander conceived the earth as cylindrical, and that the idea of the sphere emerged with Parmenides: David Furley *Cosmic Problems* (Cambridge, 1989) 14–26; M. R. Wright, *Cosmology in Antiquity* (London, 1995) 20–2. Wright notes that there was also a Pythagorean theory which held that the earth rotated round a central fire, and she has suggested to me that the notion of a central fire derives from that of a hearth.

[47] *On the Heavens* ii.2 and ii.5, cited in G. E. R. Lloyd, *Polarity and Analogy* (Cambridge, 1966) 261.

[48] The circular conception is criticized in Herodotus iv.36 and in Aristotle, *On Meteorology* 362b. A helpful map illustrating Herodotus' Athenocentric conception of the world can be found in Herodotus, *Le storie* Vol. I ed. D. Asheri (Milan, 1989) p. cxxiii.

south, Celts to the west and Scythians to the north.[49] The Greeks organized the world, as they organized the cosmos, by placing themselves at the centre, the point where axes intersect.

Vernant, in his seminal study of Greek space, has shown how Greek cosmology relates to Greek political thinking, and specifically how the idea of a centred earth held in equipoise or suspension relates to ideas of *isonomia* 'political equality'.[50] He also examined the physical space of the *polis*. The vertical dominance of the Acropolis in the pre-democratic city yielded to the level democratic Agora, from which roads radiated out to the peripheral city walls, and to the communities beyond that federated to form the *polis*. While the hierarchical Acropolis was dominated by a single patron, the democratic Agora belonged equally to all the gods. The official centre of Athens was the altar of the twelve gods in the Agora, a symbol of convergence which it is tempting to relate to the idea that Attica once comprised twelve cities.[51] Planners from Cleisthenes to Plato and Aristotle were preoccupied with preserving political balance between those who lived at the centre and those who lived on the periphery. Cleisthenes' system of tribes combated regionalism in Attica by linking demes in the hinterland and in a coastal ring around the city to demes at the core within the city.[52] The statues that emblematized the ten Cleisthenic tribes were located centrally in the Agora, facing the seat of the democratic Council, and to this central point every deme sent its representatives.

Cultic activity was also concerned to draw lines between the centre and the periphery. The great processions out to Eleusis and Brauron linked the Acropolis to the margins of Attica. Celebration of the Dionysia commenced with a procession that brought the statue of the god into the city from outside, in a journey that symbolically represented the god's first arrival from Eleutherae on the Theban border.[53] Whilst the medieval church points the worshipper

---

[49] See W. A. Heidel, *The Frame of the Ancient Greek Maps* (New York, 1937) 1–55; P. Lévêque and P. Vidal-Naquet, *Clisthène l'athénien* (Paris, 1964) 77–83; O. A. W. Dilke, *Greek and Roman Maps* (London, 1985) 22–9.

[50] *Mythe et pensée* 202–37. Vernant's essays were first published in 1965.

[51] For the tradition see R. Martin, *Recherches sur l'agora grecque* (Paris, 1951) 173; Noel Robertson, *Festivals and Legends: the formation of Greek cities in the light of public ritual* (Toronto, 1992) 69.

[52] Lévêque and Vidal-Naquet, *Clisthène* 13–18; Aristotle, *Politics* vii.10. On Plato's *Laws* in relation to the Cleisthenic system, see Vernant, *Mythe et pensée* 257–60.

[53] For the symbolism see M. Detienne, *Dionysos at Large*, tr. A. Goldhammer (Cambridge, Mass., 1989). On the spatial principles behind cult organization, see F. de Polignac, *La Naissance de la cité grecque* (Paris, 1984); R. Schachter, 'Politics, cult and the placing of Greek sanctuaries' in *Le Sanctuaire grec* ed. A. Schachter and J. Bingen (Entretiens Hardt 37, Geneva, 1992) 1–57, esp. p. 33; Robin Osborne, 'Archaeology, the Salaminioi and the politics of sacred space in Archaic Attica' in *Placing the Gods: sanctuaries and sacred space in ancient Greece* ed. S. E. Alcock and R. Osborne (Oxford, 1994) 143–60.

eastwards towards an invisible Heaven or Jerusalem beyond, classical Greek temples are designed to draw the worshipper in towards a statue at the centre, or in earlier times, it seems, to a hearth.[54] Robin Osborne has demonstrated how the design of the Parthenon presumes that the visitor will follow the frieze procession around the building before encountering the goddess within at the centre.[55] While Christian worshippers stand in front of an altar, Greek worshippers stood in a circle round it. Participants in a sacrifice described a circle around the altar in order to demarcate and purify the scene of death. Euripides' Iphigeneia, for example, imagines both her father and herself circling the altar on which she is to die; and in conformity with standard practice Achilles purifies the spot by running around it with barley and water.[56] *Periestiarchoi* performed a similar task in the *orchêstra* of the theatre, using the blood of a piglet.[57]

The word 'focus' to which I keep returning derives from a Latin term for hearth.[58] The ever-burning hearth, figured in the divine scheme as the goddess Hestia, was a powerful symbol in Greek life.[59] Mycenaean houses were centred upon the circular hearth at the centre of the covered *megaron*, illuminated by the vent above. In the democratic period, a brazier remained important as the symbolic centre of the home in rites such as the arrival of the bride, death, and the incorporation of the new-born child in the family, but the architectural centre and focus of the house became the courtyard and the patriarchal shrine of Zeus Herkeios.[60] With the arrival of democracy, the domestic hearth was necessarily marginalized in favour of the communal hearth of the *polis*. In many cities the Council dined in circular buildings with a hearth at the centre, though in Athens when a circular building was erected in the Agora for the communal eating of the Council, the official 'hearth' of the city remained in its archaic location in the ancient *agora* of the pre-classical city.[61] At a symposium the wine passed around the circle of banqueters. Their verbal contributions were placed 'into the middle'.[62] The visual focus at the centre of the

---

[54] Robert Parker, *Miasma* (Oxford, 1983) 167.

[55] 'The viewing and obscuring of the Parthenon frieze' *JHS* 107 (1987) 98–105.

[56] *Iphigeneia in Aulis* 1472, 1479–81, 1568–71; *GR* 56, 83; also Euripides, *Heracles* 926–7.

[57] *DFA* 67.   [58] See G. Nagy, *Greek Mythology and Poetics* (Ithaca, 1990) 160–4.

[59] Vernant is again fundamental: see his essay on Hestia and Hermes in *Mythe et pensée* 156–201. A major source for Vernant is F. Robert, *Thymélè* (Paris, 1939) 276ff.

[60] *GR* 255; on the classical house, see Michael Jameson, 'Private space and the Greek city' in *The Greek City* ed. O. Murray and S. Price (Oxford, 1990) 171–95. On uses of the hearth see also J. Bremmer and H. Roodenburg (eds.), *A Cultural History of Gesture* (Cambridge, 1993) 26.

[61] See Pauline Schmitt Pantel, *La Cité au banquet* (Rome, 1992) 96–7, 145ff.; on the location, 146 n.5, and Robertson, *Festivals and Legends* 31. See also F. Cooper and S. Morris, 'Dining in round buildings' in *Sympotica* ed. O. Murray (Oxford, 1990) 66–85.

[62] For Cleisthenes' banquet see Herodotus vi.129–30. For the significance of the phrase *es meson*, see N. T. Croally, *Euripidean Polemic* (Cambridge, 1994) 165.

gathering was not a hearth but a bowl in which the wine was mixed, and the blending of the wine sacred to Dionysus with a quantity of water can be seen as symbolizing the values of the mid-point.[63] In the theatre the libations must have been poured over the *thymelê*, locating Dionysus god of wine at the symbolic centre. Surrounded by the twelve choral dancers of tragedy, it is also possible to see the *thymelê* as symbolic of Hestia, supplanted by Dionysus to become the thirteenth Olympian, fixed in eternal immobility.[64]

It seems to be a common feature of circular buildings that the space at the centre leads down into the earth. An obvious example is the Tholos at Epidauros that probably housed the serpent of Asclepius. Vernant interprets Hestia not only as the centre point on the horizontal plane but also as a link on the vertical plane between the earth in which the hearth is sunk and the gods above who receive the smoke of the fire. There is a link, Vernant continues, between the idea of a hearth and the idea of an *omphalos* or navel-stone such as one finds at Delphi, for both are associated with centrality and rootedness. The navel at the centre of the body was seen as a kind of root from which new life stems, and Delphi was seen as both hearth and navel of Greece.[65] When Pindar wrote a dithyramb to be danced around an altar in the Athenian Agora, he described the Agora as the *omphalos* of Athens.[66] In the theatre we should not see the *thymelê* as an altar referring upwards so much as a stone rooted in the earth floor, with a potential for emphasizing the chthonic and maternal symbolism of the earth. The *thymelê* reinforces the notion that the floor of the *orchêstra* represents a mid point on the vertical plane, where mortals are caught between the gods of the underworld and the Olympians above.

From the Homeric to the classical period the human body was conceived as a microcosm. Aristotle, for example, describes the heart as both the 'hearth' and the 'acropolis' of the body.[67] The centre of the body was taken to be the seat of thinking and feeling. Platonist dualism which locates personal identity in the head has had such a profound influence upon the Christian tradition that it is hard for modern westerners to escape from thinking in terms of higher and lower emotions, and of mind conflicting with body. In the world of Greek

---

[63] See F. Lissarague, *The Aesthetics of the Greek Banquet*, tr. A. Szegedy-Maszak (Princeton, 1990) 19–46, especially p. 45.

[64] The immobile Hestia is included as one of the twelve gods in Plato, *Phaedrus* 247, but not in the Parthenon frieze. For references to the twelve, see *GR* 125 n.1. Rosemary Wright refers me to the temple of Vesta/Hestia in Rome, where the hearth at the centre of the circle is surrounded by twelve columns symbolizing the twelve Olympians.

[65] See *Mythe et pensée* 179–80; A. Ballabriga, *Le Soleil et le Tartare* (Paris, 1986) 6–15. Clytaemnestra calls Cassandra to the 'central-omphalos hearth' at *Agamemnon* 1056. For the distinction between high altars (*bômoi*) and low chthonic altars (*escharai*), see Yavis, *Greek Altars* 92–3.   [66] *Dithyramb for the Athenians* 3–5.   [67] *Parts of Animals* iii.7–670a.

tragedy, thinking is indisseverable from feeling. Mental sensation is associated with a series of different terms, all of which have a more or less precise physical location in the central region of the body: *cholos* (bile), *phrên* or *phrenes* (usually translated as 'mind' and loosely associated with the diaphragm), *kardia* (heart), *thumos* (notoriously untranslatable, conceived in liquid terms, sometimes rendered as 'will', 'impulse'), *hêpar* (liver), and the generic term covering all of these, *splanchna* (innards). One thinks and feels, in other words, with the centre of one's body. In sacrificial ritual, prophets paid close attention not to the brain but to the *splanchna* at the centre of the animal. In biological thinking, there was a sense of necessary movement from the centre to the periphery and back to the centre. It was assumed that the blood did not circulate around the body, but moved directly out to the veins on the surface and back to the heart.[68]

As I observed at the start of this chapter, the stage/*orchêstra* split correlates with the dualist thinking of the Hellenistic period. The sphere of reason and morality belonged to the actors in the Hellenistic period, whilst physical self-expression belonged to the dancers. In the fifth century, however, the protagonist was not elevated to the status of hero through a raised stage, high and immobilizing buskins and elongated mask, but was of a kind with the chorus. The stage nakedness of the satyr play and comedy threw the emphasis onto the body of the dramatic character, and in tragedy the mask was principally a means of blotting out expression so that the actor had to use his body to transmit visual meaning. The actors of New Comedy who stood on a stage in the Theatre of Dionysus were in shadow, so their masks could be deciphered as keys to personality,[69] but the actors of fifth-century tragedy out in the *orchêstra* were silhouetted by the low, bright, spring sunshine and had to be seen as shapes, as integral bodies rather than faces.

We must be on our guard against the efforts of Polacco, Pöhlmann and others to present us with a pictorial Greek theatre, in which space is structured by means of depth. It is all too easy for the modern eye, familiar with two-dimensional perspectival art, to see the *skênê* door as the point of focus, and the unique position of visual strength. Oliver Taplin, for example, has many valuable things to say about the *skênê* doorway as focus, but does not even consider the *thymelê* in his catalogue of the physical resources of the fifth-century theatre.[70] We are not used to thinking of our universe, our living spaces and

68 See R. B. Onians, *The Origins of European Thought about the Body, the Mind, the Soul, Time and Fate* (Cambridge, 1951); J.-L. Durand in *La Cuisine du sacrifice en pays grec* ed. M. Detienne and J.-P. Vernant (Paris, 1979) 139ff.; W. G. Thalmann, 'Aeschylus' psychology of the emotions' *American Journal of Philology* 107 (1986) 489–511; Ruth Padel, *In and Out of the Mind* (Princeton, 1992) 12ff.   69 See Wiles, *The Masks of Menander*.   70 *SA* 434–51.

our bodies in terms of a centre point. Yet the relationship of centre and periphery was the key to democratic Greek thinking about space, and the theatre must be seen as one democratic spatial practice among many. The empirical observations of modern performers working in a circular space are evidence of trans-cultural laws of perception that come into play once a culture-specific disposition of the theatrical space has been made.

In many Greek tragedies it is plain that the visual focus is an altar or a tomb.[71] An altar must be at the strongest point in numerous 'suppliant' plays: for example, the altar of the assembled gods in Aeschylus' *Suppliants*, of the two goddesses in Euripides' *Suppliants*, of Thetis in *Andromache*, of Zeus Agoraios in *The Children of Heracles* and Zeus the Saviour in *Heracles*.[72] Suppliants in these plays are the still focus of attention while the action around them decides their fate. In Aeschylus' *Niobe* the static visual focus throughout the play seems to have been Niobe sitting on the tomb of her children.[73] Euripides' *Helen* commenced in the same way with the heroine sitting on a tomb. In Aristophanes' parody of Euripides' play, a woman who fails to recognize that a theatrical reenactment is being played out curses Euripides (playing the role of Helen) for 'presuming to call the altar a tomb'.[74] Tombs are different from altars but often have a functional similarity.[75] An altar was the normal focus for choral dancing,[76] as for example in the Thesmophoria, and a tomb in the theatre could conveniently serve the same purpose. In *The Libation Bearers*, after libations have been poured, the *kommos* (lament) is danced around a tomb that is sacred, immobile and the focus of attention. We should not infer from Aristophanes' joke that the permanent *thymelê* sufficed as a sign for Helen's tomb, for in itself it was much too small.

Aeschylus' *Persians* provides us with one of our most difficult staging problems when the ghost of Darius is resurrected from his tomb in the visual climax of the play. Taplin has a good survey of the evidence, but maintains that the tomb could not be in the centre of the *orchêstra* where it would be 'an intoler-

---

[71] Arnott, *Greek Scenic Conventions* 46–51 provides a useful check-list of altars and tombs. There is some up-dating of Arnott in J. P. Poe, 'The altar in the fifth century theater' *Classical Antiquity* 8 (1989) 116–39.

[72] Rehm 'Staging of suppliant plays' (n.29 above) is fundamental.

[73] The papyrus fragment speaks of her sitting on the tomb for three days: D. L. Page, *Select Papyri*, Vol. III (Cambridge, Mass., 1970) 8; cf. Aristophanes, *Frogs* 912.

[74] *Women at the Thesmophoria* 888. The line plays on *Libation Bearers* 106, where Aeschylus' chorus promised to honour the tomb of Agamemnon as an altar, and is comic in visual terms because the altar of the Thesmophorian goddesses is brought into use as the tomb of the Egyptian king.

[75] For hero-tombs as altars see *GR* 194; Rehm, 'Staging of suppliant plays' 265 n.6.

[76] See Claude Calame *Les Choeurs de jeunes filles en Grèce archaïque* (Rome, 1977) Vol. I, and Chapter 4 below.

able obstruction', and relegates it to the edge.[77] Yet the Queen has poured libations into the earth and Darius states that he has ascended from the underworld, so the tomb should be associated symbolically and visually with the earth floor of the *orchêstra*, not with a marginal rock or raised stage. The area of the *thymelê*, as we have noted, has appropriate vertical connotations. The ghost needs to inhabit a sacred space that lends weight to his oracular prescriptions. In performance terms the climax of the play demands use of the strongest point. Taplin is wrong to think that in a space as large as the ancient *orchêstra* a tomb would be a distraction, for there can be no problem of sightlines when the audience looks down from above. The centre-point is given no other cultic associations, prior to the tomb scene, and a chariot is the major spectacular feature, leaving the structure in the centre to be identified as Darius' tomb at the due moment. The problem, of course, is that, in the absence of a tunnel as at Eretria, and assuming that there was no third actor who could be concealed inside a tomb, Darius needs somehow to enter. Since he announces upon his entry that he *saw* his wife near the tomb (684), it is perhaps easiest to conclude that he arrived as a disembodied spirit, like the ghost in *Hecuba*, and ascended to the *orchêstra* from the terrace behind.[78]

In the last part of this chapter I shall take a brief overview of some plays by Euripides and Aeschylus in order to suggest how the two strongest points of the performance space, the *skênê* door and the centre point of the *orchêstra*, were articulated in performance. The action of *Hippolytus* is organized around two statues. The statue of Aphrodite must be placed by the door, for characters greet it as they make their exit into the *skênê*.[79] The statue of Artemis must be out in the open, and a central position would have allowed it to be the focus of attention in the first scene when Hippolytus crowns it with a garland, to remain thereafter as a silent threat anticipating the goddess' appearance *in propria persona*. Artemis haunts both the forests and the salt-flats, so there is no logic in placing her at one of the two *eisodoi* which represent the two directions of shore and forest from which characters enter. It is the spatial opposition of inside and outside that distinguishes the two goddesses. Aphrodite is associated with the bedchamber, Artemis with the open spaces. In terms of the

---

[77] *SA* 117, opposing the view of Wilamowitz; discussion 116–19, 447–8. H. D. Broadhead in the standard critical edition (Cambridge, 1960) p. xliv takes the same view, though noting (n.4) the older view of Paley and Ridgway that the *thymelê* was used. We may compare the ritualist G. Gilbert Murray who opts for the centre in *Aeschylus* (Oxford, 1940) 55 with the rationalist Pickard-Cambridge who opts for the margins: *TDA* 35.

[78] In a vase painting of slightly earlier date which seems to show a comparable scene, the figure stands behind the tomb: E. Simon *The Ancient Theatre*, tr. C. E. Vafopolou-Richardson (London, 1982) 8–9 and pl.2; further discussions in *NTDWD* 52–4; *COAD* 57. On *Hecuba*, see p. 182 below.   [79] W. S. Barrett, *Euripides: Hippolytos* (Oxford, 1964) 154.

body as microcosm, Aphrodite is associated with sexual entry, hence the door, Artemis with the sealed womb. Aphrodite's position by the house associates her with the pleasures of civilization, whilst a position at the *thymelê* associated with the earth and the umbilicus would help to associate Artemis with the fertility of nature and with the pain of childbirth (161ff.). The double chaste/fertile nature of Artemis seems paradoxical to the modern mind, but makes sense when we attune ourselves to the Greek structuring of space. The relationship of the public space of the *orchêstra* to the private space of the *skênê* does not in this play define a male/female opposition so much as two different aspects of womanhood.

The setting of Euripides' *Ion* is the temple of Apollo at Delphi, the symbolic centre of Greece. Despite detailed visual descriptions offered by the chorus, it is impossible to make sense of the spatial arrangements of the play in terms of perspectival realism, for the use of space is too fluid. The *skênê* doorway conflates the steps on the east side of the real Delphic temple with the door into the sanctum twenty metres further back, creating a single schematic point of entry into the temple. Ion's job is to sweep the '*thymelê*' of Apollo, and the stage *thymelê* might here be used to suggest the great altar of Apollo before the east door. The climax of the play is a scene where Ion confronts his mother and comes to the verge of killing her. At this point in the play there is a strong implication that the action is taking place inside the inner sanctum or *adyton* (1309) beside the sacred *omphalos*, the navel-stone known also as Python's tomb.[80] Behind this scene lies a ritual archetype, for according to Delphic myth the boy Apollo shot his mother's enemy, the chthonic Python, at Delphi.[81] Emblematically Ion's bow associates him with Apollo, and it is a logical inference that Ion aims his bow at his mother just as earlier he aimed it at sacred birds.[82] The link between Ion's mother and the chthonic Python is established by a sequence of serpentine allusions: she is descended from Athenian serpent-kings, has a Gorgon's poison in her amulet, and is insulted by Ion as a viper (1262–3). The symbolism of the scene becomes clearer when we imagine it sited by the *thymelê* in the *orchêstra*. The name Delphi means 'wombs', and the Delphic *omphalos* was regarded as the umbilicus of the world. The playing of

---

[80] See R. P. Winnington-Ingram, 'The Delphic temple in Greek tragedy' in *Miscellanea tragica in honorem J. C. Kamerbeek* ed. J. M. Bremer, S. L. Radt, and C. J. Ruijgh (Amsterdam, 1976) 29–48; also G. Roux in 'Trésors, temples, tholos' in *Temples et sanctuaires* (Lyons, 1984) 166.

[81] The shooting was illustrated on fifth-century coins – *LIMC* 'Apollo' 998, 1000 – and in sculpture – Pliny, *Natural History* 34.59. For ritual commemoration see Joseph Fontenrose, *Python* (Berkeley, 1959) 455; for the Python's tomb, 374, 457.

[82] Taplin in *GTA* 137 rejects the bow on the grounds of psychological plausibility, and the doctrine of 'significant action' (see p. 5 above). He fails to consider the mythic dimension, or the dramaturgical question of why Euripides troubled to establish the bow in the first place.

this scene at the *thymelê/omphalos* of the theatre clarifies the latent structure of myth and ritual beneath the manifest tragicomedy of mistaken identity, evoking an ancient confrontation between patriarchal Olympian forces represented by Apollo and chthonic matriarchal forces represented by the Python. Theatrical space is not marshalled in order to allow the audience to conjure up a single vista in Delphi, but in order to evoke the symbolism of Delphic space. We shall see in the next chapter how the choreography of the opening chorus reinforces this symbolic dimension.

In relation to *Prometheus Bound*, Jean Davison observes that 'the outer limits of geographic description serve as a directional device by which the Greeks recognize their centrality in the Mediterranean world'.[83] We must ask ourselves, therefore, where in the microcosm of the *orchêstra* was the immobile figure of Prometheus: in the centre or on the margins? If Prometheus was placed against the *skênê* wall, which would in this case signify the wall of a ravine, the actor could conveniently be withdrawn at the end on the *eccyclêma*.[84] The evidence of the text, however, seems rather to favour the centre, since Prometheus does not seem to have a view of the *eisodoi*. He hears but does not see the arrivals of the chorus and Io, and does not remark upon the arrival of Oceanus. Hermes is noticed rather abruptly, as if he had entered to eavesdrop.[85] A central position for Prometheus is appropriate since, although imprisoned on the northern margins of the world, he is visited by Oceanus whose nature it is to circuit the world (138), and who may properly, therefore, pass silently behind Prometheus. The common assumption that Oceanus is flown in on the crane above Prometheus is a spatial absurdity, for oceans do not inhabit the air above like Olympian gods but circulate in the void around the earth. One might add that Oceanus' opening anapaests do not suggest the rhythm of flying, and that birds which really fly do not need four legs (395).[86] A central position for Prometheus lends emphasis to the cyclicity of Io's journey, which Prometheus describes at length: having come north via the Adriatic, Io will turn to the east and then head south in a vast circuit that takes her around the Black Sea and Mediterranean to the Nile, whence her descendants will return to Argos. When

---

[83] 'Myth and the periphery' in *Myth and the Polis* ed. Dora C. Pozzi and John M. Wickersham (Ithaca, 1991) 58.

[84] For the critical debate, see SA 273–4, and Suzanne Saïd, *Sophiste et tyran, ou le problème du 'Prométhée enchaîné'* (Paris, 1985) 46–63. Taplin rejects the *eccyclêma* on aesthetic grounds. Prometheus is placed in the centre by John Davidson in '*Prometheus Vinctus* on the Athenian stage' *Greece and Rome* 41 (1994) 33–40.

[85] See SA 268–9 on the 'technical anomalies' of this mid-scene entry.

[86] SA 260–2 imagines a crane, but dismisses the scene as vacuous and the play as non-Aeschylean. George Thomson in his edition (Cambridge, 1932) 150 more plausibly suggests wheels. I follow Thomson 142–4 in assuming that the chorus entered dancing.

Oceanus arrives on his winged steed, his opening words name Prometheus as his *terma* (284), like a boundary-stone to be circuited at the end of a chariot-race.[87] The stadium seems to be a visual metaphor that makes sense of Prometheus' centred position in the theatre. He is pinned to a boundary stone that is marginal in respect of the whole stadium but central in respect of the semi-circle at one end.

In the *Oresteia*, we can map out in some detail an oscillation between the two strong points of the acting space. In the first two plays we see a marked shift of focus from the centre of the *orchêstra* to the *skênê* door, while the third play sees a reverse movement from the *skênê* to the public space of the *orchêstra*. The start of *Agamemnon* is set in the public space of the city. The choreographic focus of the first and longest ode is logically an altar. Calchas interprets the dead hare as though officiating at a sacrifice, and in the climax Iphigeneia is sacrificed like an animal. A *thymelê* or central altar seems an obvious visual reference point if the dancers are to succeed in fixing the audience's attention upon the scenes they describe. In the second half of the play the focus shifts from *orchêstra* to door. Agamemnon walks ceremoniously into his palace, and Cassandra follows him through a door identified as the gateway to Hades (1291). The interior world of the house is finally opened up, the sacrificial victims are displayed, and a woman takes control of the public space of the *orchêstra*.

In *The Libation Bearers*, the focus of the first part of the play is a marker representing the pyre, altar, gravestone and burial mound of Agamemnon. Orestes, Electra and the chorus call at length upon Agamemnon who lies beneath the ground, and it is an obvious inference that the strongest point within the performance space, the *orchêstra* centre, was used.[88] If the centre was linked to Agamemnon in the first play as the site of Iphigeneia's death, then use of the same position for the tomb would have helped the audience to question the eulogizing of Agamemnon in *The Libation Bearers*. In the second half of the play the focus shifts to the door, and Orestes like Cassandra has difficulty in passing through it. The *skênê* opens, and a pair of lovers are again revealed within.[89] Orestes must move away from the *skênê* into the public space

---

[87] The 'race' motif would be particularly important if the trilogy indeed ended with the institution of a torch race: see R. Winnington-Ingram, *Studies in Aeschylus* (Cambridge, 1983) 188–9.

[88] Garvie's Oxford edition (Oxford, 1986) follows Pickard-Cambridge in assuming that the *thymelê* cannot be incorporated in the play. Sidgwick, in his edition of the play (Oxford, 1884) 47 assumed that the *thymelê* was used for the tomb; so too Karl Reinhardt *Aischylos als Regisseur und Theologe* (Bern, 1949) 110–11; J. C. Hogan in *A Commentary on the Complete Greek Tragedies: Aeschylus* (Chicago, 1984) 106; Bowen's edition of *The Libation Bearers* (Bristol, 1986) 27; Michael Ewans' Everyman edition of *The Oresteia* (London, 1995) 162, influenced by his production.   [89] *GTA* 125–6. The 'mirror scene' is one of Taplin's most fertile concepts.

of the *orchêstra* when he orders the chorus to stand round him in a circle and display the net (983). The image of encirclement suggests that Orestes has returned to the centre, so identifying himself with his father.

In the *Eumenides* the initial focus is the door of the Delphic temple, but in the body of the play the focus is the statue of Athene located in the *orchêstra* to denote the public space of Athens.[90] At the start of the play, Aeschylus justifies the presence of a statue of Athene in the *orchêstra* by having the Priestess refer to the presence of Pallas Pronaia – 'Athene before-the-temple' (21). When the *skênê* opens, the tableau displays not two bloodstained lovers but Orestes embracing a white blood-stained *omphalos*. Orestes goes out of the acting area, which shows that he has left Delphi, and returns to embrace the statue in the *orchêstra*. The chorus of Furies apparently join hands (307) in order to sing their 'binding song'. The idea of binding in the refrain implies encirclement, and the idea of an altar is implicit when the Furies sing of Orestes as a sacrificial victim (*tethumenôi*). Orestes effectively becomes a second Iphigeneia. The action mirrors the ending of *The Libation Bearers*, where Orestes perceived the black-clad chorus around him as Furies. The encirclement of a sacred space at the centre of the *orchêstra* is a motif repeated through the trilogy.

I have suggested that the statue of Athene stands at the centre of the *orchêstra*, and is used to identify the scene as Athens. Four different Athenian spaces merge into one: the Acropolis, the archaic *agora*, the new Agora and the Areopagus. Overtly, the setting is in front of the rock where the Areopagite Council sat, and where there stood an altar supposedly dedicated to Athene by Orestes upon his acquittal.[91] However, Athene addresses the jury as the 'people of Attica' (681), and they function more like common Athenian dicasts in the Agora than like Areopagites.[92] After the trial Zeus Agoraios is said to have triumphed (973). Orestes is three times said to have taken refuge at Athene's 'hearth' (440, 577, 669), a term which evokes the hearth of Athens located in the archaic *agora* east of the Acropolis.[93] Finally, when Orestes speaks of coming to the 'house and statue' of Athene (242), the obvious reference is to the temple of Athene Polias on the Acropolis where the ancient statue was

---

[90] *SA* 386 n.1 argues sensibly that 'the Erinyes surely dance *round* Orestes . . . This is evidence, though of necessity inconclusive, that the statue was somewhere in the *orchêstra*.' *TDA* 44, Sommerstein, *Aeschylus: Eumenides* 123, and Scullion, 'Athenian Stage' 117–18, take the literalistic view that the statue should be adjacent to the *skênê*, so that it can be understood as the real statue of Athene within her temple on the Acropolis. Rush Rehm misses the house/*orchêstra* dichotomy when he argues that the same aniconic marker in the centre of the *orchêstra* serves for both *omphalos* and statue of Athene: 'Staging of suppliant plays' 290–301.

[91] Pausanias i.28.5. For visual representations, see A. J. N. W. Prag, *The Oresteia: iconographic and narrative tradition* (Warminster, 1985) 49.   [92] See Sommerstein's edition pp. 16–17.

[93] Pantel, *La Cité au banquet* 146 n.5.

housed.[94] Aeschylus thus uses the statue of Athene to create a syncretic Athens in which aristocratic, political and religious centres are fused. The Athens created within the theatrical space is of a symbolic rather than illusionary nature.

The spatial opposition of *orchêstra* centre and *skênê* door articulates a conflict that is, in large measure, a conflict of male and female. The altar in *Agamemnon* is sited in a male-dominated public space. The Herald and Agamemnon greet male gods when they arrive, and the male chorus are preoccupied with Zeus. The house, however, is controlled by Clytaemnestra, and is the domain of the woman. This pattern is repeated in *The Libation Bearers*, where the *orchêstra* is dominated by Agamemnon's tomb, and Clytaemnestra still controls the house. In the third play the situation is more complex. The interior space of the temple, although dedicated to Apollo, is occupied by the female chorus, who reclaim a space that belonged to them in pre-Olympian times.[95] The public exterior space is dominated by Athene, who as a motherless warrior reconciles oppositions that have seemed absolute in the first two plays. The gendering of space in this way is typical of fifth-century Greek thinking. The woman is associated with enclosed space in accordance with her sexuality (enclosed genitalia), her reproductive functions (the enclosing womb) and her economic role (within the *oikos*, the home), while the male is associated with the public space where, according to democratic ideology, his major role lay.[96] When the patriarchal and monarchical power of Agamemnon at the centre is replaced by the sexually ambivalent and democratic power of Athene, the cycle of killing is halted. The centre is the point of equilibrium around which male and female, Olympian and chthonian, individualist and communal forces finally balance themselves. The movement of the action corresponds with that of democracy – away from the private towards the public, away from a society based on the *oikos* towards a society which put civic identity first, away from the enclosed acropolis to the open *agora*.

Although the spatial coding which I have outlined is culturally specific, the exigencies of focus relate to the physiology of perception. There is much to be

---

[94] *SA* 390.

[95] The Priestess describes how Apollo succeeded a trio of goddesses as patron of Delphi, and this female claim upon Delphi was an innovation: see C. Sourvinou-Inwood, *Reading Greek Culture: texts and images, rituals and myths* (Oxford, 1991) 217–43.

[96] Vernant, *Mythe et pensée* 182–6; Hanna Scolnikov, *Women's Theatrical Space* (Cambridge, 1994) 11–28; Eva C. Keuls, *The Reign of the Phallus* (New York, 1985) 93–7; Camille Paglia, *Sexual Personae* (Harmondsworth, 1992) 26ff.; H. Lefebvre, *The Production of Space*, tr. D. Nicholson-Smith (Oxford, 1991) 247–8. See chapter 7 below. For qualifications to the argument about women's exclusion from public spaces, see P. E. Easterling, 'Women in tragic space' *BICS* 34 (1988) 15–26.

learned in this respect from modern productions of Greek tragedy where Greek spatial forms are replicated, particularly when there is sensitivity to the political basis of the form. Peter Stein's production of *The Oresteia*, presented in an Edinburgh ice rink in 1994,[97] is exemplary in these respects, and seems worth documenting in order to conclude this chapter. A rough circle was defined by the horseshoe auditorium (constructed perforce out of straight blocks of seating) and a shallow stage served to emphasize the *skênê* door at the head of some steps. At the start, a table in the centre of the *orchêstra* evoked Thyestes' feast. The chorus used no mime, and there was thus no occasion to conjure an altar for Iphigeneia. The central table was replaced by Agamemnon's chariot, and the line of strength between *skênê* and centre was used for the line of red fabrics, allowing Agamemnon and Clytaemnestra to occupy the two strongest points of the space at the start of their great confrontation. In the second play, a raked marble slab in the centre was used for the tomb, and the chorus danced in a circle round it. In the second half the lighting dimmed on the tomb, allowing Orestes and Clytaemnestra to confront each other in front of the *skênê*, though tension between the two foci was maintained when Orestes referred to his father's curse by gesturing at the tomb. An *eccyclêma* brought on the Furies and the Delphic *omphalos* in the *Eumenides*, whilst to represent Athens an emblem of Athene was set up on top of a flat square base in the centre of the *orchêstra*. In a bold piece of direction, the *skênê* was then removed to signify the arrival of the play in a world that was both public and contemporary. In his final images, Stein reverted to a vertical organization of space, with an upper level becoming the space of the Olympians and Athenians, and a lower level the space of the Furies. We see in this production how a modern director can continue to use the power of the centre, and the articulation of *orchêstra* and *skênê* in order to structure the action.

The historian of ancient theatre often seems to be trapped in a closed circle, claiming objectivity in order to justify contingent, historically conditioned tastes. Webster, for example, clearly has a taste for stage machinery, and Taplin a distaste, a difference which probably reflects Taplin's exposure to the minimalist theatre of the sixties. To pay rigorous attention to practicalities is a necessary but not a sufficient condition for analysis, because common sense is always in the end historically conditioned. Questions of practicality have a habit of merging into questions of interpretation. Can Athene fly in on a chariot? Can the same door represent two places sequentially? Does left carry

[97] The production was originally mounted with a German cast at the Berlin Schaubühne in 1980. It was reworked with a Russian cast in 1993/4, and presented at the Murrayfield Ice Rink in August 1994.

the same significance as right? What is true of literary critics is no less true of archaeologists. What one generation *knows for a fact* or *knows from common sense* is doubted by the next: the stage, the sacrificial altar in the centre, the circular auditorium. Archaeologists, like literary critics, propose a *schema* to which the data correspond, and can never simply report what is there – because *what is there* can only be perceived in terms of *schemata*.

The structuralist methodology which I have adopted in this book will at the very least demonstrate that a closed hermeneutic circle exists. My object, however, is in some measure to break out of the circle. My premiss is that any spatial arrangement in the theatre is socially conditioned, so we must examine spatial relationships in their historical specificity. We have first to search for the outlines of a specifically Athenian, democratic spatial practice. We have then to look at the Athenian theatre space as a totality and see how the triad of actors, chorus and audience are spatially related, before turning to local detail, the working of specific plays at specific moments. Theatre space will be seen in this book as a set of parameters, and our task will be to analyse these parameters. I shall not ask atomist questions such as 'When does she enter?', or 'Where is the altar?', or 'How does the *skênê* evoke Delphi?', but structuralist questions such as: 'What is the relationship of door to altar? . . . of Delphi to Athens? . . . of the door in this play to the door in that?' One cannot reconstruct the staging of the *Oresteia* by asking: 'What is the most practical way to bring on the Delphic *omphalos*?' One has to begin by exploring the relationship of building and hearthstone in Greek spatial practices and representations of space, in the architecture of the theatre, and in the patterning of the trilogy, before looking at an isolated theatrical moment. I have begun in this chapter by analysing the parameters of centre point and periphery, *thymelê* and doorway, open space and closed, because these spatial oppositions stem directly from the archaeological conclusion that the acting space was unitary and more-or-less rounded. Before proceeding to the other major parameters, we have first to examine the principal tool at the dramatist's disposal for articulating the performance space, namely choreography.

CHAPTER 4

༄

The mimetic action of the chorus

Within the architectural space of the Theatre of Dionysus, the most important spatial relationship is that of actor and chorus. Both shared the same acting space, and there was no 'low stage' removing the chorus from the audience's field of vision at times when it took no part in the dialogue. The reader of a Greek tragedy can all too easily forget that the chorus is present. The reader of a tragedy in translation is in a particularly parlous position because the choral odes with their dense metaphors and mythic allusions often appear impenetrable by comparison with the dialogue, and it is easy to slide across the words. The fifth-century spectator was never able to forget the presence of twelve or at some points fifteen bodies placed in some kind of space relationship to the actors.

The terms in which Plato satirizes tragic performance are revealing:

In our part of the world [i.e. Athens] what happens is pretty much the same as in every *polis*. After the government has made a public sacrifice, there comes a chorus, not one group but a host of choruses. These place themselves not far from the altars, often right next to them, where over the offerings they emit complete blasphemies: speeches, rhythms and tunes in the form of lamentation. Whichever has instant success in drawing tears from the *polis* that is making sacrifice wins the prize.[1]

Although competition and choral dancing were features of many other festivals, Plato alludes to tragedy here because of the emotions that the chorus generates, and an apparent disrespect for the gods. He describes tragedy as it formally and traditionally was, a contest of choruses on the occasion of a sacrifice to Dionysus, held in the precinct of the god. Plato, unlike Aristotle, grew up in Athens and experienced fifth-century drama. He conceives tragedy as an event rather than a text. He would have danced publicly in choruses, albeit not necessarily in tragedy, and would have appreciated the skill and stamina of his peers who danced the chorus in the four successive plays of a tetralogy. He witnessed the lavish expenditure of the *chorêgos* upon the chorus, upon golden

---

[1] *Laws* 800.

crowns and victory celebrations.[2] Such experiences, far removed from the experience of reading texts, would have shaped his perception of Athenian tragedy as in the first instance a choral mode.

Greek dance was regarded as mimetic, rather than as a set of muscular extensions. The idea that dance is a form of imitation was rooted in cult, which required dancers to enact (for example) movement through the Cretan labyrinth, or the movements of Athena after her birth in full armour.[3] Plato states that composers, audiences and actors would agree without exception that 'music' (i.e. anything in the province of the Muses) is a matter of 'imitation'.[4] In *The Laws* he speaks of music imitating brave men and cowards, and of rhythms that portray women and slaves. Bacchic dancing is the 'imitation' of nymphs, Pans, Sileni and satyrs.[5] This representational aspect of Greek dance is alien to the modern mind, which tends to see dance aspiring either to the primitive Wagnerian *Gesamtkunstwerk* or to a modernism that prefers to be abstract and self-referential.[6] It is perhaps this modern conception of dance that allows one modern authority to dismiss choral odes as 'wenig mimetisch' 'scarcely mimetic'.[7]

In order to visualize the performance of a Greek tragedy, we need to confront the issue of mimetic 'imitation' during a choral ode. The question of what the chorus *does* has been an embarrassment for most modern critics. We have seen how Taplin marginalizes the chorus in favour of the actors, sliding from 'I don't know' to 'it doesn't matter'. Influenced by Taplin, C. P. Gardiner attempts to salvage the chorus by endowing it with a 'character', and she eliminates much choral dancing on the grounds that it is psychologically implausible.[8] A more literary approach disposes of the problem by regarding the chorus as disembodied singers rather than an organic part of the dramatic action. R. W. B. Burton, in his monograph on the Sophoclean chorus, sets up a distinction between two choral functions, singing and acting: 'In its role as singers the chorus is distinct from the actors. In the Greek theatre this distinction was marked visually by the dance movements which accompanied its songs and by the fact that it occupied a different part of the acting area.'[9] For Burton, movement is by implication subordinate to the language which it 'accompanied'. At the same time the chorus is subordinate to the actors, occu-

[2] Agathon's celebrations with the chorus after his first victory are mentioned in the *Symposium* 173a. On expenditure, see *DFA* 77.   [3] *GR* 102.   [4] *Laws* 668.
[5] *Laws* 655, 669, 815.
[6] See Marshall Cohen, 'Primitivism, modernism, and dance theory' in *What is Dance?* ed. R. Copeland and M. Cohen (Oxford, 1983) 161–78.
[7] Jürgen Rode, 'Das Chorlied' in *Die Bauformen der griechischen Tragödie* ed. Walter Jens (Munich, 1971) 85–116, p. 113.   [8] *The Sophoclean Chorus* (Iowa, 1987) 7.
[9] R. W. B. Burton, *The Chorus in Sophocles' Tragedies* (Oxford, 1980) 3.

pying a separate space rather like the instrumentalists in an opera or ballet. Dancing in this view helps to isolate the chorus from what is conceived as the real world of the play.

T. B. L. Webster in his study of the chorus attempts to correlate the persistence of particular dance movements in iconographic records with the persistence of particular metres in poetry. Tragedy is shown to have drawn upon a series of ancient dance forms. Subsequently, Webster declares, 'a later poet can play considerable tricks with the rhythm of the words without upsetting the rhythm of the dance'.[10] Dance remains the poor relation, for the dance is fixed while language is open to change and renewal. Webster's wife and colleague, A. M. Dale, allows more subtlety to the dance, which she sees as 'an aid to the spectators and a pictorial clarification'. She compares the relatively simple rhythms of sung lyric with the complex metres of danced choral lyric and suggests that this complexity 'with its resolutions, contractions and shifting rhythms, was first made possible by the interpretative power of dance'.[11] Although language is inspired by dance, Dale still gives primacy to language as something which dance 'interprets'. The careful reader has leisure to absorb the rhythms, and thus does not in the end need to see those rhythms clarified visually. Building on the work of Webster and Dale, William C. Scott has demonstrated how the repetition of metrical patterns in the *Oresteia* points the audience towards patterns of action and imagery. The length of the *Oresteia* allows the modern reader a unique glimpse of how a particular metre would evoke not only a mood but also a tissue of associations. Like Dale but unlike Webster, Scott allows that a metrical variant (for example, an iambic metron of short-long-short-long resolved to short-short-short-short-long) would be reflected in the choreography.[12] The primacy of language over choreography was rejected by H. D. F. Kitto, who, in an important essay on dance, argued that there was scope for a given metre to be danced in duple or triple time according to dramatic context.[13]

Lillian Lawler, Gould and Lewis, and John J. Winkler based their attempts to visualize the dance upon statements from late antiquity to the effect that the dance of tragedy was rectangular,[14] in contrast to the dance of the dithyramb

---

[10] T. B. L. Webster, *The Greek Chorus* (London, 1970) 201. The fullest attempt to codify Greek dance movements on the basis of iconography was made by Maurice Emmanuel in *La Danse grecque antique d'après les monuments figurés* (reprint: Geneva, 1987).

[11] A. M. Dale *Collected Papers* (Cambridge, 1969) 164, and *The Lyric Metres of Greek Tragedy* (Cambridge, 1968) 2.

[12] William C. Scott, *Musical Design in Aeschylean Theatre* (Hanover, N.H., 1984) 26–7.

[13] 'The dance in Greek tragedy' *JHS* 75 (1955) 36–41.

[14] Lillian B. Lawler *The Dance in Ancient Greece* (London, 1964) 82–5; *DFA* 239–42; 'The ephebes' song: *tragōidia* and *polis*' *NTDWD* 20–62, 50ff. Texts by Photius and Pollux in *COAD* 362, 394.

which was always circular. This evidence has to be treated with great circumspection. Our most detailed information comes from Pollux, whose account of tragedy relates elsewhere to Hellenistic practice, and all our other sources are late ones. Choral dancing must have undergone profound changes with the separation of actors from chorus in the Hellenistic period, a separation which caused the choral ode to become a mere interlude in the action. Plato in *The Laws* sees dance as the basis of education because dance traditionally played such an important part in Greek culture. In the Great Dionysia, one festival among many, 500 boys and 500 men danced in the dithyramb, at least 36 young men danced in tragedy, and 120 men in comedy, while many more danced in the procession. Every significant public and private event in Greece was celebrated by choral dances, whether rigorously traditional, improvised or like a Pindaric victory ode commissioned for the occasion.[15] Tragedy achieved its effects by drawing upon a rich cultural vocabulary of dance forms, such as the paean, the lament, the war-dance, or the initiation dance, and it allowed the dramatic context to give those dances a changed and often inverted meaning.[16] The importance of a received vocabulary is demonstrated by Webster and Scott in respect of metrics, and the same principle applies all the more strongly to movement.

Choral song, dance and music were, according to the traditions of the fifth century, a *Gestalt*, and none existed in isolation.[17] The dance, we are told, should not stray beyond the metre of the words, whilst the words should contain nothing that is not expressed in dance.[18] In respect of the acoustical component, Dale argues that verse is merely 'the incomplete record of a single creation, Song'.[19] Greek verse was based upon length rather than stress, and complex metres had to be sung in order that their time-values should be intelligible, while simpler metres were chanted to the accompaniment of the pipes. Only the very simplest metres, such as the iambic trimeter, could be rendered in speech. The rhythm was embodied in the words and could not be changed by a different tune or vocal delivery. The words created or echoed the rhythm

---

[15] As Helen Bacon observes in 'The chorus in Greek life and drama' *Arion* 3 (1995) 6–24, p. 15. For a cultural overview see John Herington, *Poetry into Drama* (Berkeley, 1985); Stephen H. Lonsdale, *Dance and Ritual Play in Greek Religion* (Baltimore, 1993).

[16] See for example Ian Rutherford, 'The tragic paean' *Arion* 3 (1995) 112–35; also Peter Wilson and Oliver Taplin, 'The "aetiology" of tragedy in the *Oresteia*' *Proceedings of the Cambridge Philological Society* 37 (1993) 169–80, an essay which marks a significant shift away from Taplin's hermetic view of tragedy. For the issues in a broader context, see P. E. Easterling, 'Tragedy and ritual' *Metis* 3.2 (1988) 87–109.

[17] Kitto cites Aristoxenus as the best authority for what he terms a 'triple partnership': 'Dance in Greek tragedy' 36.

[18] Students of Damon (later fifth century) cited in Athenaeus 628: *COAD* 366.

[19] *Collected Papers* 166.

of the dance without mediation, for there was no external percussion to create the beat.[20] The piper was not a leader but an accompanist, creating an extra dimension of harmony – a point made clear in a satyr play where the chorus of satyrs complain to Dionysus: 'It is song that the Muse made queen. Let the pipe dance after it, for it is a servant.'[21] Vase paintings demonstrate the close physical relationship between tragic or satyr dancers and the piper.[22] Aristotle complained of the tendency of the piper to participate in the mimetic action of the chorus, twisting himself to evoke discus throwing, or pulling at the chorus-leader to evoke Scylla.[23] It seems that the piper was a mobile figure, leading the chorus into the *orchêstra*,[24] but thereafter follower rather than leader, going where the action took him.

This *Gestalt* started to break down at the end of the fifth century, perhaps in the dithyramb more than in tragedy. Aristophanes in *The Frogs* wrote a pastiche of a Euripidean aria containing an element of coloratura: the fixed relation of word and rhythm is abandoned when the singer turns *eilissete* into a warbling *ei-ei-ei-eilissete*, and there is a hint of this technique in the extant music for *Orestes*.[25] Plato condemned the way poets began to allow verse to be heard without the pipes, and instruments without words. To use the naked pipe and lyre without the accompaniment of dancing and singing, he complained, is 'complete *amousia* [inartistry] and *thaumatourgia* [wonder-making]'. While the vocal aspect of choral performance penetrates to the soul, he argues, the aspect of movement trains the body.[26] It is a Christian and Cartesian consciousness, convinced that the body/soul dichotomy is unavoidable, which today thinks of the chorus as singers who happen to accompany their mental activity with bodily movement.

In the classic American musical, the chorus are used to reflect glory upon the star, for the genre celebrates the individual, not the triumph of the social unit. Lyrics and choreography are both subordinate to the tune, and to an outside force, the orchestra. The classical Greek aesthetic was different. The moment of performance was controlled not by a beat imposed from the darkness of the pit, but by the collective of dancers. Power, as in the *polis*, had to be visible. Greek

---

[20] See Thrasybulos Georgiades, *Greek Music, Verse and Dance* tr. E. Benedikt and M. L. Martinez (New York, 1973) esp. chapters 6 and 7.

[21] Athenaeus 617: *COAD* 338–9. See the discussion in Bernhard Zimmermann, 'Comedy's criticism of music' *Drama* 2 (1993) 39–50.

[22] *DFA* figs. 36, 42 (tragedy), and 40, 45, 46 (satyr play).

[23] *Poetics* 26.1–1461b. John Herington suggests that in a similar way a piper in the dithyramb imitated the pregnant gait of Semele: *Poetry into Drama* 153. We know that the piper followed the actors about the Roman stage from Cicero, *Pro Murena* xii.26.

[24] The scholiast on *Wasps* 582 states this: *DFA* 242 n.1.

[25] *Frogs* 1314, 1348; *COAD* 341–2. See also Georgiades, *Greek Music* 118; Zimmermann, 'Comedy's criticism' 42.   [26] *Laws* 669–73.

tragedy took for its subject matter the relationship of individual and *polis*, and the conventions of the genre demanded that chorus and actors should be in equilibrium. While the *polis* funded the star actors who played heroic individuals, it was heroic individuals within the *polis* who demonstrated their communitarian spirit by funding and training the collective, the chorus.[27] The Greek process of production differed profoundly from that of the musical. While the modern choreographer takes the lyrics and tunes and attempts to find movements that will accompany these, the Greek dramatist wrote choral odes knowing that he would be responsible for directing the production.[28] The system obliged him to conceive dance movements and a score for the piper in addition to words. Aeschylus, for example, in a play by Aristophanes, states that he invented his own choreographic *schêmata*, and these seem to be of triadic form, with movements 'this way, that way, and hither'.[29] When the Greek dramatists wrote choral odes, they were not writing for readers, but for performers.

Today nothing is extant but the words which embody the rhythm. Since we have lost the choreography and the music of the pipes, how are we to begin to reconstruct the body/soul *Gestalt* characteristic of ancient performance? Aristotle in the *Poetics* states that the medium of dance is rhythm, and that by means of rhythms in the form of *schêmata* dancers imitate character, emotion and action.[30] For a more serviceable vocabulary, we have to turn to Plutarch, who defines three key terms. (1) *Schêmata* are tableaux at the culmination of a dance movement: '"Schemata" are positions or arrangements. Movements bear upon and end in these, as when one composes with the body a "schema" of Apollo, Pan or a Bacchant and remains in that image like a picture.' (2) Whereas the *schêma* is mimetic of a shape or form, a *phora* ('transfer' or 'move') creates the 'semblance' of an emotion, action or potentiality. (3) *Deixis* is a pointing to something such as earth, sky, oneself or persons nearby. Plutarch adds that deixis can easily be mishandled and become clumsy, like the use of proper names in poetry where the rhythm is not expressive of what those names signify.[31] The idea that the dance culminates in a static image is of particular importance, and may remind us of the tableaux of the Victorian stage, or of the *mie* (poses) in kabuki.

---

[27] On the system of liturgies, see *DFA* 86–91. A book by Peter Wilson is forthcoming.

[28] *DFA* 84–5; Dale, *Collected Papers* 161–6. In *Lyric Metres* 204, Dale points out that Dionysius of Halicarnassus was confident that he possessed Euripides' own score. Unlike Aeschylus and Sophocles, Euripides does not seem to have been an actor; nevertheless, an anecdote speaks of him singing his text to his actors: *DFA* 91.

[29] Athenaeus 21d (frag. 696 Kassel-Austin).

[30] *Poetics* i.5–1447a. The terms are *ethos*, *pathos* and *praxis*. Dance is distinguished from the music of the flute, which requires rhythm and harmony.

[31] Plutarch, *Table Talk* ix.15–747. Athenaeus and Pollux offer examples of mimetic *schêmata*: see Lawler, *Dance* 83; *DFA* 249–50; Leo Aylen, *The Greek Theater* (Cranbury, N.J., 1985) 116–18.

Winkler's attempt to link tragic dancing to military dancing is unhelpful in its implications, since the chorus usually represent women or old men who are the antithesis of warriors and their dance cannot have looked overtly militaristic. He may well be right to identify the chorus as ephebes, but he fails to give sufficient attention to the inversionary nature of ephebic rituals.[32] If we today are to reconstruct a sense of fifth-century performance, our guideline must be to trust the text and fifth-century archaeological evidence. After examining the circular binding dance in the *Eumenides*, Lawler concedes 'that free, varied choreographic designs were used frequently in tragedy, and that they must have enhanced greatly the effect of the plays'.[33] Gould and Lewis concede that the binding dance may have been circular, but otherwise find evidence for circular dancing only in Aristophanes.[34] They are, however, looking at the evidence in very narrow terms. Claude Calame in his broad-based study of early dance concludes that choral lyric always took the form of a procession, or of a circular dance around a focus such as an altar, musician or solo singer. Although tragic dance is reputed to take a militaristic rectangular form, he observes that it derives from choral lyric, and that the division between choral lyric and tragic dance must therefore be less sharp than one might have supposed.[35]

The tragic chorus is linked to the dithyramb and to the choral lyric of poets like Pindar, Simonides and Stesichorus through its use of the triadic form: strophe/antistrophe/epode. Eight late texts affirm, with minor variations, that the strophe is a movement to the right (i.e. clockwise) circuiting the altar, and the antistrophe to the left (anti-clockwise) whilst the epode is delivered facing the god. The first rotation imitates the movement of the outer heavens, whilst the counter-rotation imitates the regressive movement of the sun and other planets through the zodiac. One text refers to Ptolemy's *On Stationary Poetry*, but Ptolemy is not likely to have been the originator of this theory.[36] The etymology of 'strophe' and 'antistrophe' implies turning and counter turning.[37] The triadic principle of circling one way around the altar, reversing the circle, and halting before the divine image seems an obvious way to structure a

[32] Winkler speaks of 'a complex and finely-controlled tension between role and role-player': *NTDWD* 57.   [33] Lawler, *Dance* 84.   [34] *DFA* 239 with n.2.

[35] *Les Choeurs de jeunes filles en Grèce archaïque* (Rome, 1977) 1.79–86.

[36] The texts are printed in translation in William Mullen, *Choreia: Pindar and the dance* (Princeton, 1982) 225–8. One refers to tragedy: scholiast on *Helen* 640. Mullen 229 sees no reason why this astral thinking should not date back to Pindar. For movements 'to the right' as 'clockwise', see Joseph Cuillandre, *La Droite et la gauche dans les poèmes homériques* (Paris, 1944) 229ff. For the relationship between cosmology and theatrical dance in Japanese theatre, see Kunio Komparu, *The Noh Theater* (New York and Tokyo, 1983) 121–2.

[37] There is a good survey of the terminology in F. D'Alfonso, *Stesicoro e la performance* (Rome, 1994). D'Alfonso draws the same conclusions about the circular choral dancing of Stesichorus as Mullen draws in relation to Pindar.

circular choral dance, and astral explanations might be accounted for as a later rationalization.

It would appear from Plato's myths that the rotational principle of strophic dancing made a deep impression on him, and helped to inform his understanding of the cosmos. In the *Timaeus*, he describes the movement of the fixed stars around the earth and counter-movement of the planets, and relates this principle of 'the same and the different' to the reasoning process inside the human head.[38] In the 'Myth of Er' the cosmos is likened to the whorl of a spindle, the outer rim of which rotates counter to the rest.[39] In *The Statesman* Plato pictures a cosmos which the gods rotated in one direction at the start of the golden age, but which in the age of Zeus has been left to reverse its rotation as the human race deteriorates. He cites as inspiration the myth which we also find in Euripides that the crime of Atreus forced the sun to reverse its direction;[40] and in the circular city of *The Laws*, a microcosm of the harmonious cosmos, twelve squads charged with defence and community service rotate around the twelve segments of the outer circle of the city month by month for a year, and then in the second year reverse their trajectory. They move first 'to the right', which Plato here specifies should mean anti-clockwise ('towards the dawn').[41] These strange visions confirm the symbolic importance that the form of rotation and counter-rotation possessed. In the *Timaeus* Plato specifically refers to the stars as 'choruses', and the idea that the stars are dancers is a common enough topos in Greek tragedy.[42]

The question of choral numbers is relevant to circularity. Late sources tell us that Sophocles increased choral numbers to fifteen,[43] but attribution of the change to a specific dramatist is suspect, and we cannot be sure exactly when the change took place. The text of *Agamemnon* 1346ff. appears to be written for twelve chorus-men,[44] and we have two fifth-century vases which each seem to portray six dancers.[45] On the other hand an inscription of the 430s refers to a *choregos* and fourteen *tragôidoi*, a term which refers most plausibly to chorus-

---

[38] *Timaeus* 34–7, 43–4.   [39] *Republic* 617.   [40] *Statesman* 268–74; *Orestes* 1001–7.
[41] *Laws* 760.
[42] *Timaeus* 40c; *Ion* 1079; *Electra* [Euripides] 467; *Antigone* 1147; Euripides frag.593.
[43] *DFA* 234 n.5. Some give 14, excluding the chorus-leader. Csapo and Slater argue for a change soon after the *Oresteia*: *COAD* 353. The number 14 may possibly have had Dionysiac significance, implying that the chorus were the 14 parts of Dionysus' dismembered body: see Walter Burkert, *Homo Necans*, tr. P. Bing (Berkeley, 1983) 234.   [44] See the discussion in *DFA* 235.
[45] (1) Basel krater with 6 men dancing before a tomb: *NTDWD* pl.6; early fifth century. The issue turns upon whether the actors are masked, for this could very well not be a dramatic dance but a pyrrhic dance performed by young soldiers. (2) Krater by the Niobid painter of c.460–450: *DFA* 184 and fig. 42. Gould and Lewis remark that 'it is hard to see what is represented . . . if it is not a chorus of tragedy'. A piper is surrounded by 6 dancers who exemplify 6 different postures. The 'Pronomos' vase could be evidence for 12 or 15: see *NTDWD* 45 n.72 – countering the argument in *DFA* 236; also *COAD* 70.

men.[46] Given that the chorus is more prominent in Aeschylus than in the later dramatists, it seems more profitable to consider why the change occurred than when.

The number ten is anthropocentric, being related to the body, and was the basic unit of democratic organization.[47] The number twelve is cosmic, being related to the lunar month, to the hours (as defined by the Babylonians and Egyptians), to the zodiac, to the directions of the winds and to the Olympian pantheon which recognized twelve major gods.[48] Plato restored twelve as the number-base for his traditionalist, theocentric, non-democratic ideal city in the *Laws*. While comedy is numerologically both political and cosmic (5 choruses of 24 = 10 × 12, perhaps reflecting tribal recruitment), the tragic competition seems to be numerologically cosmic, given that twelve plays were performed and the original chorus was twelve. While comedy is overtly concerned with democratic processes, the *raison d'être* of tragedy was to give political issues a divine or cosmic perspective. Number is often symbolically associated with space. The Pythagoreans always associated ten with the triangle (1 + 2 + 3 + 4).[49] Twelve is associated symbolically with the cosmic circle, while fifteen more obviously lends itself to a triangular or rectangular formation.

We can see from Pollux's account of the rectangular chorus that fifteen makes sense as a means of creating a rectangle five persons broad by three deep, with a controlling centre-front position for the chorus leader.[50] A comedy of *circa* 424 BC speaks of the middle-left position in a tragic chorus, apparently alluding to the centre-front position in a chorus entering from the audience's right.[51] The role of the leader was crucial in Ariane Mnouchkine's production of *Les Atrides* which visited Britain in 1992, when Catherine Schaub, the chorus-leader, energized the choral group from this centre-front position, and forced the difficult words of the chorus upon the audience's attention.[52] In a choral group of twelve the natural formation is a circle, and geometry offers no

---

[46] *DFA* (3rd edition, 1988) 361. The term *tragôidoi* normally refers to the chorus according to Gould and Lewis in *DFA* 127; and Winkler, *NTDWD* 37, 58–61. Csapo and Slater also opt for the chorus: *COAD* 353. P. Ghiron-Bistagne argues that the term could equally refer to all the performers: *Recherches sur les acteurs dans la Grèce antique* (Paris, 1976) 119–21.

[47] See P. Lévêque and P. Vidal-Naquet, *Clisthène l'athénien* (Paris, 1964) 91ff.

[48] M. R. Wright, *Cosmology in Antiquity* (London, 1995) 13, 15; O. A. W. Dilke, *Greek and Roman Maps* (London, 1985) 28; *GR* 125.   [49] Wright, *Cosmology* 45.

[50] See S. Melchinger *Das Theater der Tragödie* (Munich, 1973) 26–7. For texts, see *DFA* 240–1.

[51] Cratinus, *Men of Seriphos: COAD* 363. The terms 'chorus leader', 'next-stander' and 'third-stander' appear in Aristotle: *COAD* 363–4.

[52] As the one member of the cast who had experience of working in India, she was in a unique position to set the lead in the chosen style. See O. Aslan (ed.), *Le Corps en jeu* (Paris, 1993) 294–6. Demosthenes notes the dependence of the chorus on the leader: *DFA* 77 n.4.

natural position for a leader. Aristotle states that tragedy evolved out of the improvisatory activity of the leader of the dithyramb,[53] which was of course a circular dance, and it is easy to see in *Persians*, for example, how the Herald, the Queen, Darius and Xerxes function in turn as chorus leader, being both visual focus of the dance and lyric interlocutor.[54] The change from twelve to fifteen is the corollary to a progressive disentanglement of chorus from actors. It emphasizes the role of a chorus leader, who is now quite distinct from the actor as surrogate chorus leader, and it allows the dance to be increasingly frontal, pushing the text and gestures out towards an audience spread high up the hillside. The collective ethos implicit in the chorus of twelve gives way to possibilities of virtuoso individual display. Whether the dialogue sections of the chorus were spoken by a single 'leader' remains unknown. What we must envisage is not a tragic dance that is generically distinct in the fifth century from all other dances, but rather a gradual change of emphasis towards frontal presentation. Tragic dancing was not a new and radically different rectangular form, but evolved from traditional forms of circular dancing.

Strophe and antistrophe are metrically identical, yet within the whole of Greek tragedy no two strophes are alike.[55] It is a reasonable inference, given the unity of dance and song, that the choreography of strophe and antistrophe was precisely identical. The technical difficulty of writing paired verses is illustrated by Aristophanes when he portrays Agathon softening his strophes in the sun in order to bend them into the right shape.[56] Dionysius of Halicarnassus states that not only the same rhythm but also the same music was used in the antistrophe.[57] In anapaests written for a march, metrical patterning is much less precise than in passages designed for dance and song.[58] It is inconceivable that the tragedians would have taken such trouble to create subtle responsions in the text if they were not concerned to make the symmetry apparent to the spectators in the theatre. As Kitto puts it, repetition was conceived by the dramatist 'not only aurally, but visually and spatially as well'.[59]

Kitto's pupil, Leo Aylen, has explored the implications of choreographic symmetry, taking the famous example of *Agamemnon* 218–37. Both strophe and antistrophe deal with the sacrifice of Iphigeneia. The strophe begins with Agamemnon putting on 'the harness of necessity', the antistrophe with the pleas and tears of his daughter. The dance cannot in any narrow mimetic way represent the putting on of a harness, but must more broadly represent a suf-

---

[53] *Poetics* iv.12–1449a.   [54] On Xerxes, see Lonsdale, *Dance* 257.
[55] Dale, *Collected Papers* 253.   [56] Aristophanes, *Women at the Thesmophoria* 68.
[57] *On Literary Composition* 19. M. L. West, *Greek Metre* (Oxford, 1982) 5 accepts without question that the music of the strophe was repeated in the antistrophe, but evinces no interest in the question of dance.   [58] West, *Greek Metre* 79. On anapaests, see also Dale, *Collected Papers* 35.
[59] Kitto, 'Dance in Greek tragedy' 36.

fering individual stifled by a mob. From the point of view of the audience, the effect is to create a symmetry between the two figures. Agamemnon is not simply the villain, for he will in the course of the play become a sacrificial victim just like Iphigeneia. The medium of dance allows this crucial symmetry to be made apparent to the audience.[60] By analysing choral odes in this way, seeking to find which elements are repeated in the antistrophe and which are not, we can distinguish how much is represented mimetically.

Such reasoning was anticipated by A. M. Dale in 1948. Although arguing for a close interrelation of dance and song, and accepting the probability of a 'general correspondence' in the choreography of strophe and antistrophe, Dale refused to accept that identity of choreography could be an absolute rule. Gould and Lewis incline towards Dale's view, with its corollary that gesture and movement somehow followed the words as distinct from the rhythm and music.[61] Dale cites three passages as self-evident examples of the impossibility of identical choreography. I shall examine her three chosen instances in order to show why her reasoning is mistaken.

Bacchae 977ff.

After Pentheus has departed for the mountains in female costume, the mood of the persecuted Lydian Bacchants is one of vengeance. The form of the ode is: strophe – refrain – antistrophe – refrain – epode. The refrain calls for Justice to kill Pentheus, and the epode calls upon Dionysus to manifest himself in his true form. Dodds observes of the antistrophe that 'This passage is the hardest in the play, and full of textual uncertainties',[62] so I shall not hazard a translation. The outline is, however, clear. While the strophe visualizes the scene on Mount Cithaeron, the antistrophe is a *credo* of the chorus. Dale claims that identity of choreography is impossible because the strophe is 'dramatically imagined' while the antistrophe is 'reflective' in tone. It is, however, a typical pattern in Greek tragedy that the strophe sets up a concrete well-visualized image, and the antistrophe gives that image a philosophical dimension. Since the dominant metre is dochmiac (short-long-long-short-long), a metre associated with intense excitement, the idea that the antistrophe is 'reflective' must be misconceived.[63]

---

[60] Aylen, *The Greek Theater* 120–4. I have on several occasions asked drama students to create symmetrical choreography for this passage, and may therefore confirm that movement can be used to create the effect that Aylen envisages. Aylen also analyses an ode from *Antigone*, and his discussion benefits from the production at Greenwich Theatre (London) of his 'isometric' translation of that play.   [61] Dale, *Lyric Metres* 213–14; *DFA* 252.

[62] *Bacchae* ed. E. R. Dodds (Oxford, 1960) 202.

[63] See *ibid.* 199. Note in particular that the phrase in 1006–7, 'other greater, clearer things', is a run of eleven short syllables implying fast dancing. The phrase 'for a noble life' at the end of 1007 is a further run of seven short syllables.

The strophe and antistrophe (hereafter A and A') can be described in terms of four movements. The overall strategy of the dramatist is to move within A from Pentheus to the vision of Agave, and within A' from Pentheus to the vision of the chorus. The correspondences that we see are mimetically precise.

1. (Lines 1–5) A evokes the hounds of Madness running to the Bacchants on the mountain and biting Pentheus; Pentheus in female garb starts to spy. A' evokes Pentheus going to the Bacchants on the mountain with a mad resolve; the madman attempts the impossible. *The movement depicts running, the Bacchic orgy, Pentheus' madness.*

2. (Lines 6–8) A represents Pentheus being seen by his mother Agave. A' is syntactically obscure (in keeping with the state of mind of the chorus) but is concerned with the idea of divine punishment. *The movement represents a human being watched by someone stronger than a human, and the focus shifts from watched to watcher.*

3. (Lines 7–9) A represents in direct speech the shout of Agave that someone has come to the mountain. A' proclaims the creed of the chorus: 'I reject rationality. I rejoice in the hunt. Other, greater, clearer things . . .' *This is a public declamation about something seen, and the gestural action is deictic.*

4. (Lines 10–12) In A, Agave pronounces that this is no human but is born of a lion or a Gorgon. In A', the chorus conclude that they will reject an unjust way of life and reverence the gods. *The focus shifts to what is seen in the vision: common humanity is contrasted with the divine or demonic.*

There is no way that an audience could grasp the intended symmetry without the medium of dance, which generalizes the concrete narrative of the strophe and concretizes the abstract language of the antistrophe in order to draw action and thought together. The final line of A ends with the phrase 'race of Libyan Gorgons' and some kind of tableau must have fixed this idea in a visual image. The refrain then commences: 'Come, manifest Justice, come sword in hand to kill' and there is of course manifest justice in stabbing a Gorgon. A' ends with the words: 'rejecting ways that are outside Justice, reverence the gods'. The same tableau that fixed the idea of the demonic now fixes the idea of the gods. The choreographic identity of Gorgons and 'gods' calls the Bacchants' concept of the divine into question. In the repeat of the refrain, the idea that justice is manifest now has to be questioned. Through the mirror of the antistrophe, moral certainties are undermined. The reader who approaches the play as literature, particularly one who reads for semantic content rather than rhythm, is likely to be baffled by the apparent other-worldly pietism of the chorus at this point in the play.[64] In performance,

---

[64] The Greekless reader attempting to penetrate the antistrophe through the medium of Arrowsmith's translation has to run the gauntlet of paraphrase, expansion, syntactical improve-

philosophical verbiage is counterpointed against Bacchanalian movement. The nature of the gods and their relationship to justice is problematized, in preparation for the horrific messenger speech that is to follow.

Hecuba 923ff.

The form of the ode is A, A′, B, B′, epode. Hecuba and the chorus of Trojan slave-women are stranded on the shores of Thrace with the Greek fleet, and Hecuba plans to kill the Thracian King who has murdered her son. A describes in brief the physical fall of Troy. A′ begins a more detailed account, with images of sacrifice and sleeping. B and B′ focus on the figure of a young woman, creating an image of passive femininity that contrasts ironically with the violent act which Hecuba's women will undertake. The young woman, when B commences, is about to join her warrior husband in bed. It is the correspondence of B and B′ which Dale finds choreographically impossible because of the detailed 'mimetic accompanying action'. The text, broken into sections for convenience of analysis, runs as follows:

B	B′
1. I was setting my tresses one-by-one in the folds of my turban	Leaving my cherished bed, in just a *peplos* like a Spartan maid
2. gazing at the depthless light in a golden mirror	I prayed to holy Artemis, to no avail, alas.
3. ready to fall onto the covers on the bed.	I was taken off, gazing at a dead bed-mate
4. Up came a wave of sound over the city.	of mine, over the salt sea
5. The shout across Troy was this: 'Oh	looking back at the city while homeward
6. sons of Greece, when oh when after the Trojan keep	the ship made its way [lit. 'moved foot'], and cut me off from the land of Troy.
7. is sacked will you come home?'	I gave way to my grief . . .

Thus laid out, the correspondence of the phrases is clear.

ment, Christianized language, and a solemn iambic beat. The strophic patterning is entirely invisible. *Complete Greek Tragedies: Euripides V* ed. D. Grene and R. Lattimore (Chicago, 1959).

1. A girl in bedroom attire: in B looking like a Trojan, in B' like a Greek. The movement of grooming must become a movement of fear.
2. A gaze into vacuity.
3. The focus is on the bed: the falling woman, her prostrate husband.
4. A movement as of the sea.[65]
5. A movement in the direction of Troy. A deictic reference to the burning city at line 823 implies that a particular direction has been established in the play for Troy that lies over the water.
6. Away from Troy: the dancers shift their balance as the tower falls, the foot leaves land.
7. Tableau of grief. Common to both conclusions is the pathos of the person separated from home: the Greek soldier, a Trojan woman.

The hidden symmetries which the choreography brings out are those of Greek and Trojan, of male and female, of sex and death. It is an important theme in the play that Agamemnon the apparent victor is also a victim, separated from home, politically impotent, and doomed to be murdered. The Greeks entered Troy and attacked women, the women will enter the *skênê* and attack men. The strophe/antistrophe convention is an integral part of the tragic genre because of its ability to realize equal and opposite forces before the eyes of the audience. It is the relationship that Plato termed, in respect of circles that rotate in opposite directions, 'the same and the different'.

Ion 205ff.

The chorus of slave-women from Athens arrive and inspect the sculptures on Apollo's temple at Delphi. The structure is A, A', B, B'. The unique feature of this ode is that B' is interrupted by a series of remarks by the temple-slave Ion. The interruptions helpfully segment the dance into its constituent phrases. In A, the women contrast Athens with Delphi, and end with a tableau of Heracles killing the Hydra. In A' they end with a tableau of Bellerophon killing the Chimaera. It is the correspondence of B and B' that Dale rejects because B continues the description of the sculptures while B' is a request for permission to enter the temple and would seem to require different gestures. The text is as shown.[66] Asterisks mark the points where Ion interrupts.

---

[65] Collard comments that the metre marks a quickening of the action at this point, appropriate to the strophe but not to the antistrophe. He misses the point that the antistrophe builds up at the end towards the women's curse in the epode: *Euripides: Hecuba*, ed. and tr. Christopher Collard (Warminster, 1991) 179.

[66] I have followed the text in A. S. Owen (ed.) *Ion* (Oxford, 1939). Textual problems include a failure of exact metrical correspondence at 209–10=222–3, and the curious interruption by Ion

B	B'
1. Yes everywhere I let my gaze range.	Yes you by the temple I'm speaking to.
2. See on the stone walls the rout of the Giants.	Is it permitted to enter the sanctum with a woman's foot? *** No?
3. Friends, we are looking.	For you, we have a question. ***
4. Can you see, swinging her Gorgon-eyed shield at Enceladus . . .?	Is it true, the *omphalos* at the centre of the earth is in Apollo's temple? ***
5. I see Pallas, my goddess.	So indeed the story tells. ***
6. Hey now. A thunderbolt, fiery and warlike, in Zeus's far-throwing hands.	I understand. We do not transgress the law of god. The exterior is a joy to the eye. ***
7. I see it: frenzied Mimas burnt in the flames.	Our mistress permits us to look into god's sanctum. ***
8. Dionysus too with his unmilitary thyrsus! – another child of earth slain by Bacchus.	Pallas co-dwells with the nurturing house of my ruler(s). Here is the person of whom you ask.

Before analysing the choreography, we need to be aware of the sense of space assumed by the playwright. The chorus are notionally positioned in front of the east façade of the temple, but the gigantomachy described in B was located on the west pediment.[67] As was noted in the last chapter, there can be no question of nineteenth-century realism here. Representation here depends upon the dancer, not the scenographer, and mime must be used to create a sense of what the chorus see.

In terms of movement, the correspondences seem to be as follows.

1. The chorus redirect their gaze, and look towards the *skênê*.
2. A movement forwards to inspect becomes one of rout/recoil.
3. They fix their gaze. In B', Ion would be moving forward at this point.
4. The choreography must represent a circular movement representing the shield and its brandishing in B, the navel-stone and its surrounding cosmos in B'. Ion's response in B' emphasizes the parallelism, stating that the navel-stone is surrounded by Gorgons.

at 221 in the middle of a metrical and syntactical unit. A solution to the latter problem is that Ion literally overlaps the last two syllables of the phrase, covering the *oud'an* of the chorus with his own *ou themis*. His emphatic *ou* (No!) would cover the identical syllable uttered by the chorus. There is no precedent for such a device, but there is also no precedent for an actor interrupting an antistrophe.   [67] Owen 83.

5.   The chorus refer back to their own experience.

6.   Brief action of seeing; then a movement to express the fearful power of
       the divine, followed by arms akimbo to express throwing or the scale of
       open space.

7.   Peering into something that is divine and half-hidden.

8.   The gesture of slaying with a Bacchic wand becomes a gesture of point-
       ing at the new arrival, Creusa.

When Ion comes forward it is likely that he goes to the *thymelê*, and is encircled by the chorus. The *thymelê* would have been associated with the eye of the
shield in B and now in B' becomes the *omphalos* surrounded, as Ion says, by
women. After movement 5 Ion tells the chorus that they may not enter the
temple but must stay outside at the *thymelai*. The choreography in this way
helps to prepare the chorus for the climactic encounter of Creusa and Ion when
the *thymelê* becomes associated with the *omphalos*.

The final tableau is the climax of the ode, and only makes sense in the
context of the play as a whole. A and A' end with the slaying of a serpentine
monster. Although the climax of B is the slaying of another chthonic monster,
the climax of B' is the apparently pacific arrival of Ion's natural mother. The
symmetry of B/B' makes sense when we become aware that Creusa is
descended from a chthonic monster (267–9, etc.). The phrase 'Pallas co-dwells
with the nurturing house' alludes to the Erechtheum next to Athene's temple,
built over the grave of Erechtheus, Creusa's father (281–2).[68] The final tableau
of the antistrophe proffers an explicit parallel between the mythic encounter
of Dionysus and giant, evoked through language and mime, and the present
visible encounter of an armed Apolline youth and his chthonic mother. The
relationship between Dionysus and Apollo is important later in the play when
the paternity of Ion is mistakenly traced not to Apollo but to the Dionysia, and
celebrated in a Dionysiac banquet.[69]

Schematically, we might represent the symmetries established by the chorus
as follows:

---

[68] Archaeologically, there are close links between the Erechtheum and the temple of Apollo at
Delphi, for both are built over a cleft, allowing access to the earth beneath, and are said to
house chthonic serpents. See 'Trésors, temples, tholos' in *Temples et sanctuaires* ed. G. Roux
(Lyons, 1981) 163. On Creusa, see Nicole Loraux, 'Kreousa the autochthon: a study of
Euripides' *Ion* in *NTDWD* 168–206; also A. W. Saxonhouse, 'Myths and the origins of cities:
reflections on the autochthony theme in Euripides' *Ion* in *Greek Tragedy and Political Theory*
ed. J. P. Euben (Berkeley, 1986) 252–73.

[69] On the cult of Dionysus at Delphi, see L. R. Farnell, *The Cults of the Greek States* (Oxford,
1896–1909) V.186. For its place in the play, see Pozzi's discussion in *Myth and the Polis* ed. Dora
C. Pozzi and John M. Wickersham (Ithaca, 1991) 135–44.

B	B'
myth	present
Delphi	Athens
Olympian Dionysus	Ion son of Olympian Apollo
earth-born giant	earth-born Creusa

In order to appreciate the full subtlety of these oppositions, we need to return to the context established by the first strophe and antistrophe (A/A'). Three themes are introduced. (1) A commences with a comparison of Athens and Delphi; in A', the chorus compare images at Delphi with the tales they have heard while weaving in Athens. The reference to weaving ensures that an Athenian audience will relate the gigantomachy at Delphi to the gigantomachy that women of Athens wove onto the robe of Athene for the Panathenaia.[70] (2) The choreography half-way through A and A' must express the idea of doubleness. While A describes the twin façades of the temple, A' describes how Iolaus the shield-bearer shares in the labours of Heracles. The virtues of pairing emerge later in relation to the double patrons of Delphi, the double ancestry of Ion. (3) The Hydra and Chimaera which mark the climax of A and A' are both multi-bodied children of Echidne, and lend themselves to mimetic representation by a choric group. This contrasts with Dionysus' slaying of the giant in B, which requires deictic representation: the audience does not now see the monster, but sees the chorus seeing the monster. In A and A', there is no ambiguity: the monsters are evil, whilst Heracles and Bellerophon are heroic. In B the victors are not heroes but Olympians, and their victory is morally more ambiguous. Ion, the protagonist of the play, is the son of an Olympian father and a Chthonian mother. The play as a whole celebrates the myth of Athenian autochthony, the idea that Athenians, though protected by Olympian Pallas, were born of the earth. Choreographic symmetry allows the playwright to clarify binary thematic oppositions that would otherwise be obscured by the linear force of the narrative.

We have examined the three odes which Dale chose as examples of the impossibility of choreographic symmetry, and have seen that symmetry is not merely possible but dramaturgically potent. We may therefore accept visual symmetry for working purposes as a rule, a fixed convention of the genre. *The metrical identity of strophe and antistrophe means choreographic identity.* Scholars have not been trained to read with this simple rule in mind, and translations

---

[70] On the robe see Robert Parker, 'Myths of early Athens' in *Interpretations of Greek Mythologies* ed. Jan Bremmer (London, 1987) 187–214, p. 192.

are not made on this basis. The consequence is that important dramaturgical strategies are for ever being overlooked.

The antistrophe effects a transformation of the strophe, so that the same visual image receives two meanings. The transformative principle can most easily be seen at work when we look at strophic songs given to individual actors, where stage objects are often used as the focus of visual meaning. Euripides' Electra removes a pot of spring water from her head in the strophe, and in the antistrophe the pot becomes the lustral bath in which her father was murdered.[71] Ion sweeps the altar of Apollo with a branch of laurel, and in the antistrophe the branch becomes the emblem of the god, addressed as the god.[72] Aeschylus' Orestes promises to take revenge on his mother with his own hands, and in the antistrophe the chorus mime how the hands of Agamemnon's corpse were cut off by Clytaemnestra to forestall revenge.[73] The bow in the hands of Odysseus is a bow that has left the hands of Philoctetes.[74] The dance form here allows Philoctetes to mime the object that has been taken away from him. In *The Persians*, the defeated Xerxes displays an empty quiver in the strophe, his rent garments in the corresponding antistrophe.[75] Symmetry of gesture is rigorously preserved on a line-by-line basis, for a generalized reference to the remains of Xerxes' equipage becomes a reference to rent garments; the display of the quiver is answered by a generalized reference to further catastrophe.

An important question which confronts us when we look at strophic passages given to individual actors is whether the chorus danced in accompaniment. The dances of Electra and Ion occur before the entry of the chorus, so must have been unaccompanied. On the other hand, in the long antiphonal sequence at the end of *The Persians*, where Xerxes and the chorus alternate lines, it is hard to imagine that the chorus stood stock still each time Xerxes had a brief utterance. The principle of dancing to interpret the words of a singer has ancient roots in Greek culture.[76] It is hard to conceive how Heracles in *Women of Trachis* (1005ff.), when brought in dying on his litter, could perform a dance to accompany a strophic song which refers to his being lifted, moved and touched. It seems a more attractive idea that the chorus should dance in response to the song, and externalize the sufferings of the dying man. In *Alcestis* (393ff.), Alcestis' son sings a strophe which culminates in the action of his kissing her mouth; by the end of the antistrophe Alcestis is clearly being carried out. Again, symmetry of movement must be created by the chorus, not by the actor. In *Ajax*

---

[71] *Electra* 140–2=157–9.   [72] *Ion* 112–14=128–30. See pp. 204–5 below.
[73] *The Libation Bearers* 434–8=439–43.   [74] *Philoctetes* 1127–9=1150–2.
[75] *Persians* 1018–22=1030–4.
[76] For sources, see *DFA* 255 n.2. See also Calame, *Les Choeurs de jeunes filles* I.153ff. The principle found theatrical expression much later in the pantomime.

(351ff.), the hero on the *eccyclêma* surrounded by slaughtered cattle sings that a tide of blood circles racing around him; in the antistrophe he sings that he sees no helper but the chorus. There is an obvious equation between the imagined circling tide of blood and the shocked sailors who gather in a circle around their master. The source of movement is not Ajax but the chorus. In *Hippolytus* (372ff., 679ff.), a strophe sung by the chorus has its antistrophe sung by Phaedra some 300 lines later. The chorus conclude the strophe singing that there is no more mystery about the 'fate of Love, wretched child of Crete!' Phaedra concludes the antistrophe: 'I am the worst-fated of women!' The choreography is easy to understand if the chorus in the antistrophe, now silent rather than singing, repeat a set of deictic gestures which point in the direction of Phaedra. It would seem from these examples that the task of creating choreographic symmetry normally fell upon the chorus, but the actor could participate, and in the absence of the chorus render the symmetrical pattern on his own.

In choral odes performed independently of the actors, it is usually harder to discern the way choreographic images are transformed. Detailed illusionist mime – Philoctetes' handling of his missing bow, for example – does not lend itself so well to twelve-fold repetition, and the playwright has to work on a larger scale. In order to explore the difficulties and possibilities of symmetrical choreography, I shall take one further choral ode for structural analysis, the *parodos* or 'entry-ode' of *Iphigeneia at Aulis*. This play is sometimes held to herald the historical redundance of the chorus, although it was produced posthumously on the same day as *The Bacchae* where the chorus is palpably essential. The *parodos* incorporates a long description of the fleet, which many have considered to be an interpolation. E. B. England, in what is still the standard English critical edition, claims the agreement of 'nearly all editors' that the catalogue is an interpolation.[77] Webster dismisses it as 'excessively dull',[78] Barlow as 'decorative' but 'hardly justified in terms of dramatic integration',[79] Kenneth Cavander as 'little more than a catalogue of obscure names'.[80] None of those who claim the passage as an interpolation can, however, explain why it has been interpolated.[81]

---

[77] E. B. England in *The Iphigenia at Aulis of Euripides*, ed. E. B. England (London, 1891; reissued, New York, 1979) 21.　　[78] T. B. L. Webster, *The Tragedies of Euripides* (London, 1967).

[79] S. A. Barlow, *The Imagery of Euripides* (Bristol, 1986) 20.

[80] *Iphigeneia at Aulis by Euripides*, tr. K. Cavander (Englewood Cliffs, 1973) 172.

[81] D. L. Page inevitably follows England and excises the passage. He admits to puzzlement, however, as to why a long choral passage should be interpolated in an age of increasing dominance by actors: *Actors' Interpolations in Greek Tragedy* (Oxford, 1934) 141–6. Froma Zeitlin takes a more sympathetic view in an essay concerned with word-pictures: 'The artful eye: vision, ecphrasis and spectacle in Euripidean theatre' in *Art and Text in Ancient Greek Culture* ed. S. Goldhill and R. Osborne (Cambridge, 1994) 138–223, p. 165.

The chorus are young married women from Chalcis, a town across the straits from the shore where the Greek fleet is becalmed. Schematically, the ode looks like this:

The chorus enters and describes its journey from Chalcis:

A: over water	A': over land
round the shore	through sacrificial grove
Aulis	Artemis
sailing	blushing
fountain of Arethusa	mass of armed Greeks
Achaean army	Small Ajax
Achaean fleet	Ajax of Salamis[82]
Menelaus sends fleet	Protesilaus plays draughts
with Agamemnon	with Palamedes
fetching Helen	Diomedes
reedy river	throwing discus
shepherd Paris	Meriones scion of War
gift of Aphrodite	marvel to mortals
by dewy spring	from mountainous island
Hera and Pallas	Odysseus
Aphrodite wins	Nireus the most beautiful

Non-strophic interlude:

Armed Achilles races along the shore, competing against a chariot and keeping level with it.

Description of the fleet: the right wing

B: Achilles' ships	B': Ships of Argos and Athens
joyous sight	Argive ships
eyes of women	sons of warriors
Phthian Ares	son of Theseus
50 ships [of Achilles]	60 ships [of Attica]
emblem: Nereids[83]	emblem: Pallas on winged chariot

Description of the fleet: [the centre]

C: central Greece	C': southern Greece
Theban armament	Cyclopean Mycenae
50 ships	Agamemnon's 100 ships

---

[82] The text says 'the garlanded of Salamis' (194), a clear reference to Athens' naval victory.
[83] Achilles' mother was a sea-nymph and daughter of Nereus.

emblem: Cadmus' dragon
earth-born Leïtus commands
Phocis
Locrian [little] Ajax

ally: Adrastus
justice over runaways
Pylos
emblem: river-bull

Epode:

> *other groups*
>
> twelve Aenians
> Elians near them
> Taphian oarsmen
> from Snake Islands
> terror to sailors
>
> Ajax of Salamis
> binds right to left
> twelve well-turning ships
> fatal to foreign craft
> I'll preserve the memory

The first strophic pair sets up an opposition of water and land. In A the chorus describe their arrival over water, and mention the water source of their city. The sight of the fleet turns them to the seizure of Helen by the river and the judgement of Paris by a spring. In A' the chorus describe their journey through the sacrificial grove (where Iphigeneia will be sacrificed to Artemis at the end of the play) and they see the Greek sailors idling ashore. While A in the ode deals with Aphrodite and her gift of Helen, A' is concerned with the action of Artemis who has prevented the fleet from sailing, and forced warriors to be idle. The structural opposition is similar to that which dominates the *Hippolytus*, where Artemis of the forests is pitted against sea-born Aphrodite. The fact that the chorus are young women helps to explain the purpose of the Aphrodite/Artemis polarity.[84] Just as girls devoted themselves to Artemis before reaching an age where they might experience Aphrodite, so the Greek warriors must show devotion to Artemis before sailing to Troy in pursuit of Aphrodite's gift.[85] It is significant that in A the chorus speak of themselves as married (176), in A' as 'new-budding' (188).

Nireus is described by Homer as lacking stamina but more beautiful than any of the Greeks save Achilles.[86] The image of beautiful Nireus corresponds

---

[84] For archaeological and ritual links between Aulis and the Brauronia, see Lily Kahil, 'L'Artemis de Brauron: rites et mystère' *Antike Kunst* 20 (1977) 86–98.

[85] For the relationship between war and marriage in this play, see Helene P. Foley, *Ritual Irony* (Ithaca, 1985) 84ff. For the topos in general, see the references collected by Goldhill in *NTDWD* 107.   [86] *Iliad* ii.671–5.

with the image of beautiful Aphrodite at the end of the strophe, and the tableau of human beauty makes a convenient link to the handsome Achilles, a heroic individual competing against impossible odds. The non-strophic dancing suits Achilles' linear progression to the finishing post. Racing along the shore, Achilles is located between the two opposites established in A and A': water and land. As the son of a sea-goddess (whose wedding is described in a later ode), he unites in his person the opposition of land and water. He also unites the opposed goddesses of sex and chastity for by virtue of the plot he is paradoxically a bridegroom and not a bridegroom, being ignorant of the duplicitous letter that declares he will marry Iphigeneia.

Euripides' description of the fleet is based upon Homer's description of the fleet beached at Troy. In Homer, Achilles always protects the right wing and Ajax the left,[87] and Euripides duly starts with Achilles on the right. The logic of Euripides' subversion of Homer relates to the political situation in the last years of the Peloponnesian War. The prime position on the right wing, described in B and B', has a positive colouring, while the blocs described in C and C' have a negative colouring. The idealized Achilles in B is paired with Athens and her democratic ally Argos in B'. The flawed Agamemnon, as in Homer, is identified with a Mycenae distinct from Argos.[88] This Mycenaean Agamemnon is accompanied – and here Euripides throws Homer to the wind – by Adrastus, the Argive king who initiated the brutal war of the seven against Thebes. The forces from Argos in B' are controlled not by Adrastus but by orphans of the war which Adrastus initiated. The idealized figures of B and B' are implicitly young and unblooded, and the opposition of youth (in B/B') versus maturity (in C/C') echoes the Artemis/Aphrodite opposition of A'/A.

C commences with the Thebans, implacable enemies of Athens in the Peloponnesian War, and they are paired with Agamemnon whose weak character is exposed by the play. A dragon is paired with Adrastus. The force of the reference to Leïtus is that Leïtus was the patronal hero of Plataea.[89] Once the scene of a Panhellenic triumph against the Persians, and then an Athenian pro-

---

[87] *Iliad* ii.494ff. The positions of Achilles and Ajax are given at viii.224–6, xi.5–9.

[88] Later in the play, Euripides allows the distinction between Argos and Mycenae to blur, in order to capitalize on the Aeschylean association between Argos and the scene of Agamemnon's death. At 152 Agamemnon refers to Cyclopean *thymelai*, and at 532 to an Argos that has Cyclopean walls, apparently assimilating the walled Mycenae and the Argolid region. Clytaemnestra at 870 and 1192 and Agamemnon at 1267 simply refer to Argos. At the end of the play (1499–1501) Iphigeneia refers to the Cyclopean walls of Mycenae.

[89] Pausanias xi.4.3. F. Jouan in the Budé edition of the play *Euripide vol.vii* (Paris, 1983) calls attention to some of the topical aspects of this passage.

tectorate, Plataea had recently been razed to the ground by the Thebans and Spartans. Nestor's Pylos must have had similar connotations of glory and disaster, for it was Athens' last outpost in the Peloponnese, and had recently been recaptured by the Spartans.[90] There is a deliberate counterpointing of B/B' (politically positive) against C/C' (politically negative). The final tableau in B and B' must represent female emblems on the ships' prows: mermaids on Achilles' ships and Athenes on Athenian ships. The sailors seem youthful, and the choreographic image is one of female beauty. The dominant images in C and C' are chthonic monsters and monstrous men – Cyclops, the dragon, Adrastus, Paris. The closing images are provided by Little Ajax, who was noted for his smallness, and Alpheius the river-demon. In the tableau, Ajax bidding farewell to his city becomes the bull-emblem on Nestor's prow. These figures are not chaste or feminine but are sexually threatening.[91]

The epode commences with a miscellany of small contingents, northern Aenians, western Elians and piratical Taphians, illustrating the variety and comprehensiveness of the Greek fleet. It then passes to Ajax of Salamis, in his Homeric position on the left wing. The text states that Ajax links the right wing to the left, weaving them together near and furthest with his twelve ships to create an unbroken line.[92] The significance of Ajax is that he is a solidary figure, in contrast to Achilles the charismatic aristocrat. His role is to weave together the diverse representatives of the Greek world into a single entity, and the invocation of Salamis summons up the image of a united Greece fighting the foreign invader.[93] Choreographically the epode restores the chorus to a fixed central position, appropriate to the sense of the whole which it now adopts. In setting out this ode I have followed Dale and Webster in assuming that we have Euripides' text and that the final section is technically an epode.[94] Most editors, however, although the sense of the passage seems intact, assume that three lines have vanished and print the last section as a strophic pair because five lines

---

[90] In 408/7 BC, after an occupation of fifteen years: D. M. Lewis *et al.* (eds.). *Cambridge Ancient History* Vol.v: (Cambridge, 1992) 486, 503.

[91] Alpheius, the river-demon of Pylos, half-brother of Achilles, attempted to rape both Artemis and Arethusa (note the reference to Arethusa in line 170). Little Ajax was later famed for the rape of Cassandra (evoked at 751ff.). See my figure 13 for an inversion of this scene. The Locrians used to send girls to Troy in ritual atonement for the rape; see *LIMC* i.i.336.

[92] Jouan would prefer the lines to mean that Ajax links the right wing of his twelve ships to the left wing of the fleet.

[93] Note the reference to barbarian vessels as *barides* (297), a non-Homeric term used of the Persian vessels which bridged the Hellespont in Aeschylus *Persians* 553.

[94] A. M. Dale *Metrical Analyses of Tragic Choruses* Vol.ii (*BICS* supplement 21.2, London, 1981) 146; T. B. L. Webster *The Greek Chorus* 171. Also considered an epode by Wilamowitz, Krantz and Seeck.

display precise metrical repetition.[95] The twelve Aenians (changed from Homer's twenty-two) balance the flotilla of Ajax whose solidary nature is emblematized by the symbolic number twelve. The alternative nomenclature of the Elians/Epians anticipates the way Ajax's ships can turn either way. The nautical hazard of the Snake Islands anticipates the finale when the women keep their memories close and doubtless shrink back as the venomous Menelaus makes his entry.

The structure of the *parodos* anticipates the narrative of the play as a whole. Achilles the Homeric-style individualist fails to change the situation when faced with the modern democratic collective. When Iphigeneia decides to accept death, she makes an eloquent speech about the Panhellenic ideal, and declares that for the unity and supremacy of Greece it is right to sacrifice her individual life. At the time when the play was written, the rhetoric of Panhellenism was seen by some as the means to a political solution, and the triumph of Athens at Salamis could be held up to other Greeks as a glorious contrast to the current Spartan policy of rapprochement with Persia.[96] Just as Achilles resolves the oppositions of A/A' by bringing together the qualities of divine and human, aquatic and earthly, beautiful and strong, betrothed and not betrothed, so Ajax resolves the oppositions in B/B' and C/C', being monstrous but noble, marginal but unifying, Athenian but Panhellenic.[97]

The Homeric world of the story and the immediate here-and-now of the Peloponnesian War collide in this ode.[98] Critics who condemn the 'catalogue' as an interpolation, and allow only the first half of the ode to stand as Euripidean, want art to be universal and cannot readily conceive that Euripides might have preferred to be topical. They are content to admire the individualist values associated with Achilles, but not the collective democratic ethos associated with Ajax. In the Theatre of Dionysus, the world of the play was not entirely other and separate from the world of the audience. Without the

---

[95] England, Gilbert Murray in the Oxford Classical Text (1924) and Jouan print the passage as strophic. Also the Tuebner edition: *Euripides Iphigenia Aulidensis* ed. H. C. Günther (Leipzig, 1988); and most recently *Euripides: Iphigenie in Aulis* ed. Walter Stockert (Vienna, 1992), with discussion on pp. 238–9.

[96] For Gorgias' proposal of a Panhellenic crusade against the Persians to end the internecine war, see Foley, *Ritual Irony* 102; also Jouan's edition p. 42. Foley has a long discussion of the importance of Panhellenic rhetoric in the play.

[97] On Ajax and Athens, see the essays by David J. Bradshaw and John M. Wickersham in Pozzi and Wickersham, *Myth and the Polis*. Bradshaw notes that the Athenians sacrificed to Ajax after the battle of Salamis. Wickersham shows how the Athenians validated their claim to Salamis by citing Homer's placing of the ships.

[98] For the principle see Vernant's seminal essay 'The historical moment of tragedy in Greece' *MTAG* 23–8.

chorus, the *Iphigeneia at Aulis* would be a psychological narrative about public and private duties, guilt and idealism, and the audience would have been detached observers, but with the chorus, the play enters the spheres of myth, ritual and politics.

For an audience seated in a sanctuary, the myth was validated by reference to another, equally real space, the sanctuary of Artemis at Aulis.[99] There was no sharp dividing line between reality on the one hand, myth and ritual on the other. The men who acted before the audience were also co-celebrants with the audience.[100] The complex interrelation of myth, ritual and politics apprehended by the playwright was better communicated through a fusion of word, music and movement than through language alone. The logical structure of the ode, made clear by the dance, may at this point be worth summarizing:

A:	A':
water	land/grove
Aphrodite	Artemis
sexual activity	anticipation

interlude:
seashore
Achilles the bridegroom

B/B':	C/C':
pure young men	corrupt mature men
pro-Athens	anti-Athens
goddesses	monsters

epode:
Panhellenism
Ajax of Salamis

A few technical issues remain to be considered. The pattern of entries and exits in *Iphigeneia* suggests that one *eisodos* leads to the camp and the shore, the other

---

[99] A bronze plate near the temple of Artemis marked the threshold of Agamemnon's tent, i.e. the setting of the play: Pausanias ix.19.5. For references to the site, see Albert Schachter *Cults of Boeotia* Vol.1 (*BICS* supplement 38.1, London, 1981) 94–8. The site was a tourist attraction by 396 BC, when it was visited by Agesilaus.

[100] The chorus are girls at the point of transition to womanhood, and it may be that the dancers were young men engaged in a rite of passage, a significant parallelism. See the discussions by Winkler and Goldhill in *NTDWD* 36–42, 101, 113. Winkler *passim* argues that the chorus were ephebes. The best evidence is vase painting, but the role of young men in escorting the statue is also suggestive.

to the grove and the road to Argos/Mycenae.[101] The obvious inference is that the chorus enter as two groups, one from each side, and by their separate entries the 'hemichorus' and 'antichorus' define the significance of the two *eisodoi* for the audience.[102] If the whole chorus entered from the same side, one might wonder why a group of women coming along the shore from the Chalcis ferry should have gone inland in order to pass through the sacrificial grove. Split entry accords with the apparent difference in marital status between the two groups. An entry from two sides is used in *Trojan Women* and was also, according to the scholiast, used in *Alcestis.* Although some kind of processional entry to music must have preceded the singing of the text in plays where the chorus commences with strophic dancing,[103] the use of a split chorus here would allow two groups to approach each other from different sides of the *orchêstra* and merge for the chanted description of Achilles.

There is no likelihood that the dancing in this *parodos* is predominantly circular, for the sense requires that the chorus are looking forwards as if viewing a line of ships displayed before them along the beach. The steps of the dance need to communicate the idea of moving along the line of the beach. Although the description of the ships commences with Achilles on the right, it passes in the antistrophe (B′) to the citizens of Argos and Athens, and we might expect Athens to be on the left, since this is Ajax's position and Homer records Ajax as beached with the Athenians.[104] The catalogue of ships in Book Two of the *Iliad* does not list the ships in order of their position along the beach, and Euripides does not therefore have a simple linear model for his reworking of that catalogue.[105] Odysseus is said by Homer to have occupied the centre point in the line,[106] but his ships are not mentioned. The epode emphasizes not the marginality of Ajax on the left but his completing of the whole and his ability to turn either way. The choreography of the epode seems to demand an unbroken line facing the audience and representing the unity of the disparate fleet. Euripides' description of the fleet makes topographical sense in relation to the sideways to and fro of strophe and antistrophe. It is possible that he allocated this sequence again to hemichorus and antichorus, who seem as groups to have approached the fleet from opposite directions, in order to emphasize the transformation of the parts into a united whole in the epode.

The tiny scale of the actors in an open theatre with no artificial lighting created a very different sense of space to anything experienced by the average

---

[101] Hence the significance of Clytaemnestra arriving via the green meadow (422).
[102] Pollux iv.107 cites the terminology.
[103] Gould and Lewis analyse choral entries in *DFA* 242–4 and make this inference.
[104] *Iliad* ii.557–8.   [105] See Cuillandre, *La Droite et la gauche* (Paris, 1944) 25–7.
[106] *Iliad* viii.223.

western theatre-goer in the modern world. The gaze of the spectator encountered the actor as a tiny point in relation to the Athenians assembled in their thousands.[107] The visual image was semiotically complex not because of nuances of gesture and individual appearance, but because of the patterns formed by the actors' bodies both in relation to each other and in relation to the sanctuary of Dionysus where the event took place.

---

[107] Note that vision yields significant information about a very small area at any given moment: 2°–3° around dead centre. Vision is not passive but a process of selection as the eye moves about in saccades. The brain generalizes information about peripheral areas. See Daniel C. Dennett, *Consciousness Explained* (Harmondsworth, 1993) 54, 354.

CHAPTER 5

✧

The chorus: its transformation of space

Theatrical space should not be understood as an empty receptacle waiting to be filled with a content of signs, but rather as a principle of organization. Anne Ubersfeld argues that in the proscenium theatre the principle of organization is based on the referent, the supposed real world replicated on stage. While a clear boundary divides the stage from the auditorium, the on-stage world and an imagined off-stage world are taken to be homogenous. In the 'platform' theatre, by contrast, organization is based on the spatial relationships visible to the spectator. The sharp boundary here is not the boundary which divides actor from audience, but the one which demarcates the platform stage from all that is unseen. In the proscenium theatre, Ubersfeld writes, 'spatial organization is linked to the dramatic fiction, to the imagined space of which the scenic space is merely a concrete "translation"', whereas in platform staging 'space is organized in relation to the bodies of the actors who invest it'. The proportions of 'mimesis', where the emphasis is on the referent, the implied elsewhere, and 'ludus', where the emphasis is on the body of the performer, may change not only from play to play but also within a given play. In all forms of theatre, Ubersfeld argues, the mimetic and the ludic are present, and only the proportions change.[1]

The task of the semiotician must include the diachronic exploration of spatial *transformations*, for the organization of space within a performance is rarely a constant. I examined in chapter 1 the problems of a crude semiotic approach to theatrical space which would seek to differentiate a seen 'mimetic' space from an unseen or described 'diegetic' space, and I suggested that the sacrifice of Iphigeneia in *Agamemnon* was, from the point of view of the audience, not so much a narrated event in time past as a transformation of past action into present action. In Greek tragedy it is principally the job of the chorus to effect spatio-temporal transformations. In messenger speeches the audience

---

[1] Anne Ubersfeld, *L'Ecole du spectateur* (Paris, 1981) 64. On her platform/proscenium dichotomy, see p. 15 above.

not only listens to the messenger's narration but also sees the present responses of people listening to the narration of a past event, whereas in choral odes the addressees are normally the spectators. The sense of a fictional here-and-now can easily be dissolved as the mimetic gives way to the ludic, and post-war Argos becomes pre-war Aulis and the scene of the human sacrifice.

I shall examine some of the ludic transformations of space that Aeschylus seems to have effected in *Seven Against Thebes*. There is no direct evidence that a *skênê* was used to fix a sense of place, and a group of statues (which we shall examine in chapter 9) is the key to the play's organization of space. Analysis of space in the *Seven* runs into controversy with the very first words:

ETEOCLES: Citizens of Cadmus

The play's most recent editor, citing the authority of Taplin and Bain, brings on a crowd of extras to serve as addressees. The Chicago, Penguin, Methuen and Oxford translators all agree that Aeschylus could not have asked the audience to imagine themselves as the Theban 'citizens of Cadmus' addressed by Eteocles.[2] These interpreters would all prefer Aeschylus to have pre-set a host of extras. These luckless extras, supposedly representing all weapon-bearing Thebans young and old, would be required to stand silent for thirty-odd lines and then slip out with no clear exit line. The critical tradition has accepted almost without hesitation this remarkable budgetary indulgence rather than yield up its shibboleths of 'realism' and 'illusion'.

In his next line, Eteocles speaks of himself as the helmsman in the stern of the city. Addressing a crowd of extras, Eteocles would be a mere politician using metaphor. If he is a lone figure, however, addressing the audience from an unlocalized orchestral circle, bordered only by images of gods, the sense of space may momentarily become cosmic, and Eteocles could have been *seen* for a brief moment as lone sailor rather than politician. Such spatial transformations are possible when there are no visual signs to fix the spatial referent as a specific place in a historically conceived Thebes. When we try to pin down this archaic Thebes, the precise referent is elusive, just like the Athens of the *Eumenides* or the Delphi of *Ion*. The *orchêstra* may represent the entirety of Thebes, the statues being identified with the enclosing walls of the city (168, 175, 823); or it may just represent 'this acropolis' (240), which of course could

[2] G. O. Hutchinson, *Aeschylus: Septem contra Thebas* (Oxford, 1985) 41; David Bain 'Audience address in Greek tragedy' *Classical Quarterly* 25 (1975) 13–25; *SA* 129–36; *Seven Against Thebes*, tr. David Grene in *Aeschylus* Vol. II (Chicago, 1956); Aeschylus *Prometheus and Other Plays*, tr. P. Vellacott (Harmondsworth, 1961); Aeschylus *Plays: One*, tr. F. Raphael and K. Mcleish (London, 1991); Aeschylus *Seven Against Thebes*, tr. A. Hecht and H. H. Bacon (New York and London, 1973). On the play's interpellation of the audience see p. 213 below.

be interpreted as the whole Mycenaean city. At 345 the 'city' is regarded as being elsewhere. If the setting is specifically the acropolis, then it is not clear how the complex of shrines is organized, or whether the statues are located in temples. In the middle of the play the space becomes a confluence of roads leading to the seven gates, and we might imagine the *agora* as a more convenient location. In the latter part of the play, attention turns to the 'house' of Oedipus. There are 'woes at the hearth of the house' (851), the house is plundered (877), unwalled (882), pierced (895), and a cry comes from the house (915). In the finale a generalized Thebes, as in *Oedipus the King* and *The Phoenician Women*, cannot be dissociated from the palace of Oedipus. If there is no single referent, then the space that is transformed into different aspects of Thebes may equally be transformed into the ocean.

The chorus of Theban women arrive distraught (78–108), and embrace the statues of the gods. The audience are not at first in a position to know whether the women *actually* hear and see an attack, or merely imagine one, though their Bottom-like phrase 'I see a sound' (103) implies the latter. The audience at this early point in the play is denied any position of detachment and objective judgement. An astrophic sequence follows (109–50) in which the women physically transform the statues by clothing them and placing garlands on their heads. Once the statues have been dressed, a strophic section (151–80) allows a formal dance in honour of these gods. A/A' are addressed to individual statues, B/B' to the ensemble. The presence of eight statues, thus identified and honoured, creates a sense not only of a local cultic tradition but also of an entire ordered cosmos, a human world watched over by Olympian powers.

The next choral sequence (288–368) likens the rape of a woman to the rape of a city. After prayers to the gods in A/A', the linkage of chorus and *polis* is made clear in B/B':

B: Pity that the city should	B': Alas that unripe maids
be cast to Hades . . .	should be plucked . . .
Captive women	The city raped
young and old . . .	suffers woe . . .
The fate I fear.	Madness of Ares.

C/C' continues the theme: suckling children torn from the breast are linked by the antistrophe to corn poured to rot, and the pair-bonding of looters seeking plunder is linked to the copulation of victors with captured maidens. The focus of the tableau at the end of B/B' is probably the statue of Ares, transformed from a cult object belonging to Thebes into the fate menacing Thebes. The city which Eteocles claimed as a male domain is reclaimed by the chorus as an intrinsically female reproductive entity. Through its language and its gestural enactment of assault and rape, the chorus create a world that exists in three temporal dimensions: time present, because the chorus expresses present fears; time past, because verbal echoes evoke the attack on Homeric Troy;[3] and time future, because the chorus imagines the forthcoming attack.

A new theme is introduced when two strophic pairs (686–708) cover the arming of Eteocles.[4] In A/A', while the warrior arms, the women sing of fighting as a form of sexual desire, their sexual body language counterpointing a military ritual. In B/B', paired images of a demon departing help to identify the departing warrior Eteocles with the demonic Fury. To conceive the figure of Eteocles in terms of modern psychological realism is a reductive exercise.

The chorus' reference to Eteocles' house at 700 introduces a spatial transformation as the setting becomes less obviously the city and more obviously the house of Oedipus. A long choral ode follows (720–91) during which the battle is supposed to be taking place. At the start of the play the chorus imagined as time present a battle located in time future. Now, while the battle takes place in time present, the chorus return to time past, and recapitulate the history of the house of Oedipus.

A/A'. The Fury in A = steel in A'. This link is clear in performance because Eteocles has just made his exit, blade in hand. In A, Oedipus bestows curses on his sons; in A', steel allots graves.

B/B'. New evils in B = old evils in B'. Images of the thirsty earth and purification in B are linked in B' to the Delphic oracle at the centre of the earth.

C/C'. Oedipus' coupling with Jocasta = the rape of the city. The sexual act in C is transformed into waves cresting and swelling around the boat that is Thebes. Oedipus' phallic root planted in the earth becomes a slender Theban tower. Consummation with Jocasta becomes the assault on the city. The sexual basis of the choreography is very clear.

D/D'. D moves from the fulfilment of curses to the jettisoning of cargo from a prosperous ship. D' moves from divine wonder at Oedipus to his eviction of the Sphinx from Thebes. Again, ship = city.

E/E'. The controlling idea is doubleness. In E Oedipus responds to his double crime of incest and parricide; in E' he causes his two sons to carve his

---

[3] See Hutchinson's note on 287–368.

[4] See Helen Bacon 'The Shield of Eteocles' *Arion* 3 (1964) 27–38. *SA* 158–61 rejects the arming scene, as proposed by Schadewaldt in 1961, on the grounds that there is no direct textual support, even though Eteocles does call for his greaves, the first item in the ritual process of dressing, at 676. The precise timing proffered by Bacon in her article and translation is, unfortunately, not well matched to the words. B. M. W. Knox accepts the need for the arming scene in *Word and Action* (Baltimore, 1979) 83.

inheritance in two. The final image of E is of Oedipus destroying his two eyes; the final image of E' is of the fatal blade transformed to the swift-footed Fury. In the tableau the chorus probably cover their eyes and hear but do not see the messenger who brings news of the double killing, and temporarily embodies the Fury.

Hearing that the brothers are dead, the chorus turn from rejoicing to lamentation. In a strophic pair (822–47) which deals with the curse of Oedipus, the chorus sing in A of what they have heard, the song of the spear, and in A' they sing of what they can now see, for the two bodies are being carried in. As the bodies are laid down (848–60), the choreography is unambiguous, for the chorus beat their heads in ritual mourning (855). This action of beating is made to suggest also the movement of a boat, both Charon's boat leading to the underworld, and the boat of Theseus making its annual journey from Delos to Athens.[5] Thebes momentarily becomes Athens.

The statues which have hitherto been protectors of the walls are associated at 773 with the city's hearth. All the attention in the first part of the play is upon the periphery, the walls and guardian deities that separate Thebes from the enemy, but the attention in the finale is upon the centre. The corpses must be placed in a central position, for all that follows relates to their immobile presence. The chorus dance a sequence in four strophic pairs (875–960), and through the ode we can trace shifts in visual focus. In A/A' the subject is the house which the brothers have destroyed and which has destroyed them. We do not, unfortunately, know how the house was represented in the earlier plays of the trilogy. The focus of B is the maimed bodies, and of B' the *polis* embodied by the chorus gathered around the bodies. C passes from the ancestral tomb to shrieks of pain, and C' from the Theban mass grave to Jocasta's pains of childbirth. An obvious focus here is the *thymelê*, suggesting a tomb as in *The Libation Bearers* but also an umbilicus over a womb. In D/D' the initial focus is the earth floor of the *orchêstra*, for the brothers are of the same seed and share the same soil. The final image of D is Ares the divider, and of D' the trophy of Atê at the gates where the demon has been laid to rest. The statue of Ares, dressed and decorated by the chorus, is probably the focus of the tableau, transformed by the antistrophe from a symbol of victory to a demon of destruction. Although we lack precise stage directions, the general dramaturgical principles are clear. The chorus constantly refocus on different parts of the acting space, and in each antistrophe add more density to the symbolism, heaping more significance upon the fixed signifiers which comprise the acting space.

The relationship of strophe and antistrophe is precisely one of transforma-

---

[5] See Hutchinson's note to 856–60, citing the scholiast.

tion, for a visual image seen one way in the strophe is seen a different way thanks to the different words used in the antistrophe. Stage objects, parts of the performance space, and the bodies of the dancers are all available to be transformed and reinterpreted. We must not conceive the choral odes as poetry enhanced or illustrated by rhythmic movement, but rather as a sequence of visual images interpreted by words. All too many critics regard the *Seven* as a linguistic and rhetorical construct of scant theatrical interest because they are committed to the primacy of language.[6] Yet Athenaeus speaks of an Aeschylean dancer 'of such artistry that in dancing the *Seven Against Thebes* he made all the actions clear through dance'.[7] Once we recognise that the *Seven* is as much 'dance' as 'drama', we can see that Aeschylus' medium had infinite possibilities for the transformation of space, moment by moment through the performance.

In Euripides, the articulation of speech and lyric is sharper, and one can in principle distinguish movement between two polarities: a space with a single topographical referent established primarily by the actors, and an infinitely transformable space established primarily in the dance sequences. If we take *The Trojan Women* as an example, we can see how the sense of a specific location unfolds gradually. Poseidon in the prologue defines the setting as 'this land of Troy' (4), and he points to Hecuba who lies 'in front of the doors' (37), being of course the doors of the *skênê*. Hecuba declares that she is close to the tents ('skênai') of Agamemnon, and is being led from home ('ex oikôn') (138–41). With the arrival of the chorus, and their statement that they have come from the tents of Agamemnon (176–7), it becomes relatively clear that the *skênê* represents the Greek camp rather than the frontage of Priam's palace. The major spatial parameters are fixed by the *eisodoi*, one of which leads to the camp and one (established by Poseidon's prologue) to the sea. When Troy is addressed by Poseidon – 'farewell, oh *polis*' (45) – or Hecuba – 'Troy, Troy' (173) – or the chorus – 'unhappy Troy' (780) – it seems simplest to imagine that the auditorium is being addressed.

If we are to reconstruct the staging, the crux comes when the chorus see men on the walls of Troy, and the Herald instructs these men to burn the *polis* (1256–63). There seem to be two possibilities. Either the *skênê* is redefined in the course of the play so that it comes to represent the walls of Troy, or the flames are imagined and the space occupied by the audience is taken to be Troy. The first hypothesis requires that actors or dummies are visible on the roof of the *skênê*, and that clouds of smoke rise up in front of the audience; and that

---

[6] Recent structuralist approaches are no less logocentric than Hutchinson's philology and Taplin's 'stagecraft': see Froma Zeitlin, *Under the Sign of the Shield* (Rome, 1982) and P. Vidal-Naquet, 'The shields of the heroes' in *MTAG* 273–300.

[7] Athenaeus 22a, discussed in *DFA* 251.

when Hecuba attempts to rush into the flames (1282), she rushes towards the door of the *skênê*. A comparison with *Seven Against Thebes* favours the second hypothesis, for in that play, I argued, the audience are at the outset incorporated spatially in the world of Thebes. If Euripides' characters apostrophizing Troy address the auditorium, a similar sense of incorporation and involvement will occur. In *Seven Against Thebes*, Aeschylus represents an attack on Thebes that is not yet happening, and declines to represent the attack when it does happen, but offers in lieu a recapitulation of the story of Oedipus. In *Trojan Women* Euripides brings flames into the theatre at a point when Troy is not being put to the torch, for Cassandra appears at the doors with wedding torches, and the Herald fears that the women are firing their quarters. At the point when the whole city is being torched, Euripides' dramaturgical strategy – I would suggest – was to make the audience imagine fire, imagination having been stimulated by the earlier Cassandra scene. To have smoke rising behind the *skênê* may seem attractive to a stage designer with modern resources, but in a fifth-century context the *skênê* itself must remain intact, and a smoking *skênê* would seem a half-hearted compromise, committed neither to the power of imagination nor to scenographic mimesis. If, however, we accept the hypothesis that smoke does rise from the *skênê* at the end of the play, we must accept as a corollary that the *skênê* has been redefined and has changed from tent to city. In the first play of Euripides' trilogy, the setting was Troy; in the second, the Greek camp. It is interesting that in the third play Euripides should tie his trilogy together by creating a setting that in some way fuses the two.[8]

Fluid stagecraft allows the chorus to attach associations to different parts of the acting space. After Cassandra's wedding torches in the *skênê* doorway have been used as a visual metaphor for the burning city, the chorus in the following strophe and antistrophe evoke the Trojan horse placed at the gates of the city (511ff.). Deixis here could well have called the doors of the *skênê* into temporary service as the gates of Troy. Later in the play, when Hecuba mourns her city and her grandson, the chorus evoke first the beaches of Salamis and the nearby cult of Athene in Athens (strophe: 799ff.), and then the beaches of Troy (antistrophe: 809ff.). Symmetrical choreography hints at a spatial equivalence of Athens and Troy, the real temple of Athene above and behind the audience becoming an imagined Troy upon which the dancers gaze. When Hecuba beats the earth with her hands in a strophe (1306), and imagines the buildings of Troy turned to dust in the antistrophe, the beaten earth floor of the *orchêstra* is transformed for a moment into the ashes of Troy.

---

[8] On the relationship of the three plays, see Ruth Scodel, *The Trojan Trilogy of Euripides* (Göttingen, 1980).

In Euripides' *Medea*, there is on the face of it no comparable ambiguity about what the *skênê* represents. Although the messenger's words picture the interior of the house of Creon where the princess dies, the visible *skênê* represents the house of Jason and Medea. No verbal picture of the interior is offered because the symbolic aspect of the house is more important than the referential. As the *domos* of Jason it represents not so much a specific building as a family unit.[9] It is the hearth at which the princess will arrive in her wedding procession. When the chorus report that marriage to Jason has brought the princess to the house of Hades (1234), the audience would recognize the doors of the *skênê* as the doors of Hades.[10] Soon this sunless dwelling will contain a Fury within it (1260).

The opening lines of the play pictured the voyage of Jason and the Argonauts through the Bosphorus to Medea's homeland on the Asian side of the Black Sea. When Medea makes her long-awaited entry through the doors of the *skênê*, the chorus cover her entry by singing of Jason's false oath 'which brought her to Greece on the other side, over the brine at night to the Black Sea's salty key-hole so hard to pass'(209–12). Medea's passage through the *skênê* into the *orchêstra* is thus equated spatially with her passage through the Bosphorus into the Greek world. As in *Seven Against Thebes*, a journey across the sea becomes the basis of an alternative representational system. We might speak of a 'spatial sub-text', or of a 'subjunctive' rather than 'indicative' use of space. The term 'meta-space' will perhaps serve best to denominate this alternative spatial system, when the *polis* dissolves as the immediate referent and the voyage of the Argo comes to the forefront of the audience's attention. We must keep reminding ourselves that the audience is guided by language and movement, not by representational scenery. The human figures in the *orchêstra* are too small for psychological detail to be registered. Meaning is created by the movement patterns of small human figures within a large open space, and the device of a 'meta-space' allows these patterns to have multiple connotations.

Memory of the Argo's voyage is sustained when Medea finds harbourage with the king of Athens (769–70), and when Jason presents himself as the helmsman weathering the storm of Medea (523–5). It is, however, in the choral odes that the voyage is visually rendered. At 431ff., the chorus represent Medea sailing from her home through the Bosphorus, an image which equates in the antistrophe with integrity flying away from Greece. The chorus sing that Medea has come to a foreign land (strophe), and has lost her anchorage (antistrophe). The figure of Medea meanwhile remains trapped in the *orchêstra*, with no place of retreat either inside the *skênê* or out through an *eisodos*. Later

---

[9] *Medea* 77, 114, 130, 137, 139, 597, 608, 794.   [10] See p. 165 below.

the chorus construe Corinth as the antithesis of Athens, where Aphrodite can sail placidly along the river (835ff.). When Medea finally leaves the *orchêstra* and enters the darkness of the *skênê* to kill her children, the chorus sing of her passing through the clashing rocks of the Bosphorus, the same image that accompanied her one and only entry through the *skênê* doors. It is thus a consistent motif that the *orchêstra* represents the sea, and the fatal doorway with its doors that open and shut represents the famous moving rocks that are so hard to navigate.

The moment of murder occupies a strophe (1273ff.), and the responding antistrophe tells of another madwoman who killed her children and leapt off a cliff into the sea. The image of the clifftop prepares the way for Medea's final entry high above an *orchêstra* floor that meta-spatially represents the sea. In the final scene of the play, Medea in her chariot drawn by dragons has a dialogue with Jason down below her in front of the house. Jason dubs her a Scylla, and she responds that she may indeed be called Scylla (1343, 1359). The Argo, just like Homer's Odysseus, had to sail past Scylla, whose rock guarded not the Bosphorus but the straits of Messina.[11] Scylla as depicted by Homer is a monster dwelling in a cave high above the straits, with six heads that reach out to seize six of Odysseus' sailors. Medea in the play is positioned high above the *skênê* door, in some kind of chariot drawn by serpents. These long-necked dragons or serpents are not directly mentioned in the text, but are attested by all later commentators and vase painters.[12] Given the equivalence established by the 'meta-space' between the doors of the *skênê* and dangerous narrow straits, the force of the reference to Scylla becomes clear. The serpentine Medea/Scylla swings menacingly above the Argonaut, holding two bodies that she has seized from him. The transformative 'meta-space' allows the stage image to become polysemous. Medea rides in the sky because she is associated by birth with the sun-god. She has been forced into the sunlight, out of the dark house to which Greek society consigned her. Her serpents associate her with a chthonic Fury, but also with Scylla, guarding the straits through which Jason's vessel must pass. This monster, a victim of male love, is tied by her name to another Scylla who was drowned in the ocean after betraying her father for love, as Medea once did.[13]

---

[11] Robert Graves, *The Greek Myths* (Harmondsworth, 1960) II.368; *Odyssey*, xii.73ff. For visual representations, see B. Cohen (ed.) *The Distaff Side* (Oxford, 1995) 34–6.

[12] For sources, see D. L. Page (ed.) *Euripides: Medea* (Oxford, 1938) xxvii (literary) and lvii–lxvi (vases). Page remarks that a vase of *c*.500 BC representing Medea with snakes beside her head confirms that the association of Medea with a serpent chariot is not a post-Euripidean innovation. For two recently discovered fourth-century representations of the chariot, see Oliver Taplin *Comic Angels* (Oxford, 1993) plates 1.101 and 2.103.

[13] The two were taken as one by Ovid: see Graves, *Greek Myths* I.309–10.

The primary function of the chorus is to offer an alternative, transformative mode of seeing. If the same world is to be seen by the audience in two different ways, then it is a fundamental principle that actors and chorus share the same space. Peter Arnott, long committed to the idea that actors are tied to the *skênê* and chorus to the *orchêstra*, takes a traditionalist view of the chorus as privileged intermediaries:

By nature, composition and placement the chorus belongs both in the world of the play and in the world of the audience. It serves, therefore, as an intermediary in universalizing the story, and in relating the tragic action to the audience's present. As in so many ways, the structure of the theatre serves here as an architectural metaphor for the function of drama in this society. The auditorium follows the contours of the *orchêstra*, rising tier by tier into the community; the play's impact is transmitted by the chorus to the greater public, like ripples spreading out in ever-widening circles from a stone cast in a pool.[14]

Arnott's conception of the chorus as located mid-way between actors and audience quickly lands him in difficulties. He would like his intermediary chorus to be an objective moral commentator, but finds little moral material in Euripides, whom he pictures as someone waiting to invent the proscenium arch, forever finding the chorus 'an obstruction and intrusion'. The choruses of *Hippolytus* and *Iphigeneia at Aulis* are dismissed as 'a nullity . . . virtually ciphers, hovering on the periphery of the main action'. In *Medea* Euripides 'hoped to justify the presence of the chorus in purely realistic terms'.[15] Euripides seems to Arnott to be bent on a suicidal journey towards realism, leaving the *orchêstra* without a focus. Arnott cannot reconcile his spatial preconceptions with the plays that he reads.

The idea that the chorus are privileged intermediaries is sometimes propounded in terms of the chorus being, unlike the actors, dancers of Dionysus who are for this reason both inside and outside the play. Winkler, for example, conceiving the chorus as ephebes learning to be citizens, sees the chorus as 'a still center from which the tragic turbulence is surveyed and evaluated'.[16] Nagy sees the chorus as mediating between the heroes of the there-and-then and the audience of the here-and-now, and thus 'mediating' the 'reactive *pathos*' of the audience.[17] We must beware of a critical tendency which, in the name of politics or ritual, keeps the chorus in a marginalized position. Heinrichs develops

---

[14] *Public and Performance in the Greek Theatre* (London, 1989) 34. The metaphor of the stone derives from Vitruvius v.iii.7.   [15] *Public and Performance* 36–8.

[16] 'The ephebes' song: *tragōidia* and *polis*' in *NTDWD* 43.

[17] Gregory Nagy, 'Transformations of choral lyric traditions in the context of Athenian state theatre' *Arion* 3 (1995) 41–55, p. 50. Helen Bacon in the same volume p. 21 n. 3 provides a full bibliography.

a more sophisticated stance when he argues that the chorus invite the audience to participate in a more integrated experience, using their privileged Dionysiac status to create rituals proper to other occasions.[18]

We must also free ourselves from the assumption that in temporal terms the choral odes constitute 'interludes'. Taplin conceives the chorus as providing an 'act-dividing song': 'As I see it, then, the formal structure of Greek tragedy is founded on a basic pattern: enter actor(s) – actors' dialogue – exeunt actor(s) / choral strophic song / enter new actor(s) – actors' dialogue . . . and so on. Beneath the many complexities of the construction of the plays there lies, I suggest, this simple form.'[19] This for Taplin is the ground-pattern upon which dramatists felt free to work variants. His analysis implies that the basic role of the chorus is to demarcate, and he conceives the play not as a dramaturgical unity but as a piece chopped into acts like a Hellenistic, renaissance or nine-teenth-century play. Once, however, we give positive recognition to the prin-ciple that actors and chorus shared the same orchestral space, it is a corollary that sung and spoken parts of the play form an organic whole. If actors and chorus are physically interwoven, then choral odes do not cut off one part of the play from another. Their purpose, rather, is to extend what has gone before and prepare for an entry that is to be made. In a theatre as large as the Theatre of Dionysus, with long slow entrances through the *eisodoi*, we should not con-ceive of the chorus finishing its dance in order for a character subsequently to make an entry. The last lines of choral odes overlapped entries, and the first lines overlapped exits. We can examine in the *Medea* the kind of transitions that Greek theatre effected, as one segment of action flowed into another.

The first entry of the chorus in *Medea* is an informal one, which is to say non-strophic. It follows (in terms of text) or overlaps (in terms of performance) remarks of the Nurse about the disadvantages of being upper-class, and the Nurse's words position the class difference that separates the chorus from Medea. The chorus engage with the Nurse, and there is no kind of break in the action. The next strophic system follows Medea's statement about the woman-hood common to herself and the chorus.[20] She remains a focus of attention in the *orchêstra* as the chorus sing in A/A' of how all women are treated in male-authored literature.

---

[18] A. Heinrichs, '"Why should I dance?" Choral self-referentiality in Greek tragedy' *Arion* 3 (1995) 56–111, p. 59.

[19] *SA* 55. On p. 472 Taplin rejects the Aristotelian term 'episode' because it sounds too parenthet-ical to do justice to his concept of an 'act'. Malcolm Heath endorses and extends Taplin's argu-ment about the 'act-dividing lyric', arguing that the choral ode has its 'autonomous aesthetic reward': *The Poetics of Greek Tragedy* (London, 1987) 137–40.

[20] Line 407 – significantly mistranslated in Rex Warner's Chicago version.

In B/B' the chorus describe Medea as driven from her bed, preparing and covering the entry of Medea's bed-partner. In the next ode at 627ff., whilst Jason makes his exit towards his new bride, the chorus sing in A of excessive sexual desire; in A', once Jason is out of sight, the chorus turn to their own sexual aspirations. In B they cease looking into themselves, and look out to the city that they feel part of; and in B' they sing of loyalty to one's *philoi* (friends/relatives) as Medea's loyal friend Aegeus makes his entry. After Aegeus has offered Medea asylum in Athens, the ode at 824ff. creates an idealized picture of Athens in A/A'. As in the last two odes, the sharp and eloquent break is not between the spoken and choral parts of the text, but at the mid-point of the choral ode where A/A' gives way to B/B'. In B/B' the chorus turn from Athens to the woman who stands before them. There is no ambiguity about the final tableau, where the chorus fall on their knees: in B they mime the action of clasping Medea's knees in supplication, and in B' they imagine Medea's children doing the same. The tableau accompanies the entry of Jason, now acquiescent rather than aggressive, and meeting a Medea who also feigns submission. The tableau of submission thus mirrors the duplicitous stances adopted by Jason and Medea. We could continue this form of analysis through the remainder of the play in order to demonstrate that a choral ode does not divide segments of action but unites them. Taplin's theory shows itself at its most flawed when we come to the climax of the play, the death of the children at 1251ff. As Medea steps into the darkness of the house, the chorus begin to dance, and call upon the sun to see her. Theatrical shock is effected at the moment when the first antistrophe gives way to the second strophe. At the end of A', a tableau appropriate to a Fury and to Ruin is interrupted by a cry from a child. The voices of the children participate in B and are silent in B'. In no meaningful sense can this moment be conceived as a break in the action: it is an event.

Any Greek tragedy could be examined to make the same point, that there is no sharp spatio-temporal demarcation of choral ode from action.[21] The purpose of the ode is not to offer philosophical reflection, emotional relief, or the pleasure of verbal pictures. It is meshed with the action, but creates the possibility of seeing the action in terms that are not monocular and rationalistic. We could analyse any Greek tragedy in order to pick out meta-spaces which replace a referential, first-order space in front of a house, cave or temple. I shall conclude this chapter with an analysis of spatial transformation in three more choral odes.

---

[21] For some Euripidean examples of how choral odes and exits or entrances are strategically juxtaposed, see M. J. Halleran, *Stagecraft in Euripides* (London, 1985) 50ff.

The protagonist of *Hypsipyle* is another former bride of Jason, and like
Medea she is preoccupied with the voyage of the *Argo*. In the first choral ode
(the only one to survive), the enslaved Hypsipyle begins the first strophe by
lamenting that she cannot sing over her weaving like a free woman of Lemnos,
but must sing a baby's ditty. The chorus arrive and ask what she is singing: of
the Argonauts (= happy), or of her home in Lemnos (= sad)? They inform her
that the glorious army of the Seven is passing en route to Thebes (= now).
Hypsipyle in the antistrophe responds that she is singing of Orpheus playing
for the oarsmen of the *Argo*, and declines to sing of the passing army. In the
strophic correspondences, the movement of Hypsipyle's loom correlates with
the movement of the oars, and a baby's ditty correlates ironically with a false
panegyric of the army. In their continuation of the antistrophe the chorus sing
of two other journeys: that of Europa over the sea (= happy) and of Io the cow
(= sad). They return to present reality, Hypsipyle herself, and to the hope that
Dionysus is *en route* to find her (= now). The play sets up a structural parallel
between two principal journeys: (1) the positive journey of the *Argo*, which
brought Jason to Hypsipyle and subsequently brought their sons back to find
their mother, and (2) the negative journey of an army taking young men to die.
Land (negative) is opposed to water (positive). This thematic opposition has a
visible spatial correlative, for one *eisodos* leads to the valley, the other to the
spring. While the army in the valley pollutes the river, the virtuous Amphiaraus
comes to fetch water from the spring. The to and fro of the strophic dance
would have allowed Hypsipyle to mark out the two directions that signified

NEGATIVE : POSITIVE

land : water

grove : spring

army : Argo

The journey of the *Argo*, presented initially as a slave's day-dream, becomes
part of an integrated system of binary oppositions.

The opposition of land and water is equally apparent in the *Hippolytus*; or
rather, it has become so thanks to structuralist criticism. When we turn back
to Barrett's monumental edition, we find no glimmer of structural thinking,
as witnessed by his comments upon the ode that is danced while Phaedra hangs
herself (732ff.).

Now, in the choral ode before the new scene begins, the poet is not concerned to stir
up further our emotions over Phaidra's calamity: that calamity, affect us as it may, is
incidental to the tragedy of Hippolytos, and the poet's need now is not to enhance but
to play down the emotions it has aroused, to secure that her death itself, with which
the new scene must open, shall pass off with no added effect and leave us fresh to face
the new developments that are about to begin. The ode is designed therefore to draw

us away from the happenings on the stage, and to induce in us when we return to them a pity that shall not be violent but resigned.[22]

The critical stance here resembles that of Taplin which we examined in chapter 1, and turns on a series of unquestioned propositions: the purpose of tragedy is to arouse the particular emotions specified by Aristotle; the events of the play stem from a Fate to which we must be 'resigned'; the rhetorical 'we' embraces Greeks and right-thinking moderns alike; the tragedy is centred on one individual, not upon the male/female juxtaposition; the ode is entirely separate from the 'scene' which follows; there is a focus on 'the stage' and the chorus (wherever it may be) obliterates this focus, offering a kind of escape to the emotionally overburdened spectator.

The choreographic structure of the ode can be expressed as follows:

A	A'
To become a bird	Fly to the Hesperides
god-made	sea-lord halts
over the Eridanus [Po]	by Atlas mountains
dripping	fountains
sea-swell of the father[23]	chamber of Zeus
girls for Phaethon weep	gifts of earth
amber tears	blessing for gods

B	B'
Phaedra's voyage from Crete	sickness from Aphrodite
away from happiness	foundering
to ill marriage	in marriage chamber
ill omens at Crete and Athens	puts a noose to her throat
bind ship's cables at Athens	swaps shame for honour
step ashore	rid of Eros

---

22 W. S. Barrett (ed.) *Euripides: Hippolytos* (Oxford, 1964) 297. Compare Lattimore's 1956 analysis of the ode as 'a curtain between the acts' attributable to the poet in his *alter ego* as 'the escapist who sentimentalizes': *The Poetry of Greek Tragedy* (New York, 1966) 110. In the year after Barrett's edition, a structuralist essay by Charles Segal entitled 'The tragedy of *Hippolytus*: the waters of ocean and the untouched meadow' lifted criticism of the play out of its psychological quagmire: *Harvard Studies in Classical Philology* 70 (1965) 117–69. Segal, however, continues to regard the play in poetic rather than performance terms. George R. Kernodle's pioneering essay 'Symbolic action in the Greek choral odes?' *Classical Journal* 53 (1957/8) 1–6 identifies the narrative importance of this ode.

23 The meaning is difficult here. Barrett's note on 738–41 takes no account of the strophic symmetry between the 'father' and Zeus.

As Phaedra enters the *skênê* to die, the choreography in some way suggests flying westward. The chorus' destination in A is associated with the death of the young charioteer Phaethon, and the tableau thus foreshadows the death of that other charioteer Hippolytus. In A′, the flight westwards arrives at the marriage chamber of Zeus, analogue for the marriage chamber where Phaedra dies. The choreography must be conceived in the vertical plane, as the imagery passes from flying through the air to the sea or earth, and the motion of flying anticipates the motion of Phaedra as she leaps from her bed. The opposition of sea (in A/B) and land (in A′/B′) may again be related to the movement of the dance towards the two opposed *eisodoi*, one of which suggests the direction of the sea and one the hinterland.

The marriage of Zeus in A′ introduces the marriage of Phaedra, the subject of B. The dance in B starts with an image of the sea, as the chorus reenact the bride's journey from Crete. The rhythmic movement of the sea must be duplicated in B′ to signify the effects of Aphrodite, for Aphrodite is born of the sea (415, 522). As the fatal journey has a start and finish, so the cord has one end on the beam and the other at Phaedra's neck. The binding of the ship's cables to the Athenian quay mimics Phaedra's tying of the cord to her neck. The offstage action of the woman hanging herself is recreated by the chorus in explicit terms, but with an extra dimension: Phaedra is not only weaving cords but weaving her future reputation. The image of the bride stepping off the boat becomes in the antistrophe an image of leaving the waters of sexual desire. The final choreographic action of stepping ashore evokes Phaedra's physical action of stepping off the bed to hang herself, and a shriek from within accompanies the tableau.

Clearly this ode in no sense comprises an escape from the happenings of the play (as Barrett would have it), but rather continues the narrative by another means. The death that cannot be represented by the actors in direct mimetic form is represented in a different idiom through the bodies of the dancers. Choreographed images of the sea in this ode connect sea-born Aphrodite to her human embodiment and victim. Phaedra's fatal voyage counterbalances Hippolytus' fatal last journey, and the sea/land opposition relates to a series of other binaries: the two statues, the two choruses,[24] the two *eisodoi*. The role of the chorus is fundamental in establishing the sea as a meta-space, a space whence Hippolytus' destruction will finally come. Bridging the human and the divine, the chorus makes the play far more than a humanist study of psychological character.[25]

---

[24] For the significance of the male chorus in the play, see P. E. Easterling, 'Euripides in the theatre', *Pallas* 37 (1991) 49–59.

[25] The problems of a psychological approach are illustrated by Richmond Lattimore's bafflement

Sophocles' choral odes are less obviously pictorial than those of Euripides and Aeschylus, and he rarely extends a single visual image across a full strophe or antistrophe or strophic pair. From a linguistic point of view, Shirley Barlow finds Sophocles' odes more moral and metaphorical, but less 'sensuous'.[26] From a choreographic point of view, I would prefer to say that Sophocles is more geometric, being concerned to create patterns within the performance space as much as pictures. A good example is the *parodos* of *Women of Trachis*. Deianira learns that the life of her husband Heracles is in the balance, and she sends her son to seek him, whereupon the chorus of maidens enters. The strophes are concerned with the absent Heracles, the antistrophes with Deianira who stands in the *orchêstra*.

A	A'
glimmering Night	yearning heart
raped and bears	fought-around
puts to bed in flames	'Dêïaneira'
Sun!	like a bird
where is Heracles?	her sleepless eyes
beams of light	Heracles' journey
from east to west	wasting on an empty bed
power to see	fearing destiny

B	B'
south and north wind	our respect yet dissent
waves to and fro	your hopes worn down
the Theban-born whirled	not without pain
raised a life of Labours	what Zeus bestowed on mortals
like the Cretan sea	son of Cronos
god pulling him from	like the circling of the
the House of Hades	Great Bear

Epode
night fades
prosperity goes
to someone else
cling to this:
Zeus remembers his children

in face of the character of Hippolytus: 'Phaedra and Hippolytus', *Arion* I (1962) 5–18. Lattimore felt obliged to dub the play 'The prig's tragedy'.

26 *The Imagery of Euripides* (Bristol, 1986) 17–18, 136–7. Compare the rather different view in Dio Chrisostom lii.15: Dio found Euripides' choruses in his version of *Philoctetes* more gnomic and admonitory.

A begins with an address to the sun, born of night and put to bed in flaming
sunset. Where is Heracles, the chorus ask, in the Bosphorus (east), or the straits
of Gibraltar (west)?[27] The sun's rays can see. In A', the subject changes to the
wife longing for her husband. There is play on Deianira's name, meaning both
'husband-killer' and 'husband-burner'.[28] The sun going to his bed in the west
is linked to Deianira's bedding with Heracles. Deianira is associated with darkness while Heracles equates with the sun in anticipation of the finale when
Heracles' body will be consumed in flames. Strophe B develops a simile. Just
as a wave is swept to and fro according to the northerly or southerly direction
of the wind, so is Heracles whirled and exalted, but a god keeps him safe from
Hades. Antistrophe B', addressed to Deianira, criticizes her pessimism, for her
suffering is part of what the Omnipotent has dispensed to mortals: pain and
joy rotate like the Great Bear.

In order to grasp the spatial logic of the ode, we have to recall the parameters
of the space in which the play was performed. The two *eisodoi* and the wall of
the *skênê* lie on an east–west axis, whilst a north–south axis passes through the
statue and priest of Dionysus, the *thymelê*, and the *skênê* doorway. The movement of A explicitly concerns an east–west axis, whilst the movement of B
explicitly concerns a north–south axis. This must be a key to the choreography,
organized along the lateral axis in the first strophic pair and the longitudinal (or
front–back) axis in the second pair. The first movement is predominantly lateral
following the entry of the chorus from one side of the *orchêstra*. As the chorus
arrive, Heracles' son departs from the other side of the *orchêstra* to find his
father, and his direction of exit establishes a reference point for Heracles along
the east–west axis. Whilst A deals with the rising and going to bed of the sun,
A' evokes the marriage bed of Heracles. The first words of B establish the
north/south opposition that controls the second strophic pair. This axis allows
the final movement of B to be a recoil from the *skênê* door, often used to symbolize the gates of Hades.[29] B' is worded as a second-person address to Deianira,
whom we may guess to have been standing by the doorway when she
despatched her son on his mission. While in B the final movement seems to be
a veering from the door, in B' the final movement must suggest the circling of
the Great Bear. Just as Heracles never vanishes into Hades, so this constellation
circles for ever in the northern sky without sinking below the horizon into the
world of darkness. Whilst Crete is a symbol of the south, the Great Bear is a
symbol of the north in correspondence with the axis of the dance.

[27] This is now the accepted interpretation of the passage. See Malcolm Davies, *Sophocles:
Trachiniae* (Oxford, 1991) 80–1.

[28] Although Lidell and Scott offer 'destroying her spouse' as the meaning of the name, the root
seems to be *daïô* meaning in the first instance 'kindle'.   [29] See p. 165 below.

A non-strophic epode follows B′ and ties this astral image to the starting point of the ode, glimmering night. The chorus conclude that Deianira must hold on to one thought: when was Zeus unconcerned for his children? After linking cosmic flux to human flux, the epode ends by establishing a fixed point: the will of Zeus upon which Deianira must place her trust. In lieu of the toing and froing of strophe and antistrophe, the epode promises stability. Probably deixis here established the *thymelê* as an altar of Zeus, for in the course of the play many prayers are offered to Zeus, and oaths are sworn in his name.[30] As we have seen, the triadic pattern traditionally culminated in a static dance before the image of the god. This use of the epode to create a point of stability after the cyclicity and flux of strophic alternation is a device that seems particularly characteristic of Sophocles.

The *parodos* of *The Women of Trachis* transforms the acting space from the frontage of a house near Trachis to a model of the cosmos. It maps out a grid on the floor of the *orchêstra* that looks something like this:

	skênê door	
	Deianira	
	Hades	
east		west
sunrise	**Zeus**	sunset, dark
Heracles in Euboea		(Heracles' pyre)
	audience	
	Great Bear	

It is likely that the choreography not only defined the cardinal points but also rotated about the centre, for the closing images of B and B′ suggest a circling movement, as does the image of rivals fighting 'around' Deianira. Circular or elliptical movements around the *thymelê* could easily be mapped on the *orchêstra* floor by dancers arranged in a rectangle of 5 x 3. Whilst the sun should rotate in one direction, the Great Bear, considered as one of the fixed stars, should rotate in the other.

---

[30] Most notably the oath whereby Heracles' son promises to immolate his father on Zeus's mountain top at 1185–8. Deianira prays to Zeus at 200 and 303, and swears by him at 436–7. Lichas calls on Zeus as witness at 399. Heracles prays to Zeus at 983 and 995. 'Zeus' is the final word of the play.

The spatial parameters established by the *parodos* prepare for what follows in the remainder of the play. Heracles arrives from Euboea in the east, and goes to be cremated on Mount Oeta to the west. Heracles became, through his twelfth labour, the hero who escaped from Hades, and there is obvious cosmological symbolism in the play's insistence on the number twelve.[31] Heracles' litter does not stop its progress at the house, which significantly is not Heracles' own *oikos* (40). Unlike Deianira and most heroes (or corpses) of tragedy, he does not enter the *skênê* to find his last resting place,[32] for his destiny is not Hades but Olympus. His litter continues along the east–west axis towards the mountain, bearing like the sun chariot a body that is on fire.[33] His mistress and his son follow, betrothed to ensure that the cycle of life is renewed.

[31] The number twelve is associated with the time of Heracles' death (825), his absence (648), and with the oxen at his final sacrifice (760). Deianira's reference to an absence of exactly fifteen months (44–5, 164–5) presents editors with an unsolved conundrum. If the twelve labours can be associated with the zodiac, then they would commence and end with the spring equinox. A period of fifteen months would thus arrive at the summer solstice, traditional time for ritual bonfires. For ancient sources on Heracles and cosmology, see Graves, *Greek Myths* II.90, 103, 106, 205; also Jean Richer, *Géographie sacrée du monde grec* (Paris, 1967) 107–17.

[32] As Oliver Taplin notes in *Dioniso* 59 (1989) 104.

[33] Hence the particular significance of line 696, which some editors think spurious: P. E. Easterling (ed.) *Sophocles: Trachiniae* (Cambridge, 1982) 160–1.

CHAPTER 6

❧

Left and right, east and west

'The setting of *The Women of Trachis* is the patch of ground in front of Heracles' borrowed house near Trachis'. Any such formulation might sound precise but is in fact deeply misleading because it is couched in the language of realism. To set up a semiotic distinction, in the manner of Issacharoff, between the 'mimetic' space of the Trachian house and 'diegetic' spaces like Hades is unhelpful, for at a certain point in the first choral ode the *skênê* doors signify Hades. We need a critical language that does not turn upon a reductive notion of mimesis. We might more usefully say, in Gombrich's terms, that Sophocles like any artist uses and adapts received *schemata*. We might seek to understand the representational space created by Sophocles in Lefebvre's terms, in relation to a socially constituted spatial practice. We could say, in Lotman's terms, that Sophocles in his plays 'models' the universe. If we start from premises of this kind, then we shall find it impossible to relate to a single imagined referent the image that meets the spectator's eye. It will be more helpful to see the moving visual image as a structure, grid or geometric model.

The easiest way to analyse such a structure, following Saussure, Lotman and Ubersfeld, is in terms of binary oppositions. In chapter 8 I will examine the importance of the vertical axis in Greek performance. However, for an audience gazing downwards from high above the acting space, it is predominantly upon the horizontal plane that theatrical signs need to be organized. I have already examined the relationship between the centre of the circle and its periphery, and will return to uses of the *thymelê* in chapter 9. In chapter 7 I will examine the relationship between inside and outside, the private hidden world behind the *skênê* and the public seen world of the *orchêstra*. A feminist interest in the correlation between male/female and outside/inside has drawn critical attention to this important binary opposition. In contrast the opposition of left and right in the Greek theatre has scarcely been examined.

The Greek theatre offered the actors three points of entry, the central doorway leading from the house, and the two *eisodoi*.[1] The theatrical power of long entries through these *eisodoi* has been amply demonstrated by Taplin in his monumental *The Stagecraft of Aeschylus: the dramatic use of entries and exits in Greek tragedy*. Taplin recognizes that the dramatist in a given play 'may establish two different and precise directions for the eisodoi', and that such an arrangement would be helpful in a play like Aeschylus' *Suppliants* where the 'entire conflict of the play' would thus be 'given a concrete shape in the two directions of the eisodoi'.[2] The issue is left open and unexplored in *The Stagecraft of Aeschylus*, though a later article on Sophocles proposes that in suppliant plays generally one *eisodos* leads to the safety of a receiving city and the other leads to danger.[3] Hourmouziades asked himself the same question in relation to Euripides, and found that although in many plays *eisodos* A and *eisodos* B are associated with specific places, in some plays Euripides would seem to act rather casually, bringing on actors from whichever side happened to be convenient at a given moment.[4] Writing in the early 1960s, Hourmouziades was not trained to think in structural terms. Thus, in relation to the *Hippolytus* for example, he was preoccupied with questions of aesthetic balance, and of where in real life people might accidentally have encounters, not with the symbolic opposition of sea and hinterland. I shall argue in this chapter that in *every* Greek tragedy the two *eisodoi* articulate an opposition between two off-stage locations, and that these locations are opposites both topographically and symbolically. I shall examine in due course plays where Euripides appears to flout such a convention.

In the Hellenistic theatre we know that scene panels at either end of the wide, shallow stage were pictorial signs of off-stage locations such as the Peiraeus, the *Agora* and the countryside, fixing the meaning of the two *eisodoi*. A rotating mechanism allowed these panels to be changed between plays. The techniques of fifth-century tragedy became fixed and codified in the Hellenistic period, thanks to this piece of stage machinery. Much analysis of *eisodoi* has been preoccupied with making coherent sense of remarks in Vitruvius, Pollux and a commentator on Aristophanes, all of which are based upon the Hellenistic use of panels.[5] The idea that one side always leads to the city and the other to far-off parts has preoccupied critics. Klaus Joerden, for example, argued that in accordance with Pollux the city in tragedy should be

---

[1] I follow Oliver Taplin in using the term *eisodos*. Taplin demonstrates that the alternative term *parodos* is both ambiguous and post-classical: *SA* 449.   [2] *SA* 451.
[3] 'Sophocles in his theatre' in *Sophocle* ed. J. de Romilly (Entretiens Hardt 29, Geneva, 1983) 155–83, p. 158.   [4] *PIE* 128–36.
[5] For references and discussion, see David Wiles, *The Masks of Menander* (Cambridge, 1991) 41ff.

located on audience right, the country on audience left.[6] Hourmouziades' principal concern was to quash rigid systematization of this kind, and to argue that each play established its own specific topography.

In common with the majority of cultures, the Greeks regarded the right side as auspicious, the left side as inauspicious.[7] The right hand was used for greetings, pouring libations, or in ritual supplication.[8] Before a sacrifice someone moves 'to the right' to encircle the altar.[9] The wine-cup circulates to the right.[10] Omens were positive if they appeared on the right.[11] When Ajax goes mad, the chorus sing that he is in the leftward of his mind.[12] Plato in his mystical 'Myth of Er' sent the good souls upwards to the right and the bad souls downwards to the left.[13] Likewise, beneath a veil of scientific empiricism, Aristotelian science privileged the right at every opportunity. The surprising presence of the heart on the left had to be explained as a response to the natural chilliness of the left.[14] Pollux honoured the 'right-hand door' of the stage façade as that of the deuteragonist, whilst the left looks poverty-stricken, and again the right-hand door as the door of guests while the left is a prison.[15] The text is problematic because of the obvious fact that if the actor faces the centre of the auditorium, then the actor's right is the audience's left. It is usually assumed that Pollux refers to the perspective of the actor.[16]

A text from the fifth century envisages the Antipodes as a place where 'things above are below, while things below are above; there is a similar difference for things at the right and at the left'.[17] We must consider whether this is an acceptable metaphor for the actor/audience relationship in the fifth century, with directionality being merely relative and Euclidean. I shall argue in this chapter that the fifth-century theatre retained the qualities of what Lefebvre terms 'absolute space'. The theatre had not yet become a mirror of life. In Homer

---

6 'Excurs II: Rechts und Links: die Bedeutung der Parodoi' in *Die Bauformen der griechischen Tragödie* ed. Walter Jens (Munich, 1971) 409–10. Csapo and Slater agree that this is how Pollux iv.80 should be interpreted, along with a corroborating Hellenistic text: *COAD* 397, 361. The theory that audience right = real *agora* has been invalidated by recent archaeology which demonstrates that the archaic *agora* lay east of the Acropolis. The processional route to the theatre from the classical Agora passed via the archaic *agora*.

7 For comparative material, see R. Needham (ed.) *Left and Right* (Chicago, 1973).

8 G. E. R. Lloyd 'Right and left in Greek philosophy' *JHS* 82 (1962) 56–66, p. 58; E. *Electra* 812; *Medea* 21, 496, 899; *Women of Trachis* 1181 etc.

9 *Iphigeneia at Aulis* 1473; Aristophanes *Peace* 957.   10 *Rhesus* 363; Plato, *Symposium* 223.

11 *GR* 112; *Agamemnon* 116.   12 *Ajax* 183.   13 *Republic* 614.

14 Lloyd, 'Right and left' 62.   15 Pollux iv.124.

16 So assume Csapo and Slater in their translation of the text: *COAD* 396–7.

17 *De Hebdomadibus* 2.24, discussed in C. H. Kahn, *Anaximander and the Origins of Greek Cosmology* (New York, 1960) 84–5, and in J.-P. Vernant, *Mythe et pensée chez les grecs* (Paris, 1990) 206. The 'Antipodes' is etymologically a place where the feet are reversed.

space is vested with moral certainty: Achilles is on the right wing and not Ajax, because his mother is a goddess. In tragedy such certainties are open to intellectual challenge, but remain embedded in the consciousness of the spectators. Aristotle's debate about the directionality of the cosmos illustrates the problem at stake. He is troubled by the traditional Pythagorean insistence that the sun must rise on the right, since east is the positive term in relation to west, yet moves from left to right, the direction which in ritual always has positive connotations. Aristotle insists that all movement starts from the right, and therefore the sun really moves from right to left contrary to first appearances.[18]

Just as Greek culture privileged right over left, so it privileged east over west. A. Ballabriga has coined the term 'eotropic' to describe the Greeks' characteristic orientation towards the dawn.[19] The Athenians built their temples facing east, and laid their dead to rest facing west.[20] When Hector in the *Iliad* declares that he does not care 'whether the birds of omen fly to the right, towards the dawn and the sun, or left, towards the misty west', his equation of 'east' with 'right' makes practical sense because seers who interpreted omens always faced north.[21] For the spectator in the Theatre of Dionysus, looking south at the north-facing actor, 'right' is strictly speaking a relative concept. 'East' however, is an absolute concept, for there can only be one east. A movement 'to the right' is also absolute if it involves circularity, for rightwards is the traditional direction of cosmic movement. The late tradition that the chorus presented its left side to the audience stems from the tradition that ritual movement should be 'to the right', moving clockwise around the altar.[22]

The privileging of the right and of the east can be traced as a continuous cultural tradition from the classical world through to the Christian world. In Christian art, Heaven is always located on the viewer's left, because the devil must be on God's left hand. The sheep go to God's right, the goats to his left. This spatialization of good and evil determines, for example, representations of the Annunciation, where the angel always appears from the viewer's left, the heavenly side. The tradition that the virtuous character appears on the audience's left and the evil character on the right survives into modern folk-memories of Victorian pantomime.[23] It is interesting to compare the relationship of

---

[18] *On the Heavens* ii.2.284–5. See Joseph Cuillandre, *La Droite et la gauche dans les poèmes homériques* (Paris, 1944) 362ff.; Lloyd, 'Right and left' 62.

[19] *Le Soleil et le Tartare* (Paris, 1986) 61.

[20] Solon, cited and discussed in Donna C. Kurtz and John Boardman *Greek Burial Customs* (London, 1971) 194–5.

[21] *Iliad* 12.238ff. cited in G. E. R. Lloyd, *Polarity and Analogy* (Cambridge, 1966) 47n.2; GR 112.

[22] *COAD* 361–3.

[23] For example, Sue Maslen's programme note to Jim Davidson's *Sinderella* (Cambridge Theatre, London, 1994). I am not aware of any documentary evidence supporting this prevalent conception of Victorian tradition.

God and Devil in two-dimensional Christian art to that of Heracles and monsters on Greek vases. In the great majority of cases we find that Heracles is on the viewer's left, the monster on the right.[24] In lieu of Christ fighting the Devil, Heracles (who is also son of God, and the mortal who returns from Hell) fights savagery on behalf of civilization. Deep-rooted iconographic *schemata* such as Heracles = left / monster = right must have had an effect upon the organization of space in the theatre.

This articulation has narrative implications, for there is a sense that movement is naturally directed from left to right, that the relationship of left and right is the relationship of subject and object. Humans are set on the road to Hell, unless pulled back by a good angel. Christ journeys to Hell to rescue the patriarchs. The angel comes to Mary. In the processional mystery plays at York, we find that the waggons parked on the left of the road so that the stationary audience could view the Christian narrative passing before it in a left-to-right direction.[25] In the classical world, Heracles closes in on the monster, moving from the left. Having killed the boar, he approaches the cowardly Eurystheus from the left. When pictured with Athene on a chariot destined for Olympus, the movement is again towards the right. The interesting exception occurs when we see Heracles' body being rescued at the scene of the pyre and taken to Olympus. Here uniquely the chariot is moving from right to left to signify that the normal directionality of the human condition has been reversed.

In modern western theatre, it is a matter of empirical observation that entrances made from the left are stronger than entrances made from the right.[26] Since the phenomenon is largely unexplained, it seems important to take account of theatres outside the Graeco-Christian tradition, where cultural assumptions are different, and where the gaze of the spectator has not been conditioned by reading from left to right. In the Japanese Noh theatre, entries can only be made from the audience's left, along the bridge or *hashi-gakari*. Buddhism sanctifies the west, just as classical and Christian civilization sanctifies the east, for it rejects the finality of death assumed by the classical and Christian worlds. The actor enters from the west (left), and returns at the end of the play to the west. He often represents a ghost who returns from the world of death to life, and at the end returns again to death. It is interesting that on

---

[24] Checking the illustrations in *LIMC* 'Herakles', mostly but not exclusively black-figure vases, I find that in the combat with the Nemean lion Heracles approaches from the left in all but 7 of 81 Greek examples. He approaches Cerberus and the Erymanthian boar from the left in all Greek examples. For the Cretan bull there are 4 exceptions amongst 26 examples, and for Geryon 2 exceptions amongst 23 examples.

[25] See Meg Twycross 'Places to hear the play: pageant stations at York, 1398–1572' *Records of Early English Drama Newsletter* 2 (1978), 10–33, pp.18–20.

[26] Elaine Aston and George Savona, *Theatre as Sign-System* (London, 1991) 158; Earle Ernst, *The Kabuki Theatre* (London, 1956) 103.

the Jananese south-facing stage the same left-to-right dynamic obtains, although the movement of the play is cyclic rather than linear, for there is no sense of human progress in the Noh.[27] In the Kabuki theatre, the descendant of the Noh, the principal bridge-way (*hana-michi*) is again to the audience's left, giving a sense of greater weight to the left-hand side. A recent Japanese scholar has argued that audiences in the Edo period viewed from right to left, moving from the commonplace to the extraordinary, and that modern audiences fail to grasp the essential meaning of traditional plays.[28] The fact of a strong left-hand entry remains. Traditional Chinese theatre, unlike the Japanese Noh, makes full use of two doors. The door on the audience's left (*shang ch'ang mên*) is used for entries and the door on the audience's right (*hsia ch'ang mên*) is used for exits, and characters may enter from the right only if returning to a place whence they have come. The emperor, when attending a performance, used to sit by the left-hand door, and was greeted by the actors as they entered.[29] We thus observe the same phenomenon in China as in Japan: an asymmetrical weighting of the left, and a characteristic direction of movement from left to right. Chinese tradition tends to privilege the left, the *yang* side, in contrast to the classical/Christian tradition of privileging the right. The left-to-right principle seems therefore to transcend obvious cultural variables.

One human feature that largely transcends cultural difference is the asymmetry of the brain. It has been demonstrated in countless experiments that when the eye (either eye) is focussed on a central point, images from the left of the visual field will be projected initially and predominantly to the right hemisphere, and images from the right of the visual field to the left hemisphere. This applies to left-handers as well as to right-handers, and the male brain seems to be more lateralized than the female brain. Although there is uncertainty about the precise competences of the two hemispheres, there is no room for doubt that the left is pre-eminent in the processing of speech, and the right in many musical and visuo-spatial functions. The left is more competent not only in language but also in handling unfamiliar arrangements of visual icons, and is thus more adaptable than the right. While the right specializes in the recognition and application of conventional *schemata*, the left has syntactical skills that allow it to recognize and create new structures.[30] This division of the

---

[27] See Kunio Komparu, *The Noh Theater* (Tokyo, 1983) 117ff. The small door to the right is only used by attendants and the chorus.

[28] Chikuyi Simakaru, *Ways of Japanese Expression and Identity* (Tokyo, 1990) chapter 1. I am grateful to Meguzumi Kubota for supplying me with a translation.

[29] Cecilia Zung, *Secrets of the Chinese Drama* (Hong Kong, 1937) 4, 148; Tao Ching-Hsü, *The Chinese Conception of the Theatre* (Seattle, 1985) 31–2.

[30] The standard introduction to the field is S. P. Springer and G. Deutsch, *Left Brain, Right Brain*

brain has important implications for the theatre. An entry in the left visual field (right brain) will be understood in relation to the status quo, the spatial given, while occupation of the right visual field will register in the dominant left hemisphere, associated with adaptability and the power to manipulate language. Combat in the theatre will usually be combat for this position. It has also been shown that the right brain is more concerned with processing emotional information, particularly of a visual nature, and is more concerned with crying than with laughter.[31] There are thus physiological reasons why entry from the audience's left should have more theatrical impact, particularly in tragedy. Greek spectators were for the most part distant enough to embrace the whole *orchêstra* in their gaze, and the *skênê* doorway can be seen as analogous to the central fixation point used in psychological experiments designed to contrast left and right visual fields.

For all peoples in the northern hemisphere, in pre-industrial society, the movement of sun, moon and stars through the sky offers reassurance that left-to-right is the natural direction of narrative movement. It was the movement of the planets that allowed Aristotle to declare that a spherical cosmos had absolute properties of left and right.[32] The worshipper at dawn who stands to face the east will experience the sun electing to move towards his or her right hand. The south-facing spectator in the Theatre of Dionysus experienced the sun moving from his left to his right in the course of his day in the theatre, and his vision and personal comfort were determined by the sun's position. This perceptible path of the sun suggests the presence of a transhuman force that humans can either go with or go against. Although Hellenistic theatres are usually said to be orientated according to the lie of the land,[33] we should observe that the Attic theatres at Thorikos, Rhamnous and Euonymon are all south-facing, suggesting a common pattern. Ikarion is an oddity, and perhaps the most important directionality to note here is that the priest carrying out a sacrifice and facing the winter sunrise will be looking towards the centre of the *skênê*. Megalopolis and Aigai face north, not out of

---

(4th edition, New York, 1993). For adaptability of the right hemisphere in relation to unfamiliar spatial arrangements in pictures, see Dahlia W. Zaidel, 'Hemispheric memory for surrealistic versus realistic paintings' *Cortex* 25 (1989) 617–41, and 'Worlds apart: pictorial semantics in the left and right cerebral hemispheres' *Current Directions in Psychological Science* 3 (1994) 5–9.   [31] *Left Brain, Right Brain* 192–200.

[32] *On the Heavens* ii.2,5, discussed in Lloyd, *Polarity and Analogy* 261–2. E. Panofsky discusses this passage in relation to Greek space being finite and aggregated rather than abstract and the product of infinite relationships: *Perspective as Symbolic Form* tr. C. S. Wood (New York, 1991) 44.

[33] For a survey, see Clifford Ashby, 'The siting of Greek theatres' *Theatre Research International* 16 (1991) 181–201.

mere convenience but in alignment with a complex of buildings that respect the cardinal points.

Hourmouziades' axiom that 'each play creates its own "topography"'[34] is misleading in the way it isolates the 'play' from its historical and topographical performance context. The Greek spectator did not leave his real physical environment behind and through his imagination somehow enter a fictional universe where all spatial relationships are relative and the dramatic action is a closed structure. Fellow spectators were inescapably part of his visual field. So was the sun. His sense of absolute rather than relative space depended above all upon a sense of the east, the direction of the sunrise which was near enough due east at the spring equinox when the City Dionysia took place. The temple of Dionysus and sacrificial rituals in the sanctuary faced east in accordance with standard Greek practice. Comparable religio-mythic theatres such as Japanese theatre and Christian medieval theatre respect the cardinal points.[35] The *Natya Sastra* describes the elaborate rituals involved in setting up a classic Indian theatre, where the audience faced west. Each of the four sides is associated with its own colour and its own deities. The Buddha is associated with the centre and the major deities with the east.[36] The religio-mythic theatre of Athens would be an anthropological anomaly if it did not respect direction.

Due east of the Hellenistic *orchêstra* in Athens and aligned with the *eisodos* was the pinnacle on top of the Odeon, surmounted by a curious ball illustrated in an extant coin and mocked by a comic poet who likened Pericles to an 'onion-headed Zeus' with the Odeon on his head.[37] Greek tragedies often begin with an invocation to the dawn. Although in Aigai Philip II staged his entry at dawn, it seems unlikely that in Athens pre-play ceremonial would have allowed time for the plays to commence at dawn, and libations at dawn would be more plausible. The bulbous shape on top of the Odeon, deriving perhaps from a Persian emblem on top of the royal tent, would have served conve-

---

[34] *PIE* 136.

[35] For Japanese theatre and the 'four divine correspondences' of Buddhist thinking about space, see Komparu, *Noh Theater* 117–20. For medieval theatre see Elie Konigson, *L'Espace théâtral médiéval* (Paris, 1975).

[36] Bharata, *The Natya Sastra*, tr. 'A Board of Scholars' (Delhi, 1987) chapters 2–3. For a reconstruction see Per Edström, *Why Not Theatres Made For People?* (Värmdö, 1990) 54–5. For directionality in a surviving Indian form, see R. A. Frasca, *The Theater of the Mahabarata: Terukuttu performances in South India* (Hawaii, 1990) 142–3, 174.

[37] Plutarch, *Pericles* 13, citing Cratylus. The coin is reproduced as *TDA* fig. 1. All sources for the Odeon are given in A. L. H.Robkin, 'The Odeion of Perikles' (Ph.D. thesis, University of Washington, 1976). On a lead theatre ticket the Odeon is depicted without an orb but with its summit emphasized by the tent-like sag of the roof around it: F. Imhoof-Bluper and P. Gardner, *Ancient Coins* (Chicago, 1964) p. lxxviii pl.3.

niently as a surrogate or symbolic sun, ideally placed to be the deictic focus of a choral dance invoking the sunrise.

Euripides' *Phaethon* may serve to focus the issue of how the dramatic action connects to the real space of the theatre. One *eisodos* in this play leads to the nearby palace of Dawn and the Sun-god, i.e. the eastern horizon.[38] Phaethon dies in the course of the play after driving the chariot of Helios, so presumably his smouldering body must be brought in from the west. The chorus at the start of the play enter with an address to the sun that has just risen. The *parodos* follows a familiar pattern. The tableaux at the end of the first strophic pair relate to the lateral axis: the nightingale at sunrise, the swan on the stream of Oceanus who must reside eastward on the world's margin. The second pair of tableaux relate to the longitudinal axis: the wind from behind the boat, fear over the house/*skênê*, while the epode introduces a formal act of worship. We must ask ourselves whether an audience facing the sun could ever divest itself of its awareness of the real trajectory of the solar chariot, and accept that the real occident represented a stage orient, and vice versa. Given that real sacrifices were performed in the precinct of Dionysus facing east, any address by the chorus to a sunrise in the west would surely seem anomalous.

An interesting crux is the point in *Orestes* 1259–60, where the chorus divides, and one half goes east (literally: 'to the rays of the sun') and the other goes west (literally: 'to the evening'). Since there is no obvious reason within the closed system of the text why one side should be defined as east and one west, it seems reasonable to follow Willink and conclude that Euripides had the spectator's orientation in mind.[39] The fact that the text of *Orestes* makes no further reference to east and west does not mean that cardinal orientation failed to affect the spectator's response. Martin West believes that one side was the road which leads to the port, the other was the path which leads to the graves and to the assembly. Willink, on the other hand, locates Clytaemnestra's grave on one side and Agamemnon's on the other.[40] West's account suggests that the symbolic opposition is of rescue versus death, whereas for Willink the opposition is of

---

[38] For the text, see C. Collard, M. J. Cropp and K. H. Lee (eds.) *The Plays of Euripides: selected fragments* Vol.1, (Warminster, 1995). I am grateful to Christopher Collard for letting me see a copy of his translation before publication. Since the setting is 'Ethiopian', the audience are invited to imagine a south-east location in the direction of the summer sunrise. On the topography see Ballabriga, *Le Soleil et le Tartare* 212.

[39] C. Willink, (ed.) *Orestes* (Oxford, 1986) p. xlii n.52.

[40] M. L. West (ed.) *Orestes* (Warminster, 1987) 38; Willink, *Orestes* xl-xlii and notes to 796–8. Willink favours left/east as the side for Clytaemnestra's grave. Suzanne Saïd, following Willink, argues that the 'maternal' *eisodos* is used by the supporters of Clytaemnestra, the 'paternal' by the supporters of Agamemnon: see 'Tragic Argos' in *Tragedy, Comedy and the Polis* ed. A. H. Sommerstein, S. Halliwell, J. Henderson and B. Zimmerman (Bari, 1993) 167–89, p. 188.

female versus male. Lateral oppositions are fundamental to interpretation of what the play means or meant, and it seems important to explore what symbolic charge the two sides had for the Greek spectator. One might surmise, for example, that the side of the sunrise had a positive charge, either as the side of hope (following West) or as the side of the woman, giver of life (following Willink).

The other tragedy in which the chorus divides is *Ajax*. Half the chorus is sent out to the west to search for the missing hero, and half to the east (805). When the chorus-men return through their two separate *eisodoi*, we hear that the western group have been searching amongst the ships, the eastern group merely along a path (872–8). Thus the 'west' *eisodos* must lead to the Greek camp, the 'east' *eisodos* to the wilderness away from the fleet and further along the shore. The lateral opposition of wilderness and camp is crucial to the finale of *Ajax*, for Teucer obviously exits to the wilderness in order to find a discreet burial place for his brother at 1186, but takes the corpse out to the camp at the end when a formal burial is granted and the isolated hero is reintegrated with the collective. Ajax's Homeric position is on the extreme left wing of the fleet, as the fourth line of the play reminds the audience, and it also lies to the east of the south-facing fleet.[41] Theoretically, therefore, the case is less compelling than *Orestes* because the left/east of the play could be the left/east of the *Iliad* and not the real left/east experienced by the audience. In practice, however, it is hard to see why Sophocles would have chosen to divorce the two.

The principle of lateral opposition helps to explain why scene changes in Greek tragedy are possible but rare. When Ajax determines on suicide, he moves away from the fleet and exits by the *eisodos* that leads to the wilderness. Although the location changes in *Ajax*, spatial oppositions do not. One side always leads towards the camp, one side to the wilderness. Similarly in the *Eumenides*, where the trilogy as a whole represents a drive towards the present and progress, one side represents the direction *from Argos* and the other the direction *to Athens*. The change of location is indicated with the maximum theatrical economy if Orestes, Apollo and the chorus leave Delphi by going to the right and arrive in Athens by reentering from the left.

The binary opposition of the two *eisodoi* in the Greek theatre made drama a powerful vehicle for the exploration of symbolic analogies and polarities. Although many cultures develop dualistic symbolic systems, what appears to be distinctive about Greek thought is the self-consciousness with which it uses such categories of opposites.[42] Geoffrey Lloyd, in order to demonstrate how a

---

[41] Cuillandre, *La Droite et la gauche* 23.
[42] Lloyd stresses this point in *Methods and Problems in Greek Science* (Cambridge, 1991) 30–1, in the preface to a reprint of his essay on 'right and left'.

sequence of polar oppositions formed the basis of an integrated symbolic system, cites a Pythagorean table of opposites which finds analogies between the following polarities:

unlimited	limited
even	odd
plural	singular
left	right
female	male
moving	at rest
curved	straight
dark	light
evil	good
oblong	square[43]

A modern consciousness of race and gender will inevitably call attention to the bracketing of female, dark and evil. The bracketing of female with left was reflected in medical beliefs that girls were born from seed from the left testicle, and grew on the left side of the womb.[44] Nicole Loraux has called attention to the symbolism of Heracles' wounding Hera in the right breast, the breast denied to this 'supermale'.[45] We shall need to consider the extent to which the left/right opposition in theatrical performance is a gendered opposition.

The importance of binary opposition in Greek tragedy has been explored at length by Charles Segal, and his account of the basic oppositional structure will be fundamental to my own analysis of theatrical space in Sophocles.

Lévi-Strauss's view of myth as exploring and validating the opposition between nature and culture, the 'raw' and the 'cooked', is substantiated by a great deal of Greek tragedy. Here the tension between *nomos* and *physis*, culture and nature, often takes the form of a tension between the spheres of confident human authority and divine autonomy. On the one hand lies the polis and its Olympian-sponsored male-oriented institutions, the area where man imposes structure and the ordering conventions of nomos upon the potentially threatening impulses of physis. On the other hand lies the power of the gods in its elusive, unknown aspects, the chthonic divinities and the areas of human life under their supervision, the strain of impurity, the threatening realm of women, the biological processes of birth and death, the demands of nurture (*trophê*) and blood ties, and the curses produced or transmitted in the area of such blood ties.[46]

---

[43] Aristotle, *Metaphysics* I.v.986a, discussed in *Polarity and Analogy* 48–51.
[44] Lloyd 'Right and left' 60.
[45] *Iliad* v.392–4; N. Loraux, 'Heracles: supermale and female' in *The Experiences of Tiresias* (Princeton, 1995) 116–39, pp. 135–6.   [46] *Interpreting Greek Tragedy* (Ithaca, 1986) 32.

What Segal consistently fails to notice is the extent to which this oppositional structure is fixed by the architecture of the theatre. Segal's broad thesis is that in Sophocles the narrative drive is regularly associated with a transition from the natural and internecine to the political and civilized.[47] The opposition of wilderness (= audience left) versus civilization (= audience right) is, I would suggest, a characteristic device of Greek culture.

The complex of spatial oppositions that we have examined can be seen realized in the sculptures of the Parthenon, contemporaneous with the period of Greek tragedy.[48] The frieze depicts a procession, predominantly moving clockwise, but with a minority depicted in a counter-movement anti-clockwise. All converge on the privileged east side, where the twelve gods and ten tribal heroes are seated and the robe is made ready for the goddess whose statue is visible within. The east pediment is concerned with the cosmic sphere: the birth of Athene, framed by the left-to-right movement of sunrise and nightfall. The sun is on the sunny south/left end of this pediment, night on the dark north/right end. The west pediment is concerned with the human sphere, as Athene and Poseidon fight for Attica, surrounded apparently by the first autochthonous Athenians. Athene like Heracles moves from the left towards the enemy whom she will vanquish. The metopes define four basic oppositions of the civilized versus the primitive: on the cosmic east side, Olympian gods fight earth-born giants; on the west side (in contrast to the Athene/Poseidon combat above) Athenian males fight females, *viz.* Amazons; on the north side Greeks fight barbarians, *viz.* Trojans; and on the south side humans fight animals, *viz.* centaurs. The calm and continuous ritual procession of the frieze is in opposition to the discontinuous outer ring around the building formed by the metopes, which define the battles that had to be won in order for the orderly Athenian ritual to be performed. The idealized participants in the procession – male, Greek, masters of animals, and handsome as gods – represent the positive term in a set of oppositions fashioned in real, lived Athenian space. Like the Parthenon, the theatrical performance was also a work of art fashioned in space. Both Parthenon and theatrical performance are dedicated to their respective gods, and are exercises in defining a system of values appropriate to the *polis*. Greek plays studied as mere texts are like the Parthenon sculptures in the British Museum: spatially decontextualized in order that they may become aesthetic objects devoid of religious and political meaning.

Nature/culture is an important paradigm in Aeschylus. In the *Oresteia*, the

---

[47] The title of Charles Segal's *magnum opus* on Sophocles, *Tragedy and Civilization* (Cambridge, Mass., 1981) reflects this fundamental Lévi-Straussian concern.

[48] See J. J. Pollitt, *Art and Experience in Classical Greece* (Cambridge, 1972) 79ff.; John Boardman, *The Parthenon and its Sculptures* (London, 1985); Robin Osborne, 'The viewing and obscuring of the Parthenon frieze' *JHS* 107 (1987) 98–105.

eisodoi provide the means of defining a linear progression: Troy ⇒ Argos ⇒ Delphi ⇒ Athens. The journey from barbaric monarchy to progressive democracy seems to be mapped as a journeying from left to right, for there is an obvious affinity between the grand arrival of Agamemnon from the Trojan east and the rising of the sun, so often conceived in Greek thought as a chariot (254, 522, 767, 900, 969, etc.). Like Agamemnon, Athene too would have made her powerful entrance from the strong left (eastern, Trojan) side. When Troy is placed to the left/east and Athens to the right/west, the different symbolic aspects of the left/right relationship neatly coalesce.

LEFT	RIGHT
sunrise	sunset
Argos	Athens
primitive	civilized
matriarchy	male democracy
chthonic goddesses	Olympians
blood bond	citizenship

The establishment of Athenian democracy seems an evolutionary process as natural as the movement of the sun. The sense of a natural left-to-right progression must have been reinforced by the fact that the Dionysiac procession entered the sanctuary of Dionysus from the left, coming along the Street of Tripods.

The archaeological evidence gives us no grounds for thinking of the fifth-century theatre as perfectly symmetrical. The deme theatres encourage us to think of the Attic theatre as a lateralized space, with the two sides distinguished, and a dominant entry being made from the audience's left. The circular *orchêstra* for which I argued in chapter 2 yields an acting space broader than it is deep, for the *skênê* encroaches forwards into the circle, the *eisodoi* extend the acting area to the sides, and the front of the circle is not usable by actors because it is too close to the audience for a satisfactory focus or acoustic. As in a 'rectangular' theatre so in a 'circular' theatre the lateral axis predominates. To the left of the Sophoclean audience, the chorus would probably have gathered in the Odeon. The Odeon, erected a decade or so after the *Oresteia* (but perhaps replacing an earlier structure), suggests a three-fold symbolism: the sunrise on account of its orb, the barbarism of the Persian east, and the darkness of an enclosed female space. The tradition that the Odeon was built in the shape of Xerxes' tent is attested by Plutarch and Pausanias, and Vitruvius states that the roof was built with Persian materials.[49] Robkin argues plausibly that the structure was built in this symbolic eastern form for a

---

[49] Plutarch, *Pericles* 13; Pausanias i.20.3; Vitruvius v.ix.1.

planned panhellenic (anti-Persian) congress.[50] At a later date the memory of
the Persian war was perpetuated by statues of Themistocles on the 'right' of
the theatre and Miltiades on the 'left', each leading a Persian prisoner.[51] To the
right, in opposition to the symbol of barbarism, lay the Doric Temple of
Dionysus, the destination of the democratic god after the performance was
over.

Of all Sophocles' plays, lateral polarization is perhaps most obvious in
Oedipus at Colonus, where one *eisodos* unmistakably leads to Athens and one
to Thebes. The acting space becomes a liminal area between two opposed
worlds. Taplin sees the play as part of a genre in which one direction leads
abroad and one to the city that will offer the suppliant its protection, but he
adds that 'it is more important to recognise this division than to know which
was left and which was right'.[52] There is, however, a striking critical consensus
that Thebes must lie to the audience's left.[53] Although we can trace this consensus via Jebb's seminal edition of 1900 to the tradition in Pollux that right
(stage left) = city, and left (stage right) = abroad, the traditional view has always
seemed satisfactory, I would suggest, on an instinctive level. It accords with an
understanding that the strong entrances of Oedipus, Creon and the mounted
Ismene should be made from the left, and that narrative should unfold in a
left-to-right direction, with Athens as the direction of both physical and moral
progress. A Delian fresco adds weight to the consensus by representing
Antigone leading Oedipus in a left-to-right direction.[54] If we accept that the
representation of space in Sophocles is schematic rather than realist, then we
will have no difficulty in accepting that Oedipus' final exit towards his secret
tomb is an exit into the *skênê*, where he will serve as a sacred barrier between
Athens on the one side, and invaders on the other.[55]

Ismene goes to a spring on the Theban side (as is clear from the fact that the
Thebans apprehend her), and is instructed to face east as she pours her libation (477), so it is apposite that she should exit to the east for this purpose. She
goes to the spring in order to placate the Eumenides, the goddesses to whom
the grove is sacred. Out of sight on the Athenian side is located the altar of
Poseidon, where Theseus and the Athenians are sacrificing, and Polyneices

[50] Robkin 'The Odeion of Perikles' 94–5, citing Plutarch, *Pericles* 17.
[51] Scholiast on Aristeides 46.161.13, cited in G. M. A. Richter, *Portraits of the Greeks* (London,
1965) 1.95.   [52] 'Sophocles in his theatre' 158.
[53] E. F. Watling and Robert Fagles in the old (1947) and new (1982) Penguin translations, respec-
tively, and Robert Fitzgerald in the older Chicago translation (1954) envisage Thebes on the
left; likewise R. Jebb's edition of the Greek text (Cambridge, 1900), and J. C. Kamerbeek's
edition (Leiden, 1984); so too Paul Mazon's influential French translation in *Sophocle III* (Paris,
1960).   [54] *LIMC* 'Antigone' 2.   [55] See below pp. 165–6.

comes as a suppliant. These ceremonial sites link the Thebes/Athens binary to a more complex set of oppositions:

(LEFT)	(RIGHT)
Thebes	Athens
Chthonians	Olympians
goddesses	male god
nature	civilization

At the spring, the worshipper is female, and is not part of a social group. There is no man-made altar, no animal sacrifice, and no wine, and the ceremonial is thus in Lévi-Straussian terms based on the 'raw' rather than the 'cooked'. There is an emphasis upon youth rather than age, for Ismene is young, she uses the wool of a young lamb, and lays sprigs of young olive on the ground. The lateral opposition is not a simple one of bad and good, for Sophocles, like Aeschylus in the *Oresteia*, implies that Athens' prosperity and fertility depend upon absorbing the chthonic Eumenides alongside the sophisticated sky-based Olympians. Theban Oedipus is admitted from Thebes for his prophylactic value. Although the term 'left' has negative associations, the term 'east' is sanctified, and the ambivalent malign/spiritual quality of Theban Oedipus can be related to this paradox.

We know from Pausanias that the major shrine at 'Colonus of the Horses' (Hippios Kolonos) was an altar and grove sacred not only to Poseidon Hippios but also to Athena Hippia. There were also hero shrines to Oedipus, and to Theseus and Pirithous (mentioned at 1593–4) who visited the underworld. We also know that there was a shrine here to chthonic goddesses equivalent to the Eumenides but known by their Attic name of 'Semnai'.[56] Sophocles seems to have used stage iconography in order to simplify and schematize a complex of known sanctuaries for purposes of theatrical representation. Deictic references by the local inhabitant to 'this horseman Colonus' (59), 'this man's name' (60–1) and 'this god' (65) have generally been accepted as referring to a statue placed in the *orchêstra* and visible to the audience.[57] It would be odd and inconsistent

---

[56] Pausanias 1.30.7; Androtion = scholiast on *Odyssey* 11.271; André Lardinois 'Greek myths for Athenian rituals' *GRBS* 33 (1992) 313–28. The other shrine noted by Pausanias belongs to Adrastus, associated with setting Theseus and the Athenians against Thebes.

[57] Kamerbeek's note on l.59 lists those who would change the text in order to obliterate the alleged statue, first postulated by Scheidewinn in 1849. The statue is accepted by the Methuen and both Penguin translators, by Lloyd Jones the new Loeb translator, and by the original Chicago translator, though it vanishes in David Grene's new Chicago translation of 1991. On how the text invests the statue with an identity, see Francis M. Dunn, 'Introduction: beginning at Colonus' *Yale Classical Studies* 29 (1992) 1–12. I am not aware of any critics who have deemed the significance of the statue worthy of discussion.

with normal practice if the speaker were to keep gesturing to a statue visible to himself and Antigone but not to the audience. If the figure is a Sophoclean invention, then it could not have been mentioned casually as an off-stage presence. If there was an eponymous deme hero at Colonus represented by an equestrian statue, then it is odd that Sophocles should have honoured the figure by calling it a 'god', and then have made no further reference to it in the play. When Euripides' Oedipus refers to Colonus as the home of the 'hippios theos' he refers more obviously to Poseidon Hippios.[58] As a stage icon, an equestrian statue would have the advantage of evoking not just the place Colonus but its best-known patron deity, Poseidon, god of horses.

Given the existence of an equestrian statue on one side of the *orchêstra*, its identity explained by the text, there would be an aesthetic imbalance if this were the sole stage object. The obvious counterweight to the statue would be one or more stage trees to signify the grove. I shall examine the use of property trees in chapter 9. Since the *skênê* clearly did not take the form of a realistic sylvan landscape painting,[59] some other visual sign of the grove would be appropriate. Antigone mentions laurel, olives and vines upon arrival in the *orchêstra* (17), Ismene goes out 'past the grove' (505) in order to perform the rite of laying twenty-one olive shoots on the sacred soil. A revered everlasting olive tree similar to the one in the Erechtheum was located in the Academy, a precinct which the text assimilates to the adjacent Colonus.[60] One or more emblems representing olive trees would do much to clarify the text, if placed in opposition to a horseman on the right, creating the simple configuration:

entry to underworld

grove   horseman

audience

The horseman must belong on the right, the side of Poseidon Hippios and the Athenian cavalry.

We have to keep reminding ourselves that the text is simply the part of the performance which by chance happens to have survived. The visible presence of statue and tree is an inference which makes sense of the text that Sophocles wrote, explaining why the statue was more than decorative local colouring. The advantage of the iconographic opposition which I have posited is that it allows

[58] *Phoenician Women* 1707 – written a few years before Sophocles' play.
[59] See pp. 161–2 below.
[60] Pausanias i.30.2. The shrine of Prometheus (see line 56) was located in the Academy. See Jebb's note on 694–719 for the topography.

the audience to use their eyes in order to grasp the dense imagery of the chorus, particularly in the ode at 668ff. which celebrates Athens after Theseus has promised Oedipus Athenian protection. Symmetrical movement and gesture direct strophe and antistrophe in opposite lateral directions. Strophe A (right) commences with a reference to Colonus, land of horses, and the final tableau depicts Dionysus (male) with his maenads. Antistrophe A' (left) commences with flowers at sunrise, sacred to the earth-goddesses Demeter and Persephone, and the final tableau depicts Aphrodite (female) and the Muses. Strophe B (left) is devoted to the olive tree, Athena's gift to Athens, whilst antistrophe B' (right) is devoted to the gifts of Poseidon: the horses and ships that were Athens' military defence. The female gift on the left is associated with the fertility of nature, while the male gift on the right is associated with the prowess of warriors. The choreographic positioning of Athene on the left and Poseidon Hippios on the right would echo the famous image on the Parthenon of Athene (left) struggling with Poseidon (right) for patronage of Athens. It also makes sense in relation to the fact that the altar at Colonus was sacred to both deities. An equestrian statue on the right would have fixed in the audience's mind the complex associations of the right-hand polarity.

Sophocles' glancing reference to a statue in the text points us to the lateral oppositions that governed performance. Textual details like the arrival of Ismene on a pony (specifically, a female pony – 312) make sense in relation to a visible male equestrian on the opposite side. The opposition of female and male is the controlling factor in a coherent symbolic system:

FEMALE	MALE
left (east)	right (west)
chthonic goddesses	patriarchal Olympians
Athene	Poseidon
olive tree	horse
nature	city
wild Thebes	civilized Athens
individual	social

The closing image of the play confirms this gender-based opposition, when Antigone and Ismene exit to the left, whilst Theseus and the chorus of citizens exit to the right (1769ff.).

The lateral opposition also has a class basis, and might be defined in modern terms as left-wing versus right-wing. Athenian warriors supplied their own accoutrements, and we can see from Aristophanes' *Knights* (*Hippês*) the extent to which the Athenian cavalry were identified with upper-class values. The chorus in the *parabasis* of that play sing a strophe to their lord Poseidon

Hippios and a balancing antistrophe to Athene, celebrating their contribution to the Athenian military effort. However, some four or five years before Sophocles wrote his play, Athenian oligarchs chose the shrine of Poseidon at Colonus as the place where they would vote to remove the institutions of democracy.[61] As Lowell Edmunds remarks: 'Colonus was a cult centre, the only one in Attica, of the Knights, where they sacrificed to Poseidon Hippios, and, as such, the place was closely identified with them . . . The choice of Colonus for the meeting of the assembly in 411 BCE that established the Four Hundred would not have been an accident'.[62] After the restoration of democracy the disgraced elite of Athenian society, the men who could afford horses, vindicated themselves by defeating a regiment of Thebans and driving them back to Colonus from the gates of the city.[63] In Sophocles' play the Athenian cavalry accomplish a similar feat. The left/right opposition of Athene and Poseidon needs to be seen in this class context. Athene is patron of the entire unruly *demos*, whilst Poseidon is patron of the rich. Oedipus' final exit through the central door may be seen as a sign of the political balance which needed to be struck between 'left' and 'right'.

Oedipus has two major confrontations in the play, with Creon and with Polyneices. Creon appears from the Theban side, and his entrance is visually a strong one, for he is accompanied by a bodyguard. He mounts his attack upon Oedipus and Antigone in the regular left-to-right direction. Following successful rescue, the chorus meditate upon Oedipus' old age. After the to and fro of strophe and antistrophe, they focus in the conventional way upon a point of stability in the epode. They liken Oedipus to a rock battered by winds from the cardinal points of sunset and sunrise, midday and midnight (1239ff.). This is the prelude to Polyneices' entrance from the opposite, Athenian side. While Creon makes a strong entrance from the left, Polyneices makes a weak entrance from the right as an unarmed, weeping suppliant.[64] He claims the support of Poseidon (right) and blames the Erinye for his problems (left) (1285ff.). Oedipus on the left now becomes the attacker with the power of his curse, and the reversal of Oedipus' position transforms him from victim to attacker. Polyneices exits to the left, and his right-to-left trajectory in the play marks the

---

[61] Thucydides 8.67.

[62] From a monograph that is regrettably unpublished. I am grateful to Lowell Edmunds for making an extract available to me. For Colonus belonging specifically to the knights Edmunds cites Pherecrates frag. 134K. At the time when Sophocles wrote, the one officer of the cult whose name we happen to know seems to have been a future member of the oligarchy of the Thirty: *Hesperia* 32 (1963) 157–8.   [63] Diodorus xiii.72.3–4.

[64] Taplin notes the contrast in 'Sophocles in his theatre' 159–60. In the discussion following the article (pp. 175–6), Seidensticker, Winnington-Ingram and Taplin deal effectively with objections raised by Knox.

fact that he is going back, and that the journey of his life is the antithesis of progress. In both scenes of confrontation we notice that the power of language belongs on the right. The rational left brain triumphs in the first confrontation, but not in the second. Sophocles creates an Oedipus who transcends rationality, and stands for the values of tradition. The organization of the space accords with the competences of a lateralized brain.

In *Antigone* it is apparent that one side must lead to the battlefield, the other to the city, whilst the *skênê* represents Creon's house.[65] The play conforms, I would suggest, to the same bracketing of categories as *Oedipus at Colonus*:

left	right
female	male
chthonic	Olympian
nature	culture
wilderness	city

The chorus upon their first entrance address the east, and the direction of the battlefield: 'Ray of the sun, fairer than all others that have shone on seven-gated Thebes, you shone then, eye of golden day, as you passed over the waters of Dirce, upon the man who came from Argos with white shield and full armour, having turned him to headlong flight with your cutting bridle' (100–7). The obvious staging calls for the chorus to enter from the city, west, and to address the east where the sun is supposedly rising after the pre-dawn prologue. The orb on top of the newly built Odeon was available as a visual focus. Since the river Dirce lies to the west of Thebes, the implication of the lines is that the sun has swung round to the west during the day of battle, and the direction of its rays drives the attacker back.[66] The strongest entries in the play – Antigone when arrested, and Creon bringing in the body of his son – would be made from the left, while the relatively low-key entries of Haemon and Teiresias would be made from the right. The principal journey of the play is the processional exit of Antigone as she leaves on her inverted wedding procession, doomed to be the sterile bride of death. A right-to-left movement reverses the direction of nature, the visible trajectory of the sun to which the

---

[65] See for example Oliver Taplin, 'The place of Antigone' *Omnibus* 7 (1988) 13–16.

[66] Jebb spotted that the sun could not rise over Dirce, but wrote this off as poetic licence when commenting on the line in his edition (Cambridge, 1900). Subsequent commentators have passed over the issue, with the exception of R. E. Braun in his Oxford University Press translation (New York, 1973). Braun reconstructs Sophocles' use of the cardinal points, but his conception is more poetic than theatrical, and he posits an ahistorical south-facing *skênê*. A circling basis to the choreography is clear from the fact that the symmetrical lines of the antistrophe refer to Polyneices as an eagle circling Thebes and its garland of towers. There is strophic correspondence between the ray of the sun and Polyneices as eagle.

text calls attention (100–7, 415–17, 1064–5). As Richard Seaford points out, marriage in Greece was conceived as the victory of culture over nature,[67] but in this play it is nature rather than culture which triumphs.

The major confrontations of the play are between Creon, who is associated with the city (right), and Antigone, who goes into the wilderness (left) to bury the body and later returns to the wilderness to die. While Creon and the chorus acknowledge male Olympians – Ares, Dionysus, Zeus, Hades, Eros[68] – Antigone evokes an older, timeless order of gods (453ff.), and recognizes the chthonic goddesses Dikê and Persephone (451, 894). It is left to Teiresias to point out that Creon has ignored the Erinyes (1075), and to Eurydice to honour Athene, a female Olympian (1184). Eurydice, who in her death occupies the central position before the door, embodies the mid-point between an irreconcilable left and right. The relationship of Creon and Antigone accords with the two hemispheres of the brain. Creon, in the right visual field, relies upon verbal reasoning, while Antigone is preoccupied with a visuo-spatial conception of where the corpse ought to be. Whilst Creon seeks to innovate, Antigone's conception of the world is rooted in precedent, and her use of song and dance (806–82, 933–43) is appropriate to her right-brain emphasis.

Brecht in his meticulously documented production of 1948 had the acting area suggest a primitive sacrificial circle.[69] The austerity, formality and symmetry of his staging maximized the significance of stage positions. Brecht placed Creon's house to the audience's right, the battlefield to the left and the town in the centre. Creon sat on a bench when supposedly in his house, and the actors had no egress to the right. Brecht stresses that the chorus fail to learn, and there is no sense of progress in the play. The left was used for the strong entrance of Antigone with a pillory board bound to her back, for the dying messenger (a Brechtian addition) and for Creon arriving with Haemon's bloody shirt. Creon commands the right of the visual field throughout, until the end when he is crushed and reenters from the left. Antigone commands the left in her confrontations with Ismene and Creon, but moves to the right in her final scene where she becomes the authority figure in relation to the pusillanimous chorus. The organization of space by Brecht and Neher his designer turns upon unspoken intuitions about the left/right relationship. My own practical experimentation with actors confirms the extent to which

---

[67] 'The tragic wedding' *JHS* 107 (1987) 106–30.

[68] Aphrodite is mentioned at 799, but only in association with the alleged sexual power of Antigone. Female followers of Dionysus are also mentioned.

[69] See B. Brecht, *Antigonemodell* (Berlin, 1949). The version was that of Hölderlin. For the same left/right relationship in Anouilh's *Antigone*, see the photograph reproduced in George Steiner, *Antigones* (Oxford, 1984) pl.3.

Creon's power appears weakened when positions are reversed, and he is moved to the left-hand side of the visual field.[70]

Two vase paintings from the fourth century illustrate the confrontation of Creon and Antigone, reflecting a Euripidean rather than Sophoclean version of the story. In both, Heracles is the reconciling force in the middle, while Antigone is on the viewer's left, and Creon on the right. In one there is a strong left-to-right movement as Antigone and her guard move towards Heracles who in turn gestures towards Creon.[71] The other is more interesting because of the way it sets up an antithesis of wilderness and city. On the left, Antigone, Haemon and the guard stand on rocky terrain, plainly dressed; on the right are Creon, Ismene, Eurydice and a youth in a world of cultivation signified by growing plants and by the richness of the costumes. Gestures define a left-to-right movement that encounters the blocking stability of Creon.[72]

Philoctetes confronts the critic with two apparent problems: one *eisodos* appears never to be used,[73] and there are references to a cave with two mouths (16, 159, 952, 1082). The two mouths become explicable once we think of the acting space as a grid organized around the cardinal points rather than a scene from a nineteenth-century painting. This cave is a single cavity (1081), with one door facing the sun and one the shade (17–19, 1082). The cave thus pierces the promontory along a north–south axis, and the *skênê* door represents the north-facing aperture. A single *eisodos* is used to represent the path to the bay, and implicitly the other *eisodos* must represent the direction of the wilderness where Philoctetes hunts birds, in accordance with the familiar nature/culture paradigm. The choreography endows the unused *eisodos* with semantic content,

[70] Adrian Noble's production of the play at the Swan Theatre, Stratford-upon-Avon, in 1991 also placed Antigone on the left and Creon on the right. Systematic archival research would be needed to test how far this orientation has been followed elsewhere.

[71] *LIMC* 'Antigone' 15: Apulian vase of 340–320.

[72] *LIMC* 'Antigone' 14: Apulian vase of mid fourth century, reproduced as a drawing in *HGRT* fig. 117. Two boxes with recognition tokens signify that left and right will be reconciled in this Euripidean version. A third vase has been identified with the same scene. A monarch with Asiatic headgear sits on the left, whilst a young woman on the right flanked by two guards addresses him, gesturing with her left hand in the formal manner of an orator. On grounds of costume the characters are more plausibly identified as Priam and Helen, but if this is Creon with Antigone, then it is notable how Creon in the left visual field is weak in his body language and effeminate in his costume, whilst Antigone dominates through her control of language: *LIMC* 'Antigone' 12: Lucanian vase of *c.* 380.

[73] See Oliver Taplin, 'The mapping of Sophocles' *Philoctetes*' *BICS* 34 (1987) 69–77; also *GTA* 47. Taplin was confirmed in his original view that Philoctetes enters from the *skênê* by Winnington-Ingram's observation that the chorus hear but do not see his arrival: see Taplin, 'Sophocles in his theatre' 177. The argument seems decisive, despite Graham Ley's argument for a side entry in 'A scenic plot of Sophocles' *Ajax* and *Philoctetes*' *Eranos* 86 (1988) 85–115, p. 97.

creating an antithesis between Philoctetes the hunter of birds (side of the wilderness) and Philoctetes the hunted (side of civilization). A strophe which refers to Philoctetes shooting birds for food (710–11) is balanced by an antistrophe in which Odysseus ships Philoctetes back home (722–3). Philoctetes must use symmetrical lateral gestures in the same way when he sings in a strophe of the birds that he seeks in rain to catch (1090–4) and in the antistrophe of an Odysseus whom he is equally unable to hurt (1111–15). In the next strophe he sings of Odysseus in the bay mocking him and handling the bow (1122ff.), and in the antistrophe he turns in the opposite direction to sing of birds and beasts who can be happy because Philoctetes no longer handles the bow (1146ff.).

One textual reference suggests that this play is consistent with the normal *schema:* wilderness on the left and civilization on the right. Neoptolemus reminds Philoctetes of Chryse, scene of his snake-bite, and states that he will never be healed 'whilst the sun which rises here sets there', until he goes to Troy (1330–1). The 'here' of Lemnos seems to be defined by the actor's gesture as east, whilst Chryse, Troy and elsewhere are defined as west. Again we should expect the real orientation of the theatre to have been used. It is a corollary of this reconstruction that all lateral entrances would be made from the weaker right-hand side, which would be consistent with the surreptitious or duplicitous nature of the arrivals. The lateral axis articulates the major confrontations of the play. The logocentric Odysseus commands the right visual field, the visually centred Philoctetes (who has no skills in rhetoric but forever sees in his imagination birds, the terrain, his enemies and his homeland) commands the left, whilst Neoptolemus and the bow move between them.

In the plays of Euripides, the dialectic of nature and culture is never so straightforward, for all too often barbarism is located at the heart of civilization. In *Hippolytus*, for example, one *eisodos* leads towards the sea and one towards the inland wilderness. The sea, the sphere of Aphrodite and the route to Athens, is only in a very superficial sense to be associated with civilization, for out of the sea springs a monstrous force of destruction.

In *The Phoenician Women* Theban topography allows us to glimpse how Euripides deploys left and right in a play that is less obviously constructed around a controlling binary opposition. The prologue begins with a conventional address to the rising sun, and associates the east with Phoenicia where Cadmus, the founder of Thebes, began his mythic journey. The eastern *eisodos* is thus imbued with powerful symbolism as the place of beginnings. The prologue is followed by a scene in which Antigone, standing on the roof of the *skênê*, surveys the Argive army outside the walls. She is looking at a procession (120). The second and third champions are to the north of the city, the third east of the second. Fourth and fifth, Polyneices and Adrastus, are to the north-east, and they are followed by the virtuous prophet Amphiaraus and by Capaneus for whom Zeus has destined a thunderbolt.[74] Looking northwards at the audience, the actor must cast his gaze from west to east whilst the army is supposed to be circuiting in the opposite direction (the negative anti-clockwise direction). The first champion has the eyes of a star. As Antigone begins to turn to the east, she finds her brother lit up by the rising sun. Turning further east she associates the white prophet with the moon, daughter of the sun, and she must be turned fully to the east – implicitly into the sun's rays – when she has the vision of Zeus' thunderbolt. Thanks to the trajectory of Antigone's gaze, the east acquires enhanced religious and cosmic significance.

When the chorus enter, their first strophic pair is arranged along the east–west axis, recreating a journey made in the teeth of the west wind and replicating the journey of Cadmus. They have come from Tyre, their destination is Delphi, and an epode follows devoted to Delphi and its *omphalos*, requiring the chorus to assume an appropriate position of centrality and stability within the *orchêstra*. A second strophic pair goes on to create the idea of the encircled city and covers the entry of Polyneices. Polyneices probably enters from the west in accordance with the position which he subsequently takes up in the siege. An entry from the audience's right would suit the surreptitious nature of his arrival, and counterbalance the more imposing entry of Teiresias. Teiresias has come directly from Athens, and Athens lies to the east of Thebes. The direction of Athens is important because it fixes the final exit of the play when Oedipus and Antigone leave bound for Colonus.

The siege follows and is described by a messenger, who must indicate the positions of the different engagements by gesture. First described is the human sacrifice of Creon's son, which takes place at Dirce's spring where Cadmus killed the dragon (931ff.), a point located to the west of the town and already fixed for the audience by the son's exit. The messenger creates the drama of the encircled city by constantly turning from one side to another. Parthenopaeus attacks at a gate to the west, and Amphiaraus attacks a gate to the east. Hippomedon and Tydeus attack gates that archaeologists have not succeeded in positioning. Polyneices is in the south-west, at the gate associated with Dirce's spring, and his position here gains a symbolic charge from the human sacrifice at this location. Capaneus is south-east. Finally Adrastus, king of Argos, is said to be at the 'seventh gate', probably close to Polyneices on the south-west side if we may judge from the messenger's later account of Eteocles'

---

[74] Donald J. Mastronarde has a valuable appendix on 'the poetic topography of Thebes' in his edition of *Euripides: Phoenissae* (Cambridge, 1994) 647–50. See also his notes to 131, 145, and 159–60. Mastronarde comments that Euripides aims for an 'impression of particularity and verisimilitude'.

clockwise tour of the gates. The climax of the siege comes when Capaneus on the messenger's extreme right-hand side is struck by a thunderbolt, and Adrastus orders a withdrawal. It is here at Capaneus' gate that the brothers Eteocles and Polyneices fight in single combat (1570).

Theban topography thus fixes the positions for the most important entries of the play. Creon must bring on the body of his son from the audience's right, the weaker side, whilst Antigone leads on from the left the procession with the corpses of her brothers and mother. There is a symbolic logic here, for the death in the west is seen to be beneficent, and consonant with the movement of the cosmos, whilst the unnatural death of the brothers in the east has been sent by the gods. When Oedipus exits towards the east, having been disinterred from his living tomb within the *skênê*, he marches not towards natural death but towards a new beginning as protector of Athens. Since the play relates itself in this way to the topographical milieu of the audience, it is helpful to understand the play as a ceremony rather than a mere disembodied fiction. The organization of the action around parameters fixed by the sun is crucial to the sense of ceremony. If real east and the fictive east of the play coincide, Thebes can more easily be seen as a metaphor for the beleaguered city of Athens.

I have argued that every Greek tragedy creates a coherent topography framed around a binary east/west opposition. If this thesis is correct, then there cannot arise a situation in which character A exits towards location X at the same moment as character B arrives from location X, for this would create a meeting or a hiatus. I shall conclude this chapter by examining two exceptions which prove the rule.

In *Rhesus* the setting is somewhere in the temporary Trojan camp, and the parameters are established by the *eisodoi*, one of which leads towards Troy and the mountains, and the other towards the front lines and the Greek camp beyond. When the chorus depart towards the front to resume their watch duty, Odysseus and Diomedes sneak through the Trojan lines and murder Rhesus. The chorus exit at 564/5 without seeing the two Greeks who apparently enter at the same moment. Later the chorus are accused of letting the pair slip past them (809–10). In order to understand the dramatic technique, we have to recognize that the mode is tragicomedy. The chorus at the start of their first ode pray to Apollo as Apollo of Thymbra (a temple south-east of Troy), and their dance would seem to associate the *thymelê* with Thymbra where the Homeric Rhesus made his camp.[75] Later we hear that Odysseus is often to be found in disguise at the altar of Apollo Thymbraios, awaiting his chance to enter the city (507–9). This prepares the way for Odysseus and Diomedes to take cover by

---

[75] *Iliad* 10.430–4. Note the strophic correspondence between Apollo's image and the *thymelai* of Troy: 226=234.

the *thymelê*, unnoticed by the chorus in the darkness. While Diomedes must be wearing his Homeric lion skin, Odysseus is probably wearing the ludicrous wolf outfit that he has stolen from Dolon (592), going like Dolon on all fours, and merging with the altar in symbolic accord with Apollo's traditional identity as the wolf-god (224).[76]

In order to see how the two Greeks reach their place of concealment by the *thymelê*, we must turn to the choral ode which the chorus sing before they exit to the front. The strophe runs:

> Whose is the watch now? Who relieves
> mine? The early constellations
> are setting. The Pleiades' sevenfold course
> rides high, and the eagle soars in the centre of heaven.
>
> Wake. What keeps you? Wake
> from your sleep, to your watch.
> Do you not see how the moon shines?
>
> Dawn is near, dawn
> is breaking now, running before it
> here is the star.

The sense demands that the chorus direct their gaze into the sky, focussing upon the western horizon, the Pleiades, the pediment of heaven, the moon and Lucifer, and thus tracing a lateral line from west to east. The first phrase passes from the west to the 'centre of heaven', the second looks up to the moon, and the third looks east to the dawn. The antistrophe, after some intervening sung dialogue about duty rosters, is arranged along the same lateral axis.

> I hear. Perched above Simois
> she sings her murderous marriage;
> in vociferous chant the own-child-slayer
> sings her nightingale song and sorrow.
>
> Now are pasturing the flocks
> on Ida. The night-murmuring call
> of the shepherd's pipe is heard.
>
> A magic on my eyes is sleep.
> It comes sweetest
> to the lids about dawn.[77]

---

[76] So argues William Ritchie in *The Authenticity of the Rhesus of Euripides* (Cambridge, 1964) 76–7. The text at *Rhesus* 592 deviates from Homer's account, which has Dolon's costume remain on the battlefield. It is hard to see why the dramatist should describe rather than show Dolon's disguise unless he intends the costume to be used later by Odysseus.

[77] 527–37, 546–56 – adapted to reflect the Greek word order from Lattimore's translation in *Euripides IV* (Chicago, 1958) 28–9.

The direction of movement reverses that of the strophe. The first phrase looks to the source of the Simois to the east (cf. line 827), the second is concerned with the high mountain, and the third is an evasion of the eastern dawn. The next line of the chorus makes it clear that they are facing in the direction of the Greek camp, whither Dolon departed. The language points up the dramatic context, for the music of the nightingale evokes the murder that is to be committed, the reference to flocks is relevant to the animal costumes of the intruders and to Rhesus who strayed over the shepherd's mountain, and the reference to sleep evokes the failure of the chorus in their duties. The deictic focus upon the sky above is a device that allows the two intruders to sneak in unnoticed by the sleepy chorus, creeping along the ground like animals whilst the chorus look upwards. Perhaps Odysseus alone runs forward during the strophe, just as the morning star runs before the sun, leaving Diomedes in his brighter yellow attire to follow during the antistrophe. The integration of choreography and action is total, and there is no hiatus between the exit of the chorus and the entry of the spies; rather, the crossing is exploited to dramatic effect.

The words of the chorus imply that the Greeks are to be imagined as lying beyond the west *eisodos*. In terms of real and Iliadic topography, east is the side of Thymbra and of the mountains, whilst the sea lies to the west.[78] This is the conformation that we should expect, allowing the spies to sneak in from the right whilst Rhesus in golden armour makes his grand solar entry from the left. The audience's left would belong to the barbarians, the right to the rationalist Greeks in accordance with the normal pattern. The use of space in this play is schematic, for although Odysseus and Diomedes return past the chorus there is no question of the audience being troubled by the need for stolen horses to pass across. It may well be that Rhesus, having entered from the east, is directed through the *skênê* door to make his camp, a signal that he is placed *behind* the Trojan lines. The chorus' hymn to Apollo Thymbraios would thus mark an implicit scene change to the sanctuary of Apollo. Athene would be able to stand above the *skênê* to direct her protégés in to the scene of murder, and the Muse would appear above the house of death with Rhesus' corpse. I shall examine the non-realist nature of the *skênê* in the next chapter.

There can be no question of one character sneaking past another in the *Alcestis*, where Heracles exits towards the tomb of Alcestis at the same moment as Admetus and the chorus return from the tomb. We must begin by recognizing that this is not a typical tragedy, but a surrogate satyr play, duty-bound to deconstruct the hopeless binary oppositions set up by the three preceding

---

[78] Cuillandre, *La Droite et la gauche* 36.

tragedies. The *eisodoi* in *Alcestis* would seem to set up an opposition between life and death, for one leads towards the city, and the home of Pheres who opts to live, while the other leads towards the tomb, its symbolism established at the start of the play by the entry of Death. The language of the play sets up a related opposition of light and dark. Alcestis comes out of the house because she wants to see the sun for one last time, and life is again and again evoked as the act of seeing the sun.[79] The opposition of light and dark is reinforced by iconographic costume, for in the first scene Death wears a black peplos (843), while Apollo must wear his habitual white. Fifth-century mythology associated Apollo with the sun, and saw Death as the son of Night. Admetus, the attendants and apparently the chorus change into black during the play (216, 427, 818), and Admetus contrasts the black costumes of the funeral procession with the white costumes of his marriage procession (923). The corpse of Alcestis is probably dressed in white in accordance with Greek tradition, which often insisted that the corpse should be dressed like a bride.[80] The opposition of light and dark embraces even the description of Admetus' lands, which stretch from the dark stables of Helios in the west to the Aegean sunrise (593–5). A strophic opposition links Alcestis' journey to the underworld to the harvest moon and circling of the seasons (439–41=449–51).

The sun must have moved well towards the west by the time the play was performed, lending added poignancy to Alcestis' desire to see the sun for one last time. The direction of the tomb belongs symbolically to the west, the side of mortality where life gives way to darkness. There is no inconsistency with real topography, for the Larisa road down which Heracles is directed (835) must run westward out of Pherae, whilst Alcestis' marriage procession would have run in from the east (249, 915ff.). If Heracles follows the funeral procession to the west, to the audience's right, we are obliged to conclude that Euripides brings on Admetus and the chorus from the left, the east. Although the mourners could plausibly have passed through the town, this entry from the left carries no immediate semiotic significance, and appears dramaturgically inept, though not seriously troublesome for an audience. Euripides' strategy becomes clear when we see how this prepares the way for Heracles to make his reentry from the left bringing the woman whom he has rescued from Death. The iconographic tradition, although our examples are late in this instance, represents Heracles and Alcestis moving from the left towards Admetus on the right.[81] In the play, the mysterious reborn bride, silent and veiled, perhaps

---

[79] *Alcestis* 18, 82, 151, 206, 208, 244, 272, 437, 457, 472, 667, 691, 723, 852, 868, 989, 1073, etc.
[80] John Ferguson, *Among the Gods* (London, 1989) 127.
[81] *LIMC* 'Alkestis' 21, 23–5, 27–9, 47–8, though not 30.

human perhaps a *daimon* in human guise, arrives appropriately from the east, rescued from the underworld like the sun which rises at dawn. Alcestis' exit to the west, the side of death, becomes a cosmic circuit, and transmogrifies into a wedding procession that arrives from the east. The ritual preparations which Alcestis makes in preparation for death are similar to those of a bride, and culminate logically in the bridal action of unveiling.[82]

Alcestis is thus the exception that proves the rule – the rule that Greek tragedy always sets up spatial binaries. The task of Heracles, under the Dionysiac influence of wine, is to break down the binary opposition of life and death which tragedy posits as a remorseless and inescapable fact of existence. The Dionysiac finale allows death to become life, sunset to become dawn, right to become left, the rational to become the numinous, and the linear to become cyclic. The strict spatial conventions of tragedy are broken only because the structures of tragedy need to be collapsed before evening comes and the audience disperse.

The principle of lateral opposition is a key to the aesthetics of Greek theatre, but seems alien to a modern consciousness, for modern theatre takes place indoors, and the modern world no longer uses the sun to orientate itself in place and time. Binarism is not congenial to a humanist tradition that celebrates the integrity of the single, unique ego. Since the abolition of the medieval Satan, the Christian tradition has been monotheistic and has shaped modern thinking accordingly. The dominance of monism can be illustrated by three recent productions of Greek tragedy, Noble's *The Thebans*, Mnouchkine's *Les Atrides* and Stein's *Oresteia*. In all three, major entries were effected through a central, or near-central, downstage doorway. The importance of making a slow imposing entry – Oliver Taplin's legacy to no small extent[83] – was recognized, but not the distinctive Greek feature of binary opposition. In the 1990s many traditional binaries have been deconstructed – nature and culture, male and female, mind and body, self and other, and the Marxist opposition of oppressor and oppressed that gave shape to Brecht's *Antigone*. Lévi-Strauss's binarist structuralism has yielded to Derridean models of infinite erasure and regression. The difference between Greek and modern representations of space becomes increasingly pronounced.

---

[82] For the unveiling ceremony see Rush Rehm, *Marriage and Death* (Princeton, 1994) 141–2; for ritual details see also Robert Garland, *The Greek Way of Life* (London, 1990) 219–21.

[83] For Taplin's influence on production see his 'Opening performance: closing texts?' *Essays in Criticism* 45 (1995) 93–120, pp. 96–7.

CHAPTER 7

❦

Inside/outside

The *skênê* or screen erected across the back of the acting area created a space that was private, hidden and unseen. The structural opposition of inside and outside, unseen and seen, became a distinctive feature of Greek theatrical space. There has been general acceptance of Taplin's view that the *skênê* was introduced shortly before or on the occasion of the *Oresteia*. In the *Oresteia* we see fully realized almost all the techniques, conventions and structural oppositions associated with the *skênê* over the next forty years.[1] Taplin's argument that the tragic *skênê* had a single door, creating a powerful dramatic focus on the point of access between the seen and unseen worlds, seems entirely compelling.[2]

On the *skênê* was some form of scene-painting, creating the illusion of architectural features. I argued in chapter 2 that the *skênê* would not have been in place for the day of circular dancing and sacrificial slaughter, when the audience would have wanted a view of the tribal sacrifices that were the natural culmination of the dithyrambic dancing. The purpose of scene-painting was to create out of transient materials the illusion of a stone monument, in accordance with Dionysus' nature as god of illusion and transformation. There can be no question of a representational set, picturing a background appropriate to a specific play.[3] In simple practical terms, it would have been cumbersome to have changed sets between plays.[4] There is no evidence in the art of the period for pictorial backgrounds. In plays set before a cave, the text refers in conventionalized form to a 'house' or 'roof'.[5] The dramatist who notionally

---

[1] *SA* 452–9. Techniques are catalogued in 458 n.2.   [2] *SA* 438–40.

[3] See *PIE* 35–43; A. L. Brown, 'Three and scene-painting Sophocles' *Proceedings of the Cambridge Philological Society* 210 (1984) 1–17; Ruth Padel, 'Making space speak' *NTDWD* 336–65.

[4] *PIE* 44–50 analyses Euripidean plays performed on a single day.

[5] *PIE* 13. For Sophocles, cf. also *Philoctetes* 147, 159, 1453, *Ichneutae* (ed. Page) 281. See also Peter Arnott, *Greek Scenic Conventions* (Oxford, 1962) 99, 101. Compare also Menander's *Dyskolos*, where a cave of Pan in the middle of an Attic cliff face is set between two doors of houses that must, in topographical terms, have lain in the valley beneath. New Comedy remained visually schematic.

sets his play before a tent has no scruple in evoking a solid barred doorway.[6] Detailed verbal descriptions, like that of Apollo's temple in *Ion*, are not surrogate stage directions to the scenographer.[7]

The hidden world behind the *skênê* could be revealed by means of the *eccyclêma*, which rolled forward through the doorway to extrude a tableau. Taplin opposes both the ancient and the modern critical consensus when he argues that the *eccyclêma* was probably not used in the *Oresteia*. He sees it as 'an extraordinarily contrived device', and argues that 'after the introduction of the skene a need would have to be established for its use'.[8] This is to see the matter the wrong way round. The *skênê* blocked off the audience's view of what had previously been visible. The ideology of democracy held that all things should be made visible, that power should never be hidden. Thus councillors ate publicly in the Tholos, the *Agora* had no walls, nor did the early Pnyx, the laws were displayed in an open *stoa*, male bodies were bared in the gymnasium, statues were removed from their temples and paraded through the streets, and the tragic performance was open to all citizens. The *Oresteia* depicts a familial vendetta brought into the public space of the Athenian law court. We should understand a theatrical device that allowed the hidden world to be exposed in relation to this socio-spatial requirement to see the whole. I argued in chapter 2 that the *skênê* masked off part of the orchestral circle, and did not comprise a separate building tangential to the circle. The *eccyclêma* should not be conceived as revealing a hidden interior beyond and outside the public circle, but as restoring the wholeness symbolized by the circular dancing of the ten democratic tribes. To put the matter another way, the erection of the *skênê* was predicated upon the possibility of its removal. Taplin conceives of the *eccyclêma* as a clumsy proto-realist device, that only emerged in the later fifth century. I would suggest, rather, that Aristophanic parodies mark not the introduction of the device but the moment when it became self-conscious, and that in the last years of the fifth century the device is conspicuous by its absence.[9]

---

[6] Arnott 100; Brown 9.

[7] On the way verbal pictures problematize the act of seeing, see Froma Zeitlin, 'The artful eye: vision, ecphrasis and spectacle in Euripidean theatre' in *Art and Text in Ancient Greek Culture* ed. S. Goldhill and R. Osborne (Cambridge, 1994) 138–223.

[8] *SA* 442–3; cf. 369ff. Another sceptic is Pickard-Cambridge in *TDA* 106–8. S. Melchinger regards the *eccyclêma* as indispensable in the *Oresteia* in *Das Theater der Tragödie* (Munich, 1973) 31. For representative modern views, see John Gould in *Cambridge History of Classical Literature*, Vol. I: *Greek Literature* ed. P. E. Easterling and B. M. W. Knox (Cambridge, 1985) 270; H.-J. Newiger, 'Ekkyklema e mechané nella messa in scena del dramma greco' *Dioniso* 59 (1989) 173–85. The idea of evolution towards realism is challenged by G. Canotti, 'Scenografia e spettacolo: le machine teatrali' *Dioniso* 59 (1989) 283–95.

[9] The last well-attested instances are the two *Electra* plays, where the device self-consciously replicates the staging of *The Libation Bearers*. Euripides' play is dated to 413 BC.

In *Agamemnon*, the *eccyclêma* is plainly the simplest way to bring on the tableau of Agamemnon in his bath, wrapped in a net and embraced by Cassandra. Taplin's solution of carrying on the bodies requires a hiatus in the action, and negates Clytaemnestra's statement that she stands where she struck (1379), destroying also the visual focus for her precise account of how she ensnared her husband. Pickard-Cambridge's prim objection that Cassandra would not have been in Agamemnon's bathroom points up the fact that what is revealed on the *eccyclêma* is not the scene immediately behind the threshold (where we might rather expect to find a courtyard with separate access to the women's quarters) but a schematic representation of what lies behind doors.[10] The interiority of the setting is rapidly forgotten in the ensuing scene with the chorus and the intervention of Aegisthus' bodyguards. In the parallel scene in *The Libation Bearers*, Orestes calls upon the sun soon after his entry on the *eccyclêma*, allowing the indoor/outdoor distinction to dissolve.[11] The Greek audience did not trouble itself with nineteenth-century canons of realist representation, and the *eccyclêma* was perceived as a dramatic convention, not as an attempt to replicate a fragment of real interior space. In *The Eumenides* the *eccyclêma* allows Orestes to appear as he is described, on the navel-stone in the recesses of the temple, clutching a sword and olive branch, with the Furies before him, draped across the prophetic tripod.[12] It allows the chorus to be brought on asleep, and in accordance with the text to be woken by Clytaemnestra. When the chorus begin to dance (143), they must necessarily take to the *orchêstra* floor, and the inside/outside distinction dissolves. The withdrawal of the *eccyclêma* (234) is a convenient sign to the audience that the setting has changed even though the chorus have not left the *orchêstra*. The setting is now Athens, and the democratic and open cult of Athene replaces the secretive indoor cult of Delphic Apollo.

Once we recognize that the *eccyclêma* is in the first instance a device, we can more easily visualize a play like *Ajax*. The first part of the play is a long build-up

---

[10] See *DFA* 106; A. M. Dale, *Collected Papers* (Cambridge, 1969) 119–29.

[11] *SA* 326 n.2 notes that the same technique appears in the *eccyclêma* scene in Euripides' *Heracles*.

[12] Pickard-Cambridge and Taplin are content to ignore the navel-stone, a powerful symbol as we see in vase iconography: see *LIMC* 'Orestes' 28–53. A. H. Sommerstein's commentary in his edition of *Eumenides* (Cambridge, 1989) 92–4 seems to me correct, apart from his denial that the 'thrones' of line 47, shown on the *eccyclêma*, are to be identified with the prophetic tripod, the 'thrones' of lines 18 and 29. Sommerstein assumes (with the scholiast) that there is space for the Furies on the *eccyclêma*, against *TDA* 108, *SA* 370 and Dale, *Collected Papers* 123. He follows A. L. Brown, 'Some problems in the *Eumenides* of Aeschylus' *JHS* 102 (1982) 26–32, p. 28. Peter Stein brought in eight Furies on an *eccyclêma* about seven feet wide, with two more concealed in the *skênê* behind (see p. 85 above). The *eccyclêma* in *Heracles* must have been equally cluttered.

to the revelation of Ajax on the *eccyclêma* surrounded by the animals he has slaughtered and now restored to his senses. Descriptions in advance of the revelation help the spectators many metres away to interpret the image placed before them. Prominence is probably given to two rams taken to be Agamemnon and Menelaus.[13] The play falls structurally into two parts, and a second use of the *eccyclêma* for the death of Ajax creates an aesthetic balance. The same sword is responsible for both scenes of carnage. Ajax must use the *skênê* door when appearing for his final speech in the wilderness, for the chorus have just used both *eisodoi* to leave the *orchêstra*. The haft of his sword is already planted in the ground when he delivers his first line, and deictic references to 'this sword' (828, 834) certify that the sword is visible. The entry of the actor on the *eccyclêma* would have the further advantage of signifying (like the departure of the *eccyclêma* at *Eumenides* 234) a change of location. A logical reconstruction of the staging would have the *eccyclêma* withdrawn at the end of Ajax's final speech, and reintroduced twenty-five lines later bearing Tecmessa and a dummy impaled on the sword. This frees the actor of Ajax to make up the complement of three actors later in the play and avoids an unprecedented visible killing. It also avoids awkward visual compromises. Suggestions that the sword is planted in the doorway or that Ajax falls behind bushes placed on the *eccyclêma* do not take account of the angle of vision of the audience, and the need in a huge theatre to use large effects. Bethe's suggestion in 1896 that the *eccyclêma* was introduced, withdrawn and reintroduced has been dismissed in the twentieth century as the extravagant fantasy of a by-gone theatrical age.[14] If however we see the *eccyclêma* as a symbolic rather than realist or spectacular device, allowing perhaps a single tree to serve as the iconographic sign of a grove, we can see how the withdrawal of the *eccyclêma* is appropriate to Ajax's final words: 'Daylight! Sacred plain of my homeland Salamis! Base of my ancestral hearth! Famous Athens and race I grew up with! These springs and rivers! – to the Trojan plain also, I say "farewell", O my nourishers. To you Ajax cries this final word. The rest I shall recount in Hades to those below' (859–65). Language correlates with the space of performance. Ajax is pulled away from the light into the darkness of the *skênê*, away from the audience of Athenians

---

[13] Pickard-Cambridge is one of the few to dispute the *eccyclêma* here: *TDA* 109–10. The consequence of this puritanical objection to spectacle is that Ajax remains behind the *skênê* at 348ff., when he should be the visual focus.

[14] E. Bethe, *Prolegomena zur Geschichte des Theaters in Altertum* (Leipzig, 1896) 127–9. Subsequent scholarship on the suicide is summarized in J. S. Scullion, 'The Athenian Stage and Scene-setting in Early Tragedy' (Ph.D. thesis, Harvard, 1990) 133–69; and in Fiona Macintosh, *Dying Acts* (Cork, 1994) 130–3. See pp. 50–1 above for Pöhlmann's assumption that there were two doors.

(with Salaminians amongst them), and away from the sacred plain of the *orchêstra*, with its central hearth, and drainage course around it. The earlier *eccyclêma* scene established the *skênê* as a place of animal sacrifice, and the *skênê* which Ajax now enters becomes the house of Hades, just as it was for Cassandra in *Agamemnon* (1291). The retreating *eccyclêma* allows the actor to be removed towards the real sacrificial altar, and a dummy to be brought back to the audience when the deed is accomplished. Ajax's death is not presented as a single momentary act, as in renaissance and modern conceptions of death, but rather as a slow journey to another place.[15] The *skênê* is neither tent nor grove but the House of Death.[16]

We should see the space of Greek tragedy in geometric terms, as a grid upon which symbolic oppositions are organized, rather than in pictorial terms, as an image of the reality perceived by a single human eye. The non-representational nature of the *skênê* allows it to be polysemous, and open to transformations of the kind that were examined in chapter 5: a Greek shack can become the towers of Ilium, the door can become the Bosphorus, the darkness of the *skênê* becomes the darkness of the underworld. The schematic nature of Greek theatre space must be grasped if we are to make sense of a play like *Oedipus at Colonus*. As I showed in the last chapter, complex oppositions are articulated along the lateral east–west axis. Oedipus' tomb is to be a barrier between Thebes on the one side and Athens on the other. At Colonus Oedipus has effectively reached his journey's end, and a final entry into the *skênê*, neither left nor right, seems to be indicated. Taplin accepts that the *skênê* should be used, interpreting the acting area as a place where three roads meet, the third road into the *skênê* being a cul-de-sac. Bernard Knox, on the other hand, takes the realist/pictorial view that the *skênê* represents the grove and the grove is inviolate.[17] We must see the topological referent of the *skênê* door as not only the grove of the Semnai but also the brazen threshold, the cave-mouth in the nearby Hill of Demeter that

---

15 For death as a process, see Macintosh, *Dying Acts* 19–23.

16 For the representation of Hades by a house, see Ruth Padel *In and Out of the Mind* (Princeton, 1992) 98–100. For Hades as the *skênê*, note how the chorus refer back to the *skênê* at *Ajax* 607; compare Euripides, *Electra* 1144; *Helen* 69; Sophocles, *Electra* 109–10; also *Hippolytus* 56–7, where Aphrodite may exit through the door as through the 'gates of Hades'; also *Women of Trachis* (see p. 130 above), *Medea* (p. 122 above), *Hecuba* (p. 182 below). *Frogs* 460ff. may involve parody of Euripides, *Pirithous*.

17 Oliver Taplin 'Sophocles in his theatre' (with discussion appended) in *Sophocle* ed. J. de Romilly (*Entretiens Hardt 29*, Geneva, 1983) 155–83 pp. 158, 183. David Seale, although his conception is pictorial, sees no alternative to a *skênê* exit: *Vision and Stagecraft in Sophocles* (London, 1982) 143 n.52. Adrian Noble in his Stratford production of the play (Royal Shakespeare Company: the Swan Theatre 1991) used a large silent sliding *skênê* door to excellent effect for the exit, demonstrating that Taplin's instincts were theatrically sound. The door was non-representational, and was used also for *Antigone* and *Oedipus the King*.

was taken to be an entry to the underworld.[18] Oedipus' reference to his destination as 'this' ground is repeated four times, implying a gesture towards the threshold before him rather than somewhere beyond the *eisodos*. He declares that he leaves the light and hides himself in Hades (1552), equating the *skênê* as in *Ajax* with the House of Hades. A short choral sequence follows, allowing little time for a funeral procession to leave down an *eisodos*, and the messenger to return by the same lengthy, visible route. In their dance sequence (1556ff.) the chorus evoke the Stygian House of Hades and the gates guarded by Cerberus, an image which gains its force from the fact that the audience are looking at a doorway. Sophocles is able to use the *skênê* in a flexible way, allowing the audience to envisage an outdoor space behind the *skênê*, because he is working within a performance tradition accustomed to using the *skênê* to symbolize the House of Hades, the place of darkness. The chorus pray to the 'unseen goddess' and to the 'chthonic goddesses', imbuing the *skênê* with female associations appropriate to the Semnai and to Demeter. A final departure in the direction of Athens would have destroyed the play's careful polarization of gender.

Feminist criticism has interested itself in the inside/outside polarity, and may be said to have pioneered the theorization of Greek tragic space.[19] Froma Zeitlin, for example, demonstrates how the *oikos* (house) is owned by the male, but its space is controlled by the feminine 'other'.

Thus, in the conflicts between house and city or between domestic and political concerns that are the recurrent preoccupations of tragic plots, the woman, whether wife or daughter, is shown as best representing the positive values and structures of the house, and she typically defends its interests in response to some masculine violation of its integrity. As a result, however, of the stand she takes, the woman also represents a subversive threat to male authority as an adversary in a power struggle for control which resonates throughout the entire social and political system, raising the terrifying specter of rule by women.[20]

There can be no doubt that the opposition of *oikos* and *polis* is a recurrent motif in Greek tragedy, and is related to a structural tension in democratic society.[21]

---

[18] The fusion is signalled at lines 56–8. Jebb in his edition (Cambridge, 1900) p. xxxi believes that the Hill of Demeter, whither Oedipus goes after his final entry, is the knoll to the north of the knoll of Colonus, i.e. in the opposite direction to Athens. Topography would thus make a final exit in the Athenian direction even less likely.

[19] See p. 84 above. It is perhaps no coincidence that it was a female critic who first placed the seen/unseen dialectic on the critical agenda in 1956: A. M. Dale 'Seen and unseen in Greek tragedy' reprinted in her *Collected Papers* (Cambridge, 1969) 119–29.

[20] *NTDWD* 76–7 – from the essay entitled 'Playing the other: theatre, theatricality and the feminine in Greek drama' first published in 1985.

[21] For a good anthropological account, see S. C. Humphreys, '*Oikos* and *polis*' in her collection *The Family, Women and Death* (London, 1983) 1–21.

A critical line can be traced back from Zeitlin to Hegel's famous dialectical reading of *Antigone* as the paradigmatic Greek tragedy.[22] Hegel traced a structural opposition between two moral forces: on the one hand the male, the *polis* and gods of light, and on the other the female, the *oikos* and gods of darkness. Zeitlin's analysis differs mainly in its sociological and performative emphasis.

In the last chapter I argued that the Creon/Antigone conflict is mapped primarily on the east–west axis, an axis with strong connotations of gender. The death of Eurydice in the finale of *Antigone* is liable to perplex readers preoccupied with unity of plot, or with character development, but in spatial terms the ending is entirely appropriate. The left/right opposition culminates in the rupturing of the centre. The death of Eurydice represents the destruction of Creon's *oikos*, for she both controls the house and allows it to reproduce itself. The *skênê* is associated with Eurydice, the woman as mother, the woman as container, and not with Antigone, the woman as sister, the woman who renounces reproduction (*anti-gonê*). The *eccyclêma* here is no mere indulgence in spectacle. The text indicates that Eurydice has stabbed herself at an altar (1301), and that she is no longer in the recesses of the house (1293). This altar must be the altar of Zeus Herkeios (mentioned at 487), the altar in the courtyard that symbolized the link between *oikos* and *polis*. To punish Creon for destroying her sons, she pollutes not the female hearth but the patriarchal altar which symbolizes Creon's power to rear citizen sons.[23] The finale of *Antigone* confirms Zeitlin's broad account of Greek tragedy: a world in which the protagonist is male (Creon, not Antigone), and in which the woman's role is to be the 'radical other' lurking behind the *skênê*.

In an essay on the *Hippolytus*, Zeitlin develops a more elaborate argument. The woman's body and the house/*skênê* are 'isotopic', and the door correlates with the mouth as the passage through which secrets are made public. When Hippolytus claims that his 'tongue swore, but not his mind (*phrên*)' (612), or when Phaedra says that her 'hands are clean but the *phrên* is polluted' (317), Zeitlin discerns a duality of self, the interior self being differentiated from external appearance.[24] A similar account of interior female space is offered by Ruth Padel, who stresses the importance of the *eccyclêma* in opening up the unseen world, breaking the seen/unseen boundary upon which the tension of the play depends. She links three 'unseen interiors': house, underworld and

---

[22] A. and H. Paolucci (eds.) *Hegel on Tragedy* (New York, 1975) 178, 325. Hegel's views are summarized and attacked in Brian Vickers, *Towards Greek Tragedy* (London, 1973) 526–7.

[23] On the altar, see *GR* 130, 255–6. On its use in *Antigone*, see Oliver Taplin's note in *Dioniso* 59 (1989) 105.

[24] 'The power of Aphrodite: Eros and the boundaries of self in the *Hippolytus*' in *Directions in Euripidean Criticism* ed. P. Burian (Durham, N.C., 1985) 52–111.

mind.[25] Tragedy, she argues, creates a frightening, unseen space in the audience's mind which is linked at all levels to the idea of the woman, source of
anxiety to a male citizen audience. The 'mind' in Padel's analysis is not an
abstraction, but is related to the inner organs of the body.[26] Despite this fundamental proviso, the argument that the *skênê* is somehow to be equated with
'the self' risks assimilating Greek tragedy to the nineteenth-century proscenium theatre of Ibsen. In Ibsen, the dominant spatial parameter is depth,
and a distant view of a murky fjord, a father's portrait or a wild duck is overtly
suggestive of inner psychic forces. Drama of psychological realism is concerned
with externalizing an interior,[27] and we must be cautious of reading Greek
drama in terms that are so familiar to us. It is important to recall that the *skênê*
was a small screen below the audience, and not a massive architectural structure confronting the audience as in Fiechter's influential reconstructions.

In Aeschylus there is little evidence for a dualist notion of self. Aeschylus
portrays an animist universe where demons can possess both people and places.
The 'house' of Atreus is repeatedly personified in *Agamemnon*, and its identity
is inseparable from its human occupants. Behind the quasi-Homeric world of
the play lies a social reality in which membership of the democratic community was bound up with place. The citizen had an altar of Zeus in his courtyard, and was attached to a phratry with an altar of Apollo. He belonged to a
deme with its deme altar, and a tribe with its cult statue in the *Agora*. He knew
where the graves of his ancestors lay, and he knew that Athenians had never
migrated from elsewhere. The citizen's bond with sacred places determined his
social and thus personal identity, just as the bond between Dionysus and his
sanctuary determined the place of theatrical performance. Space was, in
Lefebvre's terms, not abstract but absolute. The returning Agamemnon greets
Argos and the gods within the land, and at the end of his oration proposes to
greet the gods of his house and hearth, while Cassandra prays to Apollo of the
entrance-way (1081). As in fifth-century Athens, so in Aeschylus' play all spaces
have their divine overseers. Space can never be abstract or inanimate.

The *skênê*/house is in a sense the protagonist of *Agamemnon*. The watchman
wonders if the house might have a voice (37), and the cries from within the
house may have seemed in performance like the cries of the house itself.[28] In
much the same way, the trail of red tapestries may have suggested that the

---

[25] 'Making space speak' in *NTDWD* 336–65, p. 346.

[26] *In and Out of the Mind* 12ff. Compare Zeitlin, 'Aphrodite' 200 n.80, citing Starobinski on
Homeric interiority.

[27] One of the best accounts is B. O. States, *Great Reckonings in Little Rooms* (Berkeley, 1985).

[28] For the personalization of the *oikos* see John Jones, *On Aristotle and Greek Tragedy* (London,
1962) 82ff.

house itself was bleeding from its wounds.[29] The house 'does not know how to be poor' (962), it is 'hated by the gods' (1090), it has its 'ancient sins' (1197). It seems to be inhabited by semi-animate forces, like Strife (1461), a Demon (1468), or a revel of Erinyes (1190), but not by 'Justice' (773). *The Libation Bearers* represents the failed resuscitation of the house. When Orestes enters to kill his mother, the chorus identify Orestes both as the eye of the house (934) – in other words the part of the corpse where life can still be discerned – and as the personification of Justice. As the bolts are withdrawn and the *eccyclêma* comes forward, they sing of the bit being removed from the house, the house seeing the light and rising from the ground (961ff., 972). Exits into the *skênê* are visual metaphors. When Agamemnon vanishes, Clytaemnestra evokes the wine harvest, suggesting that Agamemnon tramples the tapestries as if they were grapes, and that the interior of the house is cold like a wine cellar in winter (970–2). The fact that the north-facing *skênê* lay in shadow is evoked in the exits of both Agamemnon and Cassandra. Agamemnon is likened to shade against the Dog Star (966–7), the dog motif suggesting the Furies above the house. Cassandra declares that the fortunate are but shaded, and the unfortunate are obliterated as by a sponge; framed in the doorway, she vanishes from view when she has spoken (1329).

The house cannot be construed as a symbol for part of the self in the *Oresteia* because it has its own material and animate identity, as vividly rendered as any of the 'characters' played by masked actors. What is important about Orestes is not what lies within him but whether he is the human embodiment of Justice. In a sense the *skênê*, like the dramatic character, is a mask with nothing behind it. When the character exits, the actor changes his mask and the character ceases to exist. Just as the character is a mask, so the *skênê* is a façade, and both alike have meaning laid on them by the dense language of the play. The *skênê* remains a façade in accordance with the Homeric and classical understanding that only our visible lives on earth have meaning. Life is not predicated upon an unseen paradise or nirvana. When Cassandra proclaims that her image is expunged, she implies that as a slave no one will remember her, and immortality consists only in being remembered on earth.

In Euripides' reconceptualization of the *Oresteia*, a generation later, we find the stage façade being used in a rather different way to emphasize that theatre is the space of illusion. His *Electra* (413 BC) is preoccupied by the gap between identity and appearance. Electra looks like a slave but is a princess; she is formally married, but virgin; her husband is noble, but a peasant; Apollo is wise,

---

[29] For the tapestries and blood see R. F. Goheen, 'Three studies in *The Oresteia*' *American Journal of Philology* 76 (1955) 113–37, pp. 115–26; for a survey of scholarship on the scene, *SA* 308–16.

offers unwise prophecies. The play is and is not set in the world of ,chylus. It is full of visual quotations from the *Oresteia* – Orestes and Pylades ...ding, the recognition scene, the invocation of Agamemnon below the earth, stepping down from the chariot, the revelation of Clytaemnestra and Aegisthus on the *eccyclêma*. The *skênê*, I have argued, was not painted representationally, and thus the peasant cottage looks the same as the palace at Argos, helping the actions to seem familiar despite their new context.[30] After Electra has ushered her mother into the place of sacrifice and 'House of Hades', the peasant setting dissolves. The chorus recall the return of Agamemnon to his Cyclopean walls, and when they see the bodies they bewail the fate of the house of Tantalus (1158, 1176). The hovel fuses with the palace of Tantalus and Agamemnon. The play is set in a world of social mobility where wealth can shift and fly from the house (941–4), and it relates to a democratic Athens where the hegemony of the aristocracy was insecure, and the most famous Athenian aristocrat, Alcibiades, had just been exiled as an alleged conspirator. Very many citizens would have been absent in Sicily, unable to attend the play at the Dionysia. Many would have lost the use of their lands in the countryside. The bonds which tied the Athenian to his hearth and city were loosening. Through its setting on the margins of the state and away from its cult-centres, the play creates a sense of spatial dislocation. People's identity can no longer be defined in terms of the place to which they and their forebears belong, and reference has to be made instead to some kind of human 'nature' (368, 941). Orestes and Electra pray to Agamemnon beneath the ground, but there is no visible marker of his presence. Space has ceased to be 'absolute', and words can quickly redefine it.

In *Orestes* the setting is no longer the margins of the state but the centre of the city, and the protagonists seem to be surrounded and trapped (444, 762, etc.). Orestes lies on his bed in the *orchêstra* in the first part of the play, defining a playing space that is neither clearly inside the house nor outside in the hostile world of the democratic mob.[31] The straightforward dichotomy of *oikos* and *polis* which we find in the *Oresteia* and *Antigone* is no longer applicable. The *oikos* is divided within itself, and the *polis* has different political constituencies, with its actions reflecting the skills of the demagogue rather than a corporate will. Later in the play Orestes and Electra retreat into the *skênê*, barring the door, and the conventional inside/outside boundary is restored. At this point the *skênê* acquires new connotations. A Trojan slave issues from it, and describes the situation in Homeric terms, making comparisons with the

---

[30] In the most recent edition of the text (Warminster, 1988), M. J. Cropp envisages some form of scene-painting (p. xli), and thus finds evidence for pomposity of character when the peasant refers to his double doors – p. 122, note to 357.

[31] See Willink's helpful comments in his edition (Oxford, 1986) pp. xxxix–xl.

fall of Troy.[32] Helen of Troy is trapped within, while Menelaus outside speaks of a siege (1574, cf. 1568). As those within prepare to torch the building, the unlocalized *skênê* wall suggests the walls of Troy. Spartan Menelaus must also have evoked for the Athenian audience in 408 BC the Spartan invader close to the gates of Athens. Euripides seems to be portraying an Athens weakened not by the enemy without but by the frustrations of its own aristocracy within. Euripides portrays the implosion of a democratic community. There are hints also that, as in the *polis*, so in the microcosm of the individual, Euripides envisages a destructive interiority. The Furies have become a kind of pathological fantasy. Orestes declares that his body has departed; awareness destroys him (390, 396). 'Nature' is an evil in people like Helen (126). Electra has taken leave of her mind (*phrenôn* – 1021). The hands of Menelaus are clean, but not his *phrenes* (1604). Froma Zeitlin in her essay 'The closet of masks' rejects the notion of an inner self and argues that Orestes, in the absence of any secure role-model, is condemned to play a disparate sequence of roles.[33] This conclusion seems consistent with the way the theatrical space is used. The world behind the *skênê* has a momentary existence – when Helen is described spinning flax, for example – but there is no sustained attempt to make the audience envisage an interior space. As in Aeschylus, all that is significant lies before the eyes of the audience.

The last example that I shall consider is *The Bacchae* because of its implications for the festival of Dionysus as a whole. For Zeitlin, the tragic process 'puts insistent pressure on the facade of the masculine self in order to bring out that which resides unacknowledged and unrecognised within'. The *skênê*, in other words, must be identified with the ruler of the house, Pentheus. Pentheus attempts to seal and enclose his city, his house and his psyche against the incursions of Dionysus. The male thus takes possession of the house while women, the normal custodians of the house, abandon the precincts of the city. The cost of this spatial inversion is that Pentheus inside the house is transformed into a woman.[34] Zeitlin's analysis draws heavily upon Charles Segal. Segal's guiding theme is that Dionysus is the god whose property it is to dissolve boundaries: 'As Dionysus invades and destroys the sheltered space of the house, so even more radically does he open the bounded limits of the city to the forces of the wild alien to it.'[35] Richard Seaford, in an analysis more concerned with the political than the psychic dimension, likewise stresses that Dionysus does not

---

[32] See Christian Wolff, 'Orestes' in *Oxford Readings in Greek Tragedy* ed. E. Segal (Oxford, 1983) 340–56, p. 348.

[33] 'The closet of masks: role-playing and myth-making in the *Orestes* of Euripides' *Ramus* 9 (1980) 51–77. [34] *NTDWD* 77–8.

[35] *Dionysiac Poetics and Euripides' 'Bacchae'* (Princeton, 1982) 97.

mark boundaries but crosses them. For Seaford, it is characteristic of Dionysus to destroy the household in order to assert the communality of the *polis*.[36]

The visual neutrality of the *skênê* is essential if it is to suggest three inter-dependent levels: Pentheus, *oikos* and *polis*. In the final scene, with the return of the women and the fragments of Pentheus' body, the *skênê* becomes pre-emi-nently a sign of Cadmus' family which is to be dispersed. As Dionysus stands above it to assert his power over Thebes, the house can no longer be identified with the city but is rather a symbol of broken monarchical power. The signif-icance of the *skênê*, as I argued in chapter 3, must be understood in relation to the significance of the *orchêstra* centre. As Saïd points out, Euripides merges into a single theatrical space two real Theban spaces: the tomb of Semele and her bridal chamber in the ancient palace.[37] Dionysus in the prologue identifies for the audience 'this memorial near the house' still smoking from the thun-derbolt which killed his mother, and he praises Cadmus for consecrating 'this ground' (*pedon*), the 'precinct' or 'enclosure' (*sêkos*) of Semele, which he himself has hidden within a vine (6–12). Iconographically, an altar and memorial pillar surrounded by a vine and set in the middle of the *orchêstra* would seem suffi-cient for the purposes of performance. When Dionysus inside the *skênê* cries that the house of Pentheus must be burnt by a thunderbolt, the chorus focus on the former house, and see flames around the tomb of Semele (596–9). This is an interesting moment in respect of audience response, for the audience cannot have known whether or not they should understand the house of Pentheus to be physically falling, given the absence of realist scenography. In a play about the god of illusion, the stability of dramatic convention comes into question.

When the chorus arrive and devote a long ode to Dionysus, they say that they are 'bringing home' (*katagousai*) Dionysus through the streets (84–8), and they describe his bull-headed image in the corresponding antistrophe. Their *parodos* takes the form of a dithyrambic procession,[38] and it seems altogether probable that the procession brought on an image of the god. The chorus would have carried it in during the astrophic prelude, processing with it or around it during the two strophic pairs, and focussing upon the image in the epode. Such use of a statue would seem to be normal festive practice, exem-plified by the bringing in of Dionysus from the Academy at the start of the

---

[36] 'Dionysus as destroyer of the household: Homer, tragedy and the polis' in *The Masks of Dionysus* ed. T. H. Carpenter and C. A. Faraone (Ithaca, 1993) 115–46.

[37] Suzanne Saïd, 'L'Espace d'Euripide' *Dioniso* 59 (1989) 107–36, p. 129; on the evidence of Pausanias, see E. R. Dodds' edition of the play (Oxford, 1953) 62–3. On the cult see A. Schachter, *Cults of Boeotia* (*BICS* supplement 38.1, London, 1981) 185–95.

[38] On this subject see Richard Seaford's forthcoming critical edition (Warminster, 1996).

Dionysia, by a similar ceremony at the rural Dionysia at Peiraeus,[39] by the 'bringing home' (*katagôgia*) of Dionysus at the Anthesteria,[40] and by the Eleusinian procession. In *The Frogs*, which is strikingly similar to *The Bacchae* in its presentation of Dionysus, there is no doubt that the chorus of Eleusinian initiates bears an image of Dionysus in his aspect as Iacchos.[41] Vases depict the god in procession on a ship-cart, and as a mask on a column worshipped by maenads.[42] I would suggest therefore, that an image of Dionysus was brought in and set up within the central space demarcated as the precinct of Semele. Such a position would connect the god to his mother, to the ruins of the old palace and to his gift of the grape. The presence of some image or symbol of the god gives the chorus a necessary focus at four crucial moments: at the beginning when they introduce the worship of Dionysus to Thebes, at the 'earthquake' when the ruins of the old palace help suggest the ruin of Pentheus' palace, when Pentheus is being dressed and the chorus assert the power of the god, and when Pentheus is upon the mountain and the chorus call on Dionysus to give him his just punishment. An image also helps to mark complex shifts in the chorus' relationship to their god. For modern directors it can be a frustration that the revels on Cithaeron are 'off-stage' rather than 'on-stage',[43] but if some image of the god is visible to the audience then the relationship of 'here' and 'there' becomes more fluid. Spatial boundaries dissolve because the god is present in Thebes as well as on Cithaeron. One obvious form for the image to take is bull-horned (100), differentiating the brutal Theban deity from Dionysus Eleuthereus whose image is present in the *orchêstra*, contributing to the interplay of competing realities. Though the pillar at the centre could have stood alone as an emblem of Dionysus, known in Thebes as the 'pillar-god',[44] some ritual transformation of the pillar would have made a stronger visual statement.

   Whether mask, statue or aniconic column, an emblem of the god at the

---

[39] *DFA* 44 n.2.   [40] *DFA* 12.

[41] Kevin Clinton, *Myth and Cult: the iconography of the Eleusinian Mysteries* (Stockholm, 1992) 64–7. K. Dover in *Aristophanes: Frogs* (Oxford, 1993) 37–41 believes that Aristophanes probably drew his conception of Dionysus from the comic tradition, but could have had forewarning of Euripides' intentions.

[42] For the ship-cart see *DFA* 12 and figs. 11–13; for the vases, *DFA* 5–6, 30–4; Walter Burkert, *Homo Necans*, tr. P. Bing (Berkeley, 1983) 235–8. Note also the statues carried in the Sikyonian Dionysia: Pausanias ii.7.6; and the colossal statue of Dionysus carried in the Dionysiac procession of Ptolemy Philadelphus: Athenaeus 198a.

[43] I have in mind, for example, Nancy Meckler's fine production for Shared Experience (1988), where the sense of a Theban location vanished. The set was dominated by the painted image of a bull.

[44] *DFA* 32 n.2; Schachter, *Cults of Boeotia* 187–8. The phallic symbolism of such a pillar would recall that of the tree which Pentheus climbs.

centre of the public space of the *orchêstra* would polarize the opposition between Dionysus, god of communality, and Pentheus, the monarch who rules from his palace. There is a careful parallelism between Dionysus and Pentheus, the two competing heirs to Thebes, both dismembered according to the myth. When Agave brings on the head of Pentheus impaled on a thyrsus, she brings on the theatrical mask of the actor, and the mask was a symbol of Dionysus, as is clear from vase paintings that have no concern with theatre.[45] Agave seeks to attach the head of Pentheus to the façade of the palace (1213–14, 1239), and later probably joins it to the fragments of corpse placed before the house (1217). We may imagine the visual opposition of two inanimate heads: one of Pentheus heir to the *oikos*, one of Dionysus in the public space of Thebes. The *skênê* has been the main concern of critics searching for psychic interiors, but the focus in performance, I would suggest, passed as in the *Oresteia* from the *skênê* to the centre. That site in the centre has complex significations: the centre of Thebes, the site of royal power in an earlier regime, the sacred chamber where god and mortal once met, the site of the grape given to rich and poor alike, the centre of a cult open to women and foreigners, the birthplace of Dionysus. The importance of the *skênê* lies not in its hidden mysteries but in the fact that it is transient and can be discarded. The question of human interiority vanishes when Pentheus' body lies before the audience dismembered and in fragments, demonstrating that nothing lies hidden within. The head remains, but the centre belongs to Dionysus.

---

[45] Walter F. Otto, *Dionysus: myth and cult*, tr. R. B. Palmer (Bloomington, 1965) 86–91.

CHAPTER 8

❧

The vertical axis

For Lefebvre, the most important dimension of 'absolute space' is the vertical. Although different cultures have different practices, it is normal that 'horizontal space symbolizes submission, vertical space power, and subterranean space death'.[1] This tripartite *schema* is of obvious application to classical Greece, where the Olympian gods were deemed to live on Olympus above and the dead in Hades below, a world also inhabited by 'chthonic' deities, more ancient and less anthropomorphic than Olympians. For the worship of the gods above, sacrifices were burnt on raised altars so that the fumes could pass upwards, but for the worship of chthonic gods and the reverencing of buried heroes, hollows were cut in, and libations were poured into, the earth.[2] In tragedy the antithesis of light and dark is ever-present. To die is to leave the light for ever.[3] In a performance lit by the light of the sun, a performance to which many would have travelled in darkness, such imagery has a meaning that cannot be replicated in a modern indoor theatre.

The idea that 'horizontal space symbolizes submission' is ill phrased in relation to democratic fifth-century society. Whilst the archaic city was centred upon the towering Acropolis, site of royal power, the democratic city was centred on the level plane of the Agora. Within democratic society, the relationship of centre and periphery was more important than vertical, hierarchical structuring. The Parthenon may be regarded as paradigmatic.[4] At the highest points of the building, the rising lines of the pediments are overtly hierarchical: on the west, crouched Athenian heroes frame the giant figures of Athens' divine patrons, and in the east the birth of Athene is set amidst the sky. Around the frieze, however, Athenians are set in a single horizontal plane,

---

[1] H. Lefebvre, *The Production of Space*, tr. D. Nicholson-Smith (Oxford, 1991) 236.

[2] C. G. Yavis, *Greek Altars: origins and typology* (Saint Louis, 1949) 92–3. On the passing of fumes from the altar to the gods, see Vernant in M. Detienne and J.-P. Vernant, *La Cuisine du sacrifice en pays grec* (Paris, 1979) 67–8.

[3] For references, see Fiona Macintosh, *Dying Acts* (Cork, 1994) 98–103.

[4] See p. 144 above.

and they share this plane with the twelve Olympian gods. There is no marking out of individual faces or bodies, because these Athenians are first and foremost a community. The viewer does not climb up but walks around the frieze. The frieze is, however, above the viewer, and the viewer is already at the highest point of Athens, for these god-like men are the best of the Athenians, probably victors at Marathon. Horizontality and verticality are thus locked in a complex dialectic. Having viewed the frieze, the viewer passes to the centre, where verticality is decisive. The viewer stands on a level not with Athene but with the fallible Pandora beneath her feet. The colossal statue of the goddess with her winged helmet represents both her own divine power and the power of the community. Within this centripetal building the Olympians at once do and do not share the horizontal plane of the Athenians, being strictly anthropomorphic, but separated by their immortality and power. The same ambivalence about the mortal/immortal distinction characterizes the theatre.

The theatre disposed of few resources to map the vertical dimension, and we should not expect to find here the thematic complexity that characterizes the east–west axis. The vertical axis is nevertheless crucial in demarcating the tripartite universe of immortals, mortals and dead. The roof of the *skênê* and the crane were available to create a higher level when required, and the focus of the auditorium upon the earth floor of the *orchêstra* allowed the world under the earth to be evoked as a space full of meaning. I have suggested that the *thymelê* was more a hearth rooted in the earth than an altar rising towards the heavens. In some Hellenistic theatres we find in the *orchêstra* floor a tunnel known as the 'Charonian steps', i.e. steps to the underworld, though no such tunnel was constructed at Athens.[5] Dionysus was an Olympian, but he also had a chthonic aspect, exemplified by the cult of the dead in the Anthesteria, by the cemetery beneath his theatre at Thorikos, by his Athenian sanctuary 'in the marshes' and by the hearth-altar used at the start of the Dionysia.[6] Some who have retreated from the idea that the fifth-century theatre had a 'low stage' assume that steps nevertheless led up to the *skênê* doorway.[7] This conception confers hierarchical grandeur upon the figure who stands in the doorway, but negates the important idea that an entry into the *skênê* is metaphorically an entry into the underworld of the dead. In practical terms, steps would make the operation of the *eccyclêma* harder to envisage.

The most important vertical relationship in the Greek theatre is necessarily

---

[5] *TDA* 51; *COAD* 398.   [6] *DFA* 60.

[7] *TDA* 42–3. Such steps are depicted on the cover of *GTA* (first edition).

that of audience and actor. The Greek theatre is almost unique in its demand that all spectators look downwards. Iain Mackintosh is emphatic that the Greek model is not one which the modern architect should seek to imitate.

When an audience looks down on the actor it is more likely that its attention will have been precisely predetermined by a director who has organized the pattern of production. The audience looking down will then be contemplating the performer critically as did the director at the rehearsal. If the attention of the audience wavers the actor is in a weak position . . . If, on the other hand, the audience looks up to the actor, the actor is in control, can elicit responses and can manage the audience because he or she is, quite simply, in the dominant physical position. Actors and comedians generally prefer this.

Mackintosh prefers a theatre which, like the Elizabethan, sets half the audience above the actor's eye-line and half below, and he criticizes many modern theatres for setting the centre of audience gravity too high: 'This inevitably makes it more difficult for the actor to move an audience to tears or laughter. The Greek influence is partly responsible: at the Olivier Theatre the balance and sightlines were markedly improved when the stage was raised.'[8] It follows from Mackintosh's analysis that the fifth-century theatre empowered the audience rather than the actor, and Plato's term 'theatrocracy' seems apposite.[9] The emergence of a raised stage in the fourth century coincided with the rise of the actor as the dominant creative artist. We notice a similar transformation in the political arena, with the reorientation of the Pnyx at the end of the fifth century. Fourth-century politicians were able to stand on the rising slope at a height that Mackintosh would have approved, and could control their audience with their rhetorical performances. In the fifth-century theatre, the vertical sightlines encouraged a critical response rather than emotional surrender, and allowed the author/director to be the dominant creative force 'orchestrating' the action. Whatever emotional charge the spectator missed in terms of eye-to-eye contact with the actor was compensated for by the fact that thousands of pairs of eyes were focussed on the same choreographic patterns beneath, generating a different kind of intensity.

Charles Segal's structuralist analysis of *Oedipus the King* has much to say about verticality, and we can compare the structures which he perceives in the text with those which articulated the performance space. Segal draws up a convenient diagram in order to define Oedipus' identity, pulled apart by the tensions of the play.

---

[8] *Architecture, Actor and Audience* (London, 1993) 135, 137.
[9] *Laws* 701 (= *COAD* 305).

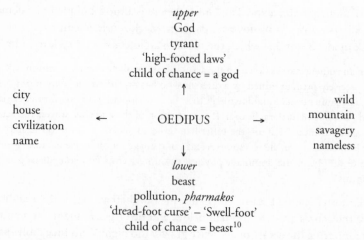

upper
God
tyrant
'high-footed laws'
child of chance = a god

↑

city				wild
house	←	OEDIPUS	→	mountain
civilization				savagery
name				nameless

↓

lower
beast
pollution, *pharmakos*
'dread-foot curse' – 'Swell-foot'
child of chance = beast[10]

Segal has placed the character of Oedipus at the central point of intersection, but in performance the centre point is a place not a character, and must be the position of the altar at which young Thebans supplicate in the opening tableau. There is a strong initial suggestion that this altar belongs to the quasi-divine Oedipus. This is 'your' altar, he is told (18). The children are not in the *agora*, but seem to have come to Oedipus' hearth (*ephestioi* – 32). The chorus are probably by the altar when they call upon 'god' and Oedipus emerges from his house to answer them (215/16). It is only when Jocasta brings on her ritual incense and garlands that the altar is defined as belonging to Apollo (911ff.). At this point in the play god replaces man as the dominant force commanding the centre, within the microcosm of the performance space.

On the horizontal plane it is reasonable to surmise that one *eisodos* (used by Creon and the Corinthian shepherd) leads outside the *polis* and one (used by Teiresias and the Theban shepherd) leads into the *polis*. This spatial opposition corresponds with Segal's Lévi-Straussian antithesis of civilization and savagery. The 'house', however, is set on an axis at right angles to the *eisodoi*, and Segal's conflation of city and single house obscures the political concern of the play with *tyrannis* – the rule of the city by a single man. In the final scene of the play Oedipus wants to go to the mountain, but Creon insists that he return inside the house. It seems reasonable to assume that gaze, gesture and movement all served to associate the Athenian Acropolis, the mountain on which the audience were seated, with Cithaeron. When, for example, Oedipus speaks of 'this my Cithaeron' (1452), he would be looking at the audience. A movement away from the *skênê*/house necessarily takes Oedipus towards the

---

[10] *Tragedy and Civilization* (Cambridge, Mass., 1981) 227. I have translated the Greek citations.

Athenian audience. That audience would have known that in myth Oedipus was destined to leave his house in Thebes in order to come towards Athens. The longitudinal axis (back/front, *skênê*/Athenians) is at the same time a vertical axis. The *skênê* door below is the site of darkness in which Oedipus hides from the sunlight, whilst the space above inhabited by the audience becomes honorific and vested with divine attributes. The statue of Dionysus is set on the same longitudinal axis, and fosters a sense that the god's fellow viewers view from a position of divine omniscience.

At the start of the festival the statue journeyed into the city in token of the god's original journey from Eleutherae at the foot of the Cithaeron ridge, a ritual that helps to differentiate the positive nature of Athens from the negative nature of Thebes, birthplace of Dionysus.[11] The final tableau of the *parodos* incorporates Dionysus, god of Cithaeron, into the world of the play (209–15). As the chorus are praying to Dionysus, Oedipus appears in the *skênê* doorway in answer to their prayers, articulating in space the opposition of god and man. The god in the theatre belongs spatially to the world of the audience, and defines the separateness of the audience from the tragic hero who stands beneath them, reaching up at their emotions.

The vertical axis is crucial to a play that deals with a man who aspires to divinity, a man who can solve all problems, but is in political terms over-powerful. The theatrical rendering of verticality turns to a large extent upon movement and choreography. At the start of the play the children crouch at altars, and the priest bids Oedipus set them on their feet (50–1). Oedipus in turn kneels to Teiresias who seems to have divine knowledge. When the chorus sing in a strophe that certain laws exist in the heavenly ether, begotten by Olympus (865ff.), and in the answering antistrophe sing of how a tyrant's *hybris* climbs to the heights, the dance must have created an image of height in order to yoke together the gods and Oedipus the *tyrannos*. Likewise ecstatic leaping must connect Olympus, Cithaeron and the full moon in a strophe to Pan the mountain-goer in the responding antistrophe (1086ff.). In this instance the chorus sing in the strophe of dancing for their *tyrannos*, and in the antistrophe of Dionysus on the summits (1093 = 1105), again using the vertical dimension to tie together Oedipus and the gods. There is no iconographic evidence to suggest that Oedipus was represented in performance as lame, and thus in symbolic terms unable to aspire to Olympian status.[12]

[11] See M. Detienne, *Dionysos at Large*, tr. A. Goldhammer (Cambridge, Mass., 1989) 31ff.; F. Zeitlin, 'Staging Dionysus between Thebes and Athens' in *The Masks of Dionysus* ed. T. H. Carpenter and C. A. Faraone (Ithaca, 1993) 147–82.

[12] The exception which proves the rule is a single 'phlyax' vase depicting a grotesque Oedipus: *LIMC* 'Oidipous' 70. Vidal-Naquet draws on fourth-century material when following up Lévi-Strauss' notorious analysis of the Oedipus myth in 'The lame tyrant' *MTAG* 207–27.

In the Oresteian trilogy, the first play is principally concerned with the horizontal plane. The arrivals of beacon, sunrise, herald and Agamemnon from over the sea give way to a focus on the polysemous *skênê*. The world below the earth is not of immediate concern, and in the pivotal scene of the play it is significant that Agamemnon never makes contact with the earth of Argos. Equally the world above the earth is not sharply visualized. The chorus imagine that gods in the air can send an Erinye (55–9), and 'Zeus' is evoked in vague monotheistic terms as a name for the unknown (160ff.). The world above is delimited by the watchman who does not reach upwards but crouches on the roof. In the second play the world below the earth becomes the centre of concern. Electra pours into the earth the libations that Clytaemnestra failed to pour in *Agamemnon* (*Ag*.1395–8). The body below the earth is the force that drives Orestes to kill. When Orestes enters the house the chorus slowly turn their attention from mother Earth (722ff.) to Olympian Zeus (783ff.), and they worship the power of the sky-gods as they imagine the house rising up (960ff.). In the third play, with the appearance of Apollo and black-clad Furies as characters, the spheres of earth-gods and sky-gods are demarcated, and the position of humans within a tripartite universe is clarified.

The representation of the Olympians in the *Eumenides* is not altogether clear from the text. When Orestes is revealed on the *eccyclêma* clinging to the *omphalos*, Apollo probably stands above on the roof of his temple. Hermes may or may not appear as his escort. The most interesting problem is the entry of Athene, for most editors have found the text unacceptable at the point where the goddess describes her arrival. She has come from Troy, she states, claiming her share of territories on behalf of the Athenians (an abrupt interpellation of the imperial world of the audience):

> Thence I came chasing my unwearied foot
> Without wings, flapping the fold of my aegis,
> To prime (*akmaiois*) steeds harnessing this chariot.   (403–5)

The normal view has been that the final line should be excised as an interpolation written in by an ambitious Hellenistic stage director.[13] The Aeschylean Athene would thus enter on foot through an *eisodos*. Critics unhappy with a minimalist staging at such an important moment have tended to excise line 404, in order to bring Athene in on a chariot.[14] Yet the subsequent removal of

---

[13] *SA* 388–90. Alan Sommerstein in the Cambridge edition (Cambridge, 1989) 153 concurs. Pickard-Cambridge in *TDA* 44–5 is another minimalist.

[14] A. J. Podlecki in the Aris and Philips edition (Warminster, 1989) 164 finds a chariot iconographically appropriate. He follows P. D. Arnott, *Greek Scenic Conventions* (Oxford, 1962) 74–5.

such horses and chariot would cause a hiatus in the action, and it is hard to see what is gained iconographically. Agamemnon's journey from Troy was a tortuous one, but Athene has come directly. The idea that Athene arrived on the crane is no longer fashionable amongst classical critics, yet Peter Stein had no such compunctions, and in his production a touch of comedy did not detract from the seriousness of his political concerns; he flew in Athene over the auditorium, recognizing the need at this point in the trilogy for spectacle, speed and use of the upper register.[15] The received text does not seem to pose any difficulties if Athene is flown in on some kind of platform. Athene's foot has not been wearied, she has no wings but her costume ripples in the wind, the platform is 'this' chariot, and steeds are an admissible metaphor for the crane because the adjective *akmaios* implies the idea of height or zenith. The flying entry also makes sense of Athene's next line: 'I see this novel crowd on land.' Iconographically the great advantage of the flying entry is that it clarifies the three vertical levels of the play's cosmology. Athene's entry is cued by a tableau in which the chorus demonstrate their provenance in the lower world: 'separate from gods in sunless light, steep and impassable for sighted and sightless alike' (strophe: 385–8) = 'ancient privilege not without honour, though my place is below ground in unsunned murk' (antistrophe: 393–6). The chorus introduce themselves to Athene as children of Night with homes beneath the earth (416–17). An entry from above defines in visual terms the spatial opposition of Olympian and chthonian that needs to be reconciled in the final settlement for the sake of mortals caught between.

Donald Mastronarde rightly concludes his study of the *mêchanê* or crane in Greek tragedy by stating that it is 'a powerful visual token of the social, ethical and psychological separation between mortal and divine'.[16] Aristotle attacked the *deus ex machina* convention because he did not wish to admit the irrational into the world of the play,[17] but the fifth-century dramatists, and Euripides in particular, did not share Aristotle's rationalist views. Gods could appear on the *skênê* roof to demonstrate vertical dominance, and we need only envisage the crane where separation from the earth is at issue. In *Philoctetes* there is no reason why Heracles should not stand on the *skênê* roof, as if standing on the mountain above the cave, and the same is true of Hermes in *Antiope*. In *The Bacchae* (where the text is unfortunately lacunose) Dionysus at the end of the play may have stood on the roof of the house to which he is heir. In *Iphigeneia*

---

[15] See p. 85 above. Stein used the *skênê* roof for Apollo at 64–93, which avoided overcrowding the *eccyclêma*.

[16] 'Actors on high: the skene roof, the crane and the gods in Attic drama' *Classical Antiquity* 9 (1990) 247–94, p. 280. The fullest previous discussion of the *mêchanê* was in *PIE* 146–69.

[17] *Poetics* xv.7–1454b.

in Tauris Athene probably stood on the temple roof, since she is concerned with the founding of temples, and Iphigeneia's journey is at issue rather than hers. Likewise in Euripides' *Suppliants* Athene may appropriately stand on top of the *skênê* wall as she evokes an assault upon the walls of Thebes. In *Heracles*, however, where the gods appear mid-play, there is a clear spatial separation required when Madness tells Hera's messenger: 'Go to Olympus, Iris, lifting your noble foot; I unseen will sink into the house of Heracles' (872–3).[18] The raising of Iris above the *skênê* emphasizes the remoteness of the gods, and the fact that Heracles in this play is mortal not divine.

The upper level is never, it seems, used by gods in a prologue, for in a prologue gods come to communicate with mortals rather than proclaim their separateness. The ghost of Polydorus at the start of *Hecuba*, however, does apparently appear on the roof.[19] There is no iconographic reason for his body to be airborne on the crane, for he has come from Hades through the 'gates of darkness' (1–2), and his presence on top of the *skênê* helps to establish Hecuba's tent as the house of death. The villainous Polymestor subsequently takes the 'road to Hades' (1031–2) and encounters 'Bacchants of Hades' (1077) inside the *skênê*. When the ghost declares: 'Now above my dear mother Hecuba I am floating, separated from my body, for three days hovering' (30–2), the audience see the *psychê* represented in Homeric terms as a simulacrum of the body that lies unburied.[20]

In some of Euripides' later plays we find a rather different conception of the afterlife, according to which part of the self descends but part rises to the stars. In *Helen* the doubleness of Helen as phantom in Troy and reality in Egypt becomes an extended metaphor for the duality of the self. The presence of Menelaus as a ritual simulacrum of the Menelaus destined for burial helps to extend the metaphor of replication. The audience are shown an Egyptian idol that has fallen from the ether (865ff.), and it is stressed many times that the 'image' of Helen in Troy was likewise created from the 'ether' or upper air (33, 44, 584, 1219), an idea which connects with the notion of Anaximenes and Anaxagoras that the cosmos was created from the consolidation of ether.[21] The non-phantasmic Helen herself has etherial origins (216) and has travelled

---

[18] I follow Mastronarde 'Actors on high' 269–70. Madness' chariot must be imagined by the chorus; there is no practical alternative.

[19] See J. Mossman *Wild Justice: a study of Euripides' 'Hecuba'* (Oxford, 1995) 50.

[20] See J.-P. Vernant, 'Psuche' in *Collected Essays* ed. F. Zeitlin (Princeton, 1991) 186–92.

[21] For the philosophical background to this passage, see M. R. Wright, *Cosmology in Antiquity* (London, 1995) 112–24. In Aristophanes, *Women at the Thesmophoria* 14–15, a play which contains a parody of *Helen*, Euripides is concerned with how life stems from the division of the ether.

through the ether to Egypt (246). When she dies she is destined to join her brothers in the ether as a star. The Egyptian priestess proclaims a philosophy that has strong roots in Egyptian thinking and connects with Greek mysticism in the late fifth century: 'There is a reward for [good deeds] for all humans both below and above. The mind of the dead does not live but it has awareness in perpetuity when it enters the perpetual ether' (1013–16). In this cosmological context the presence of Castor and Pollux, Helen's brothers, suspended in space at the end of the play, must be understood as far more than a routine use of the *deus ex machina* convention. The crane allows Euripides to offer his audience a concrete image of the Egyptian idea later popularized by Plato that the *psychê* or soul of the dead person becomes a star. Since the 'three actor rule' meant that only one of the twins could speak, it seems likely that the crane offered the audience another dualist image: the live human being and a dummy that is his indistinguishable replica.[22]

The use of the crane in *Orestes* and *Electra* reflects similar concerns with the cosmos and with the reliability of visual perception. In *Orestes* Electra longs to join her ancestor Tantalus suspended in the ether with a rock above him dangling on golden cords from Olympus (982ff.).[23] The rock, it seems, is the sun, threatening to fall at any moment. This improbable half-modern, half-Homeric image anticipates the finale when Electra, with Orestes, Hermione and Pylades, stands on top of the *skênê* while Apollo the sun-god dangles above them, accompanied by Helen, Castor and Pollux (1631ff.). There is a symmetry between the four figures in the sky and the four on the roof. Apollo and Helen mirror Apollo's protégé and Helen's daughter beneath, whilst Pylades and Electra carry torches that turn them into beacons like Castor and Pollux, the twin stars who guide sailors. The juxtaposition of a harmonious cosmos and a disharmonious humanity striving to escape its destiny makes an eloquent theatrical statement. In *Electra* the chorus cannot reconcile the ordered cosmology of Achilles' shield with the disorder of his death on account of Helen (452ff.), nor can they accept the story that the cosmos responded to Thyestes' crime (726ff.). Castor and Pollux appear on the crane as gods (or stars) but they have no power to intervene, and dismiss the god Apollo as a liar. By creating empty space between mortals on earth and gods in the sky, Euripides creates

---

[22] In *Electra* Castor speaks on behalf of his brother. In *Helen*, probably performed in the following year, Euripides would have needed to work a variant, and his obfuscation of the speaker would be deliberate.

[23] Ruth Scodel, following the scholiast, relates the play to the cosmology of Anaxagoras in 'Tantalus and Anaxagoras' *Harvard Studies in Classical Philology* 88 (1984) 13–24. Edith Hall cites the cosmology of Empedocles in 'Political and cosmic turbulence in Euripides' *Orestes*' in *Tragedy, Comedy and the Polis* ed. A. H. Sommerstein *et al.* (Bari, Italy, 1993) 263–85.

an image of absolute separation. There can be no interconnection between humans and cosmos. If the device of the *deus ex machina* seems to be an imposition on the narrative, then equally preposterous is the pious idea that stars could intervene to save the Athenian fleet.

We shall end by examining what is perhaps Euripides' most remarkable use of the vertical axis: the suttee of Evadne in *Suppliants*. Evadne leaps to her death from a crag into the funeral pyre of her husband Capaneus. The orthodox interpretation of the staging, proffered by Hourmouziades and Collard, holds that some representation of crags was set on top of the *skênê*, and that Evadne disappears to her death behind these crags and behind the *skênê*.[24] This reconstruction owes more to nineteenth-century conventions of pictorial realism than to any consideration of why the scene belongs in the play, and is unsatisfactory on every count. It is theatrically weak since Evadne is gone in a moment, and there is no focus for her father's grief. It is topographically illogical since the Hall of the Mysteries, the main architectural structure at Eleusis, is built into the cliff, and there is no gap behind. The *skênê*, which is never entered, is reduced to a meaningless façade. Most importantly this reconstruction makes nonsense of all the deictic references in the text, presuming that Capaneus' pyre lies out of sight. Euripides is at pains to arrange that Capaneus' tomb will be erected by slaves 'beside this building' (*par' oikous tousde*), while Theseus and his escort create a pyre for the other champions 'outside the sanctuary' (*chôris hieron*) (935–40). Both the chorus (1009) and Evadne (1065) subsequently refer to 'this' pyre. Evadne's father from within the *orchêstra* is able to see the tomb and pyre (1058). The pyre must be visible, and it is far better to assume that it is brought on by the available means, the *eccyclêma*. The cue is clear.[25] After the removal of the corpses, the chorus sing a strophic pair about their childless state, followed by an epode about mementoes of the dead left in their houses, at the end of which they must follow the text and cover their eyes with their garments. The rhythm then changes to anapaests as the chorus turn to look at the theatrical 'house': 'Yes, I do see now this chamber of Capaneus, and his sacred tomb, and outside the temple Theseus' monument to the dead, and the famous wife of this victim of lightning close by – Evadne, child begotten by King Iphis. Why does she stand on the airy rock which towers over this dwelling, taking this path?' (980–9). The *skênê*, as we have seen, is non-repre-

---

[24] Christopher Collard (ed.) *Euripides: Supplices* (Groningen, 1975) 16; *PIE* 32–3. Rush Rehm floats the idea that Evadne might leap off the sheer side of the auditorium, an idea that belongs more to twentieth-century environmental theatre: *Greek Tragic Theatre* (London, 1992) 159 n.6.

[25] T. B. L. Webster explains the metre in relation to use of the *eccyclêma* in this passage in *The Greek Chorus* (London, 1970) 159.

sentational and can signify a cave as well as a house or temple, the same vocabulary being used.[26] At Eleusis the obvious setting for a suicidal leap is the overhanging rock that faces the Callichoron well (apparently visible to Theseus at 392) beside the entry to the precinct. Underneath this overhang is both a narrow cave and a natural seat in the rock, and the location was evidently used for a mystery drama in which was enacted the return of Persephone to her mother Demeter. The cave was taken to be Persephone's point of entry to Hades.[27] This ritual context allows us to grasp the symbolism of Evadne's leap. She seeks blissful release in Hades (1004–6), a suitably positive Eleusinian concept of death, and then, dressed in her wedding dress, she envisions herself as Persephone bride of Hades, the tomb becoming her wedding chamber (*thalamos*) (1022).[28] The iconographic link to Persephone may be emphasized by a torch, an attribute both of weddings and of Persephone (993ff., 1025ff.). Evadne's suicide is an inversion of the Eleusinian mystery play: instead of returning to her mother by ascending from a pit and passing through a false cave entrance, she descends and abandons her father. The *skênê*, according to a familiar spatial logic, represents the entry to Hades.

Euripides' logic in setting Capaneus' tomb beneath an overhanging rock must relate to the fact that a building was set up in the late fifth century partly beneath the overhang, creating the sense of an enclosed sanctuary. The building is traditionally thought to be a temple of Pluto, though its precise function remains unknown,[29] and it is in exactly the position where we must imagine Capaneus' tomb to be sited. Capaneus' corpse impaled by Zeus's thunderbolt is presented in the play as a kind of sacred effigy (*agalma*) (631 – cf. 371, 373, 1161); he is 'delicate' (860); his corpse has not been crushed (503); and it is placed in the 'treasury of Zeus' (1010). Capaneus' presence at the head of the funeral procession arriving in Eleusis might encourage us to see him as an inversion of the youthful Iacchos, the Dionysiac effigy carried at the head of the true Eleusinian procession. As a sacred corpse, Capaneus could have been carried in the vertical position in which he died, climbing a ladder which in the play symbolizes hybris (495–7, 728–9). Unfortunately we know too little about the ritual context of Eleusis to understand precisely what his pyre

---

[26] See pp. 161–2 above.

[27] See G. E. Mylonas, *Eleusis and the Eleusinian Mysteries* (Princeton, 1961) 147, 197–8; Kevin Clinton, *Myth and Cult: the iconography of the Eleusinian Mysteries* (Stockholm, 1992) 87–9.

[28] On the inverted Persephone motif, see Rush Rehm, *Marriage to Death: the conflation of wedding and funeral rituals in Greek tragedy* (Princeton, 1994) 113.

[29] On the date and identity of the temple, see Clinton, *Myth and Cult* 18–19. Clinton goes on to argue convincingly that the rock beside the cave must be the famous 'mirthless rock' of Demeter.

signified for the Athenian audience, and why in the play only Capaneus'
remains are buried in Attica (1210).[30] Some connection with the 'Plutonion'
seems clear.

If Evadne's leap was effected in full view of the audience, then the most convenient method would be use of the crane. The actor would not so much leap
as fly, like Perseus in Euripides' *Andromeda*. Evadne likens herself to a bird
lightly poised to hover (*aiôrêma*) (1046–7). The actor is given three lines to
cover his descent: 'No matter. You cannot reach and catch me with your hand.
My body passes – not kin to you but to me and the husband who burns with
me'(1069–71). When the burning is done the chorus sing: 'Ether holds them
now, melted to ashes in the pyre. On wings they have reached Hades' (1140–2).
The relationship between a flight of the *psychê* up into the ether and a flight to
the underworld is troubling in strict logical terms, but the image of a flight to
Hades makes perfect visual sense in relation to Evadne's downward flight.[31]
Evadne's suicide was not conceived as a fleeting theatrical spectacle but as the
journey of her soul to the underworld. The vertical axis is the key to the theatrical image. Capaneus tried to climb too high and was struck down by Zeus.
The destiny of mortals is to descend.

---

[30] Euripides rejected the orthodox Aeschylean version that had the commanders buried together
near Eleusis: Plutarch, *Theseus* 29. This spot was visited by Pausanias: Pausanias i.39.2.
[31] Collard 401 notes the apparent confusion.

CHAPTER 9

❧

The iconography of sacred space

Perhaps the most important polarity in Greek spatial practice is that of sacred versus accessible (*bebêlos*) space. Religious sanctuaries are found everywhere in the Greek *polis*. Within the house the hearth is sacred to Hestia and the court-yard to Zeus Herkeios. The route into the house is controlled by images of Hermes, Hecate and Apollo Agyieus. The city as a macrocosm of the house has its own sacred hearth at the centre and its shrine to Zeus Herkeios by the gateway, and major sanctuaries mark the entry-points of the city's territory. Christiane Sourvinou-Inwood rightly comments: 'The Greek *polis* articulated religion and was itself articulated by it; religion became the *polis'* central ideology, structuring, and giving meaning to, all the elements that made up the identity of the *polis*, its past, its physical landscape, the relationship between its constituent parts.'[1] The identities of tribes and phratries are defined by their altars and cult images, and every democratic activity takes place in a sacralized space. Both the Pnyx and the Council-chamber have their altars and sacrifices. When Aristophanes has a law-court established anomalously outside a private house, the comic hero sets up domestic objects to serve as the blazing altar and as the statue of a wolf-like founding hero, and the trial starts with prayers, libations and a paean to Apollo.[2] A democratic process must take place in a space devoted to a particular god, so that it can be located within the structure of the sacred *polis*. At Rhamnous we have seen how the acting area is overseen by the image of the founding hero who gave the deme of Rhamnous its own identity within the larger collective of Athens. The audience at Rhamnous looked across at the temple of Nemesis, a sanctuary located here to mark the north-ern reaches of Attica, in a sense personifying the remote and wild location. At Athens as we have seen, the playing area was sacralized by sacrificial slaughter and roasting (which must have changed the quality of the air in the auditor-ium), by the gaze of the wooden statue and its priest, by libations of wine

---

[1] 'What is *polis* religion?' in *The Greek City* ed. O. Murray and S. Price (Oxford, 1990) 295–322, pp. 304–5. On sacred space, see also *GR* 84ff.; Robert Parker, *Miasma* (Oxford, 1983) 160–70; F. de Polignac, *La Naissance de la cité grecque* (Paris, 1984).   [2] *Wasps* 818ff.

poured onto the *thymelê* or *orchêstra* floor, and by the purifying blood of a baby pig dripping onto the earth. The audience wore wreaths which helped to transform the space of the auditorium into a space dedicated to Dionysus.[3]

Sourvinou-Inwood defines a Greek sanctuary as, in essence, 'a sacred space centred around an altar, sometimes including another sacred focus such as a tree or stone, a spring or cave'.[4] The boundary wall and the temple housing the image of the god are secondary, historically and conceptually. Within the fictive world of theatrical performance it is likewise an altar that serves to define part of the acting space as a sacred location, not a boundary line or the façade of a temple. As I argued in chapter 3, the site of the *thymelê* at the centre of the *orchêstra* is already imbued with a religious charge and the focus of the theatre makes this the natural place to site the tomb or suppliant's altar required in so many plays. Although suppliants in normal historical practice might take refuge anywhere within the bounds of a shrine, in the schematic and simplified world of the play the suppliant must cling to the stage object that represents the altar or the statue of the god.[5] In *Oedipus at Colonus* Sophocles does not have the resources to mark a boundary wall, and plans the action around a single block of rough stone. Here Oedipus sits (19, 101) and is challenged by a demesman. As the chorus enters, Oedipus goes to hide in the shadow of the *skênê* in order to clear space for the dancers. Urged by the chorus he slowly returns during the next dance sequence to his original position, which now defines the margin of the ground that is taboo (192). Having learned his identity, the chorus rescind their permission to stay at this rock (232, 263).[6] A single marker at the centre of the *orchêstra* suffices for purposes of performance to define which part of the space is sacred.

The symbolic system which articulated the sacred spaces of the *polis* was a complex one, for spatial forms were determined by the diverse cultic uses made of those spaces. Because our play-texts have no stage directions, we must turn to the art of the vase painter in order to see how sacred space was represented in performance. As is now widely recognized, vase paintings do not illustrate tragedy.[7] They may depict actors before and after performance, but never the

---

[3] *DFA* 272.

[4] 'Early sanctuaries, the eighth century and ritual space: fragments of a discourse' in *Greek Sanctuaries: new approaches* ed. N. Marinatos and R. Hägg (London, 1993) 1–17, p. 11.

[5] See Ulrich Sinn, 'Greek sanctuaries as places of refuge' in Marinatos and Hägg, *Greek Sanctuaries* 88–109.

[6] It would be literalistic to assume that performance *requires* two unhewn rocks. In his production of the play at the Swan Theatre, Stratford-upon-Avon, 1991, Adrian Noble demonstrated that only a single, central block of stone is needed.

[7] Important theoretical statements include J. M. Moret, *L'Ilioupersis dans la céramique italiote* (Geneva, 1975); F. Lissarague, 'Why satyrs are good to represent' *NTDWD* 228–36; J. R. Green 'On seeing and depicting the theatre in classical Athens' *GRBS* 32 (1991) 15–52.

actuality of tragic performance. Vase painting and tragedy are two parallel art forms, either of which may in different ways influence the other. What we can glimpse in vase painting is an iconographic vocabulary which, because of its economy, could also be deployed in the theatre. Moret has shown, following the fundamental insight of Gombrich, that the artist never simply paints what is there, but always works by adapting pre-existent *schemata*. Bérard has demonstrated that meaning is created through the innovative combination of fixed elements.[8] The visual art of the tragedian must have followed the same principle.

Although vase painters do not depict tragedies or satyr plays in performance, we have a large corpus of south Italian vases which do depict a mode of comic performance. As Oliver Taplin has shown, these vases can be closely related to the comedy of Aristophanes, even though the chorus is conspicuous by its absence, and Taplin argues that the vases usually depict specific moments of plays in performance.[9] Moreover, this corpus of vases contains a number of parodies of tragedy, the humour of which depends upon having tragic performance as the referent.[10] We learn much from Aristophanic parody about devices such as the *eccyclêma*, and we can learn more from these comic vases about the symbolic techniques of tragic performance. The comic vases help us to determine which elements in paratragic vase painting had a theatrical correlative.

Let us look at a typical comic vase from Sicily in order to assess the nature of the evidence. Heracles abducts a heroine from a shrine, while a priestess and slave look on complaisantly.[11] The action is set on a stage, apparently part of the equipment of travelling players. The tights, phalluses and masks of the actors affirm that this vase depicts a play in performance. Four slender columns at the rear of the stage help signify that the location is a temple, but are less obviously theatrical appurtenances. From the architrave or vase decoration hang cups, crowns and votive tablets which confirm the temple setting, and from the base of the stage hang bands and censers suggesting that the action is in the interior of a sanctuary. The woman at the centre of the image seems half

---

8 Moret 2–4; C. Bérard, 'Entering the imagery' in *A City of Images* ed. C. Bérard and J.-L. Durand, tr. D. Lyons (Princeton, 1989) 23–34. On Gombrich, see above p. 4.

9 *Comic Angels* (Oxford, 1993) 32–52. Taplin seeks the chorus at 56, 75–6.

10 On the issue of 'paraiconography', see Taplin, *Comic Angels* 79–83. The difficulties of analysis are exemplified by Taplin's fig. 1, depicting a comedy in which a *chorêgos* brings on a figure from tragedy. Having no established *schema* for representing a tragic mask, the artist follows the iconographic convention of 'melting' the mask into the face.

11 Vase from Lentini: *HGRT* fig. 488; *LIMC* 'Aleos' 4. There is a full description of the vase in E. Z. Fiorentini, 'Il cratere di Leontini con scena di commedia' *Memorie della Pontificia Accademia Romana di Archeologia* 6 (1943) 39–52.

Figure 10 Heracles seduces a girl (krater from Lentini)

reluctant, half acquiescent, and Heracles is in the act of removing her veil. She gestures at an idol which stands before an altar. This is necessarily a property altar since it stands off-centre and is mounted on the trestle stage. Four laurel branches abut the altar indicating that the altar is in a sacred grove. It is a sign of theatricality that the 'trees' are not free-standing but are supported by the altar. The idol seems to represent Artemis, and should logically be inside the temple, but the stage has no direct means of signifying an indoor location. The idol holds an empty tray, and extends a crown towards the retreating heroine. On the reverse of the vase the image is non-theatrical: a beautiful half-naked courtesan has a fan in one hand, and in the other holds a plate of fruit and a crown, while one attendant is about to remove her headscarf and another proffers a large basket of fruit. The vase itself would have been used for mixing wine at a symposium. Its lip is adorned on the comic, theatrical side with Dionysiac ivy and on the other side with Apolline laurel.

The comic scene is explicated by the image on the verso, and is a celebration of seduction appropriate to a gathering of male wine-drinkers. The heroine is lured away from her devotion to chastity personified by Artemis, and will enjoy the fruits of sexual gratification. The comic scene is no random snapshot of a performance, but a construct composed in order to fit the Dionysiac milieu of the symposium. The grotesque world of comedy where all virgins are available to the male is counterpointed against the real milieu of the symposium dominated by the figure of the prostitute. Although we have to read the comic vase with due caution as an iconographic construct, the vase only makes sense if it represents the kind of activity that one might see in a comic performance.

We may fairly conclude from this and similar vases that the Sicilian theatre deployed property altars. We have confirmation of property altars in the third-century records of Delos, and elsewhere.[12] It is a reasonable inference that the fifth-century Athenian theatre also disposed of such altars, and that in the fifth century these might be placed by or over the *thymelê* as required. Altars on theatrical vases are of different shapes and sizes, suggesting that in the theatre there was no single, standardized theatrical sign for an altar, and that the semiotics of the Greek altar largely elude modern scholarship. The vase painter would never confuse a hewn altar with an unhewn stone of the kind required in *Oedipus at Colonus*, so we may infer that in the theatre a specific theatrical property would be required to signify a natural shape. Particularly interesting is a vase fragment which depicts a comic actor as Electra at the tomb of Agamemnon.[13] A tall *stêlê* with a head-band tied around it to secure offerings is reminiscent of several mid fifth-century renderings of the tomb.[14] Since tomb-stone and altar are physically distinct on comic vases, we are encouraged to reject the possibility that a permanent stage *thymelê* served unaided as the tomb in the *Oresteia*.

The difficulties of using vase painting as evidence for tragedy are exemplified by a vase of circa 400 BC which seems to have been inspired by Euripides' *Children of Heracles*, written some thirty years earlier.[15] Iolaus stands on a large low altar surrounded by four sons of Heracles, and they bear wreaths and branches to signify that they are suppliants. On the left of the image stands the predatory Argive herald and on the right Athene, who thus replaces the king of Athens, his retinue and the chorus of Euripides' play. Iolaus leans

---

[12] *COAD* 272. Plutarch, *On the Glory of Athens* 348 refers to poets carrying altars along with other theatrical devices. Various altars were carried in the Dionysiac procession of Ptolemy Philadelphus: Athenaeus 197f, 200a, 202b. Pollux distinguishes an altar on the Hellenistic stage from the thymelic altar in the *orchêstra*: *COAD* 396. In Aristophanes, *Peace* 938 the comic hero fetches an altar needed for the dedication of the statue. A. Sommerstein in his edition (Warminster, 1983), subscribing to Arnott's vision of a raised stage, supposes that a permanent stage altar is used here – note to 942. I would suggest, rather, that the comedy turns on the known fact that tragedy used surrogate altars. D. MacDowell takes a similar view to Sommerstein in his edition of *Wasps* (Oxford, 1971) 24, 125.

[13] From Apulia 375–350 BC, reproduced as Taplin, *Comic Angels* fig. 21, *LIMC* 'Elektra' 1.50.

[14] See A. J. N. W. Prag, *The Oresteia* (Warminster, 1985) 51–3 and pls.F2–6. For the column/altar convention see S. Gogos 'Das Bühnenrequisit in der griechischen Vasenmalerei' *Jahreshefte des Österreichischen Archäologischen Institutes* 55 (1984) 27–53.

[15] Taplin, *Comic Angels* fig. 104= *LIMC* 'Herakleidai' 2.

Figure 11 Electra at Agamemnon's tomb (fragment from Apulia)

against an Ionic column that supports a statue, and bears an old man's stick, but his face is less aged than we might expect from Euripides' play, and a fifth youth, ungarlanded, seems to emerge from his head. The messenger in Euripides' play describes Iolaus' rejuvenation, and the artist must be depicting this process, with Iolaus' sagging body topped by a mature head and youth emerging above. The statue of a naked, garlanded young man cannot represent Zeus Agoraios, patron of the altar in the text (70, 238), for the figure is not patriarchal but young like Apollo. Apollo, however, never has such muscular thighs, a spear is not his normal weapon, and he has no relevance to the context.[16]

The vase does not 'illustrate' Euripides' play, but it does encourage us to think about the visual riddles that Euripides may have been constructing with the aid of the same iconographic resources. The broad organization of the space

left = wilderness   right = Athenian civilization
                        centre foreground = altar

relates in a very obvious way to the organization of theatrical space. The suppliants' wreaths and branches are standard theatrical accoutrements (71, 124). The statue, however, raises more difficult problems. The setting at the start of the play is specified as the Tetrapolis, the four federated villages that made up the deme of Marathon (32, 80). The female suppliants are inside the *skênê*

---

[16] *LIMC* opts for Apollo; so following the consensus does John Wilkins in his edition of the *Heraclidae* (Oxford, 1993) xxxi. One possibility might be Marathos, eponymous hero of the deme – see Plutarch *Theseus* 32.4, and Pausanias 1.32.4. Another image of the scene from the same region and period depicts Alcmene holding the statuette of a bearded Zeus – *LIMC* 'Herakleidai' 3.

Figure 12 The Heraclids (*pelikê* from Herakleia)

which represents a temple (42). The suppliants have entrusted themselves to
Zeus Agoraios (70). In Athens, the altar of Zeus Agoraios was in the Pnyx
because the god in this aspect was patron of assemblies.[17] Any statue that
Euripides used should therefore portray Zeus Agoraios, symbol of Athenian
democratic debate. At Marathon, however, we know of no temple to Zeus in
any of his aspects, and there is no sacrifice to this figure in the deme calendar.[18]
After line 82 there is no further direct mention of the local setting, and references are all to the *polis*, rather than to the deme. The chorus, for example,
evoke the dancing of girls on the Acropolis at the Panathenaea (777).[19] If we
ask ourselves what temple the audience would have expected to find within the
deme of Marathon, the answer is beyond question: the temple of Heracles.
Here the Athenians made their camp at the battle of Marathon, and they associated him with their victory.[20] The temple of the play is implicitly but unmistakably associated with the battle of Marathon when Iolaus dons a suit of
captured armour that is said to be hanging on pegs inside the temple (695–6).

[17] The altar of Zeus Agoraios seems to have been moved to the Agora after the Pnyx ceased to
be the main place of assembly: see R. E. Wycherley *The Athenian Agora*, Vol.III: *Literary and
Epigraphical Testimonia* (Princeton, 1957) 122–4. For the cult, see also L. R. Farnell, *The Cults
of the Greek States* (Oxford, 1896–1909) I.112.

[18] David Whitehead, *The Demes of Attica* (Princeton, 1986) 191; Wilkins, *Heraclidae* 60.

[19] See Wilkins, *Heraclidae* xxvii, 52–3.

[20] Herodotus vi.116. Athene, Heracles and the eponymous hero Marathos featured in a fifth-
century painting in Athens: Pausanias 1.15.4. For possible sites of the Herakleion, see J. A.G.
Van Der Veer, 'The battle of Marathon: a topographical survey' *Mnemosyne* 35 (1982) 290–321,
pp. 292–7.

At the end of the play Iolaus is reported to be setting up a fine statue of Zeus Tropaios – Zeus as turner of armies and god of trophies (936–7). This is suggestive of the famous monument on the battlefield that took the form of a white marble Ionic column, probably topped by a statue.[21] The column on the vase is in iconographic terms an unusual base for a statue, so it is tempting to associate it with this well-known Marathonian landmark. The burly image in the vase could suggest Zeus Tropaios, the wreath being an emblem of victory, but is still too young. More plausibly, it represents Heracles, now divine and husband of Youth (851, 915), standing shoulder to shoulder with the young man who represents the rejuvenated Iolaus and level with the face of the Argive. In the course of apotheosis he has lost his normal insignia of a lion-skin. The provenance of the vase in the town of Herakleion makes it the more likely that Heracles should have pride of place. The statue in the vase is a complex sign, and cannot be translated into a direct theatrical equivalent. It prompts, however, important questions about Euripides' stage iconography. The chorus pray to Zeus Tropaios, god of trophies, after the battle (867). The messenger speaks of captured weapons (787) and perhaps a weapon is brought on to transform an image of Zeus Agoraios into Zeus Tropaios. Perhaps the figure of Zeus is represented in a way that evokes his son Heracles. It was within Euripides' scope to create a polysemous image of such a kind.

In *Children of Heracles* the use of space is schematic, and does not in any realist sense portray a single location. Athens, the deme *agora* and the temple of Heracles are all evoked by the placing of the action around an altar. The altar was supplemented, I would suggest, by a victory column and polysemous statue that fixed the sense of place and provided a focus for the choreography. The result is to allow three different levels of reality to interpenetrate: the mythic battle against the Argives, the historical battle against the Persians, and recent fighting against the Spartans who, it seems, had lately advanced into Attica as far as Marathon. The sons of Heracles were ancestors of the Spartans, and the Spartans spared Marathon on this account.[22] The vicious behaviour of Heracles' sons and wife at the end of the play and the prophylactic burial of the Argive king in Attica anticipate the contemporary reality of the audience at the start of the Peloponnesian War, when Spartan invaders followed in the

---

[21] Eugene Vanderpool 'A monument to the battle of Marathon' *Hesperia* 35 (1966) 93–106; Van Der Veer 'Marathon' 307–8. *LIMC* 'Herakleidai' 3 also contains an Ionic column, suggesting a shared iconographic tradition.

[22] G. Zuntz, *The Political Plays of Euripides* (Manchester, 1955) 85. Wilkins, *Heraclidae* xxxiv follows Zuntz's dating. The play may also draw upon the murder of Theban prisoners by Plataean allies in 431 (Thucydides ii.5.7), and the murder of Spartan envoys in 430/29 (Thucydides ii.67.4).

footsteps of Persian invaders sixty years before. By presenting Iolaus in (as we must infer) the exotic armour of a Persian, Euripides created a deliberately ambiguous iconographic image of the man whom Athens risked all to defend.

The altar in the vase also merits comment. As a wide, low altar it is compatible with Euripides' references to 'Zeus's *eschara*' (121, 341). While one tradition associated the Heraclids with Marathon, another and subsequently dominant tradition associated them with the Altar of Pity in the Athenian Agora.[23] Euripides' evocation of 'Zeus of the Agora' in a play notionally set far from the Agora helps unite the two traditions. One scholiast cites Euripides' play as though it were set at the Altar of Pity, not Marathon,[24] an oversight which points up the deliberate topographic blurring. Euripides' strategy is to link a setting on the margins of Attica, distant in place and time, to the here-and now of the audience gathered at the urban centre. The vase painter portrays blood on the altar, but the Altar of Pity was not used for blood-sacrifice,[25] so it seems that the painter chose to place his emphasis on the Heraclean setting rather than the city of Athens.

Statues dominate the visual action in Aeschylus' *Suppliants*. The chorus of daughters of Danaus take refuge at a shared altar (*koinobômia* – 222) or rock (189), and there are statues by this altar tall enough for the women to hang themselves, and shaded by suppliant olive branches (354). The women threaten suicide, likening themselves to votive offerings hung in a shrine (463). The statues must be physically present, because otherwise we should have to imagine the miming of olive branches, which would begin to strip the play of all visual interest. The normal and obvious inference is that there were twelve statues representing the canonical twelve Olympians, creating a symmetry with the twelve members of the chorus who propose to hang themselves.[26] The attraction of this inference is that it assimilates Aeschylus' altar with the Altar

---

[23] For references I have benefited from a conference presentation by Emma Stafford. She cites Philostratos, *Epistolai* 39 (70) which associates the Heraclids with the foundation of the cult; also Apollodoros, *Bibliotheka* 2.8.1; Philostratos, *Life of Sophocles* 2.1.8; Zenobios 2.61; scholiast on Demosthenes, *Olynthiac* 2.6; Lactantius on Statius 12.487. Noel Robertson, *Festivals and Legends: the formation of Greek cities in the light of public ritual* (Toronto, 1992) 35, 51–4, sees the association with Marathon as specifically Euripidean, and argues that Zeus Agoraios was in some way patron of the Altar of Pity. Wilkins xix, 52–3, 60, however, maintains that Euripides did not invent the association, and sees the link to the Altar of Pity as a later 'regularization'.   [24] Scholiast on Aristophanes, *Knights* 1151.

[25] Statius, *Thebaid* 12.487–8.

[26] See the edition of H. F. Johansen and E. W. Whittle (Copenhagen, 1980) ii.166. In the Liddell and Scott, *Lexicon* (fifth edition, Oxford, 1864) under *agônios* it is suggested that the term *agônioi theoi* refers to Zeus, Poseidon, Apollo and Hermes as the four gods mentioned by the chorus and associated with competitive sports. It is hard to see the relevance of this conception to the play.

of the Twelve Gods in the Athenian Agora, virtually the only known *koinobômia* in the Greek world.[27] That altar was set up by Peisistratus, and the Plataeans were famous refugees there in the sixth century. It was rebuilt in the fifth century, probably following damage by the Persians.[28] Since it was placed at the centre of the city and was the point from which distances were measured, it seems reasonable to link its symbolism to the unity of Attica, formed by the amalgamation of twelve cities.[29] It stood at the centre of a square enclosure, and was visited by the Dionysiac procession, perhaps because it was the physical centre of the democratic *polis*.[30] The gods in Aeschylus' play are termed *theoi agônioi* (189, 242, 333, 355), which implies a connection with assemblies and perhaps the *agora*.[31] By setting his play around a 'common altar' Aeschylus' strategy must have been to encourage his audience to view Argos as an analogue of Athens. The setting of Aeschylus' play, however, is not in the Argive *agora* but outside the city, and does not relate to any known Argive cult,[32] so we must recognize that Aeschylus is engaged in a complex manipulation of signs.

We should infer that the altar of the *theoi agônioi* is central in the *orchêstra*, being the focus of the action. When coaxed away from the altar by the king of Argos, the women probably dance round it in order to act out the circuitous journeying of their ancestor Io. They return to it when the Egyptian herald arrives, and are torn away by their hair in a standard iconographic motif.[33] A

---

[27] For the iconography of the altar, see L. von Sybel, 'Zwölfgötteralter aus Athen' *Mittheilungen des Deutschen Archäologischen Institutes in Athen* 4 (1879) 337–50. For the archaeology, see L. M. Gadbery, 'The sanctuary of the twelve gods in the Athenian Agora: a revised view' *Hesperia* 61 (1992) 447–89. For references, see Wycherley, *Athenian Agora: Testimonia* 119–22; and C. R. Long in *The Twelve Gods of Greece and Rome* (Leiden, 1987) 62–83. The only other known *koinobômia* in Greece is at Altis near Olympia – Pausanias 5.15.1.

[28] Thucydides vi.54.6–7; Herodotus vi.108.4.

[29] Long, *The Twelve Gods* 173. Roland Martin in *Recherches sur l'agora grecque* (Paris, 1951) 173 prefers to see the altar as a symbol of the judicial powers of the *dêmos*. Many have held that the altar should be identified with the Altar of Pity, the principal resort of suppliants in Athens. See Homer A. Thompson, 'The Altar of Pity in the Athenian Agora' *Hesperia* 21 (1952) 47–82. However, Robertson, *Festivals and Legends* 51–4, places the Altar of Pity in the archaic *agora*, and associates it with Zeus.

[30] *DFA* 62 n.6; *COAD* 115. The text refers to a visit circling the Agora. Pindar's dithyramb is usually thought to refer to this altar: see p. 76 above.

[31] Martin, *Agora* 161 n.6 sees *agônioi* as a synonym for *agoraioi*. E. Fraenkel in his edition of *Agamemnon* (Oxford, 1950) ii.260–2 defines the term as 'gods *in* assembly'.

[32] The Danaids were supposed to have landed at Lerna, but there are no cults in this area relevant to the play; see M. Piérart (ed.) *Polydipsion Argos* (Paris, 1992) 119–23. Also Ken Dowden, *Death and the Maiden: girls' initiation rites in Greek mythology* (London, 1989) 148, 156.

[33] This post-Homeric *schema* is analysed in Moret, *Ilioupersis* 234. Those who believe in a raised stage naturally locate the altar there – e.g. H. F. Johansen and E. W. Whittle ii.1–2. The violation of the altar by barbarians may in the context of Aeschylus' play have hinted at the desecration of the Altar of the Twelve Gods by the Persians.

position in the centre emphasizes the vulnerability of the suppliants, and there is no mention of any temple, which might have suggested placing the statues by a *skênê*. The statues must be close to the altar – because otherwise the threat of pollution would have no force – and would have served to demarcate the sacred area of ground.[34] We are free to imagine clusters of statues, or statuettes mounted on pedestals, since there is no requirement that the audience recognize the individual attributes of individual statues. The chorus identify four of the gods through their insignia, but there is no need for the audience to discern these details. We must not posit a redundancy or overload of visual information, with many gods being identifiable yet having no part in the action.

Although the gods may not be identifiable, the audience would certainly have assumed that half or nearly half of such a collective were female. Yet the suppliants name only male gods, and are neglectful of goddesses. They pray at one point to Artemis, goddess of chastity, but spurn Aphrodite at the end of the play, and view Hera, patroness of Argos, as their enemy. Moreover, they make their repeated prayers not to the collectivity of gods but to the single patriarchal figure of Zeus, lord of lords (524). Their monotheism echoes their monarchical attitude to politics, for they urge that the king of Argos is the one who rules the altar and public hearth (372). 'You are the *polis*, you are the people' they declare (369). Although the king protests that he is democratic, it transpires that he has in practice the control of a demagogue (623). The image of a single altar dedicated to an assembly of gods is thus a complex icon, in ritual terms unprecedented. It asks a question of the audience which goes to the heart of the play: single or collective? The chorus, who refuse to separate themselves from their father, see the altar as dedicated to a single patriarch, and will not acknowledge the collective ethos embodied in the Hellenic pantheon. When Danaus spies the Egyptians from 'this suppliant-receiving viewpoint' (713), he must be standing on top of the altar, causing the chorus as they pray to assimilate their father with the father of the gods (631).[35]

In *Seven Against Thebes*, an assembly of statues defines the centre of the *polis* as a sacred space. At the start of the play part of Thebes seems to lie outside the acting area, and the messenger leaves for the battlements while the women enter from their homes; but as the play goes on, acropolis (240) and city fuse

[34] In Athens one statue base survives from the Aeschylean period. It is placed just outside the small enclosure, but Gadbery, 'Sanctuary of the twelve gods' surmises that it may have been moved. Long, *Twelve Gods* 11 notes that archaic statues found in the *agora* at Delos seem to be associated with the cult of the twelve gods.

[35] The phrase 'Zeus-born gods' is an inaccuracy on the part of the chorus for Poseidon is not Zeus-born.

into a single space and the *orchêstra* becomes the encircled city of Thebes.[36] At the start of the play Eteocles establishes the parameters of the city by praying to Zeus above, Earth beneath, and the 'city-holding' gods (69ff.). The chorus then enter, cling to the statues and undertake to dress them with robes and garlands in a ritual act of supplication. They ask one of the idols, Ares of the golden helmet, if he will betray the city. The next choral sequence evidently accompanies the dressing of the statues, and each statue is addressed as soon as it has been adorned. After nine lines directed to omnipotent father **Zeus**, the chorus move on to Athene:

And you, Zeus-born, battle-loving power, be our city-saver, **Pallas**; and horseman, sea-lord, king with fish-hitting device **Poseidon**, release from fear, grant release. And you, **Ares**, oh, oh, guard your eponymous city of Cadmus, in visible form tend it. And **Cypris**, progenetrix of our race, help rid us, for we are born of your blood; with pleas for gods' ears we approach you to cry out. And you **Wolf [Lycian] king**, be a wolf to the enemy army. And you **daughter of Lato** prepare your bow.   (128–50)

As soon as the dressing is physically complete, formal strophic dancing commences with an invocation of the last goddess to be made ready, **Hera**. We can reconstruct from the text, therefore, the sequence of statues that the chorus decorate: Zeus, Pallas Athene, Poseidon, Ares, Cyprian Aphrodite, Lycian Apollo, Artemis, and Hera.[37] The strophic section must be addressed forwards to the audience, and the chorus now evoke the gods in name only: Hera and Artemis in the strophe, Apollo and Ares in the antistrophe. The force of the tableau depends upon the fact that the chorus are actually facing the Athenian Acropolis, for the strophe ends: 'What does our city suffer, what will become of it? To what end does god lead it?'; and the antistrophe: 'You, blessed Queen Onka [i.e. Athene], before the city support your seven-gated sanctuary' (156–7, 164–5). A gesture towards the Athenian Acropolis, site of Athene's temple, assimilates the protectress of Thebes with the patroness of Athens, and the people of Thebes with the audience.[38] In the final strophic pair (166–80) the chorus address the gods as 'guards of the battlements' (strophe), 'surrounding the city' (antistrophe), before calling attention to their own posture of supplication.

---

[36] S. Symeonoglou, *The Topography of Thebes* (Princeton, 1985) 34–7 argues that in the archaic period the seven-gated walls surrounded the acropolis, not the wider city.

[37] My reconstruction follows W. G. Thalmann, *Dramatic Art in Aeschylus' 'Seven Against Thebes'* (New Haven, 1978) 87–9. Thalmann does not, however, examine the significance of strophic patterning.

[38] On the spatial affinity between Thebes and Athens in this play see Nurit Yaari 'Anchoring Thebes: defining space and place in ancient Athens' in *Griechisch-römische Komödie und Tragödie (=Drama 3)* ed. B. Zimmermann (Stuttgart, 1995) 94–110.

By the end of the *parodos*, therefore, the chorus have established the idea that the gods constitute an encircling protective wall separating themselves within from the enemy outside. We must imagine a semi-circular distribution of the gods around the *orchêstra*, looking something like this:

                    Ares   Aphrodite
            Poseidon   Apollo
        Athene   Artemis
    Zeus   Hera
                    AUDIENCE

The beauty of this arrangement is that it creates seven gaps between the eight statues, an ideal configuration for locating the seven exits of the seven Theban champions in the course of the lengthy pageant that comprises the centre-piece of the play.[39] This schematic organization of the acting space allows Aeschylus to suggest that each champion who passes between a pair of statues is in fact passing through one of the seven gates of Thebes. It appears that the statues are not free-standing but are backed by some kind of setting or portico (96, 278, 319), which would enhance the sense of an enclosing wall. The focal central position is reserved for Eteocles, who must first arm himself and then determine, probably by casting lots, which champion will leave by which gate, and it must be Eteocles who at the end makes the strongest exit through the centre. The prominent central position of Ares and Aphrodite relates to the fact that Eteocles and the brother who awaits him beyond the gate are descendants of Ares and Aphrodite. Ares is the 'eponymous' founder of the city because the first Thebans were born from his dragon's teeth. When Aristophanes describes the play as 'filled with Ares',[40] he probably had in mind the visual dominance of the golden-helmeted statue.

The visual image as I have reconstructed it in *Seven Against Thebes* is not mere background establishing the sense of place, or gratuitous spectacle. It offers the audience an argument, or a set of questions. The formal symmetry matches the symmetry of the two corpses that occupy the centre in the finale. The balance of male and female matches the conflict between Eteocles and the

---

[39] See David Wiles, 'The seven gates of Aeschylus' in *Intertextualität in der griechisch-römischen Komödie* (=*Drama* 2) ed. N. W. Slater and B. Zimmermann (Stuttgart, 1993) 180–94. The misprinted diagrams are corrected in *Griechisch-römische Komödie und Tragödie* (=*Drama* 3) 190. Here I develop at length the correlation between the sequence of exits and the gates, the evidence for lot-casting, and the supposed problem of Eteocles' tenses which dissolves in performance. On the presence of the champions see Helen Bacon, 'The Shield of Eteocles' *Arion* 3 (1964) 27–38. G. O. Hutchinson in the Oxford edition (Oxford, 1985) 104–5 follows *SA* 149–52, denying that the champions appear, and thus stripping the play of its major visual interest.   [40] *Frogs* 1021.

Figure 13 Parody of the rape of Cassandra (fragment from Campania)

chorus. Passing between the statues of his ancestors, Eteocles returns to his
origins. More complex symbolism must have been apparent to the eye when
Theban champions with emblems on their shields went through the 'gates' to
meet Argive champions whose emblems are pictured in words.[41] The ensemble of Theban statues creates the sense that Eteocles' fate is controlled by the
gods, and that Polyneices' invasion of the city would be an act of sacrilege. The
gods and the institutions of the *polis* are indisseverable.

With the establishment of the *skênê* as a necessary part of the performance
space, dramatists did not again use statues in such an elaborate way to articulate the space, but statues continued to be an essential resource. A parodic vase
which depicts Ajax seeking refuge from Cassandra offers us an image of a
typical tragic statue of Athene: clothed but obviously rigid, raised but slightly
smaller than life size. We have seen how the action of *Hippolytus* is organized
around a pair of statues at the centre and door.[42] Euripides' most ambitious use
of a statue is in the *Andromache*, where the *skênê* represents the house of
Neoptolemus and in the centre is the shrine of Thetis the sea-nymph, grand-
mother to Neoptolemus. The shrine comprises a sacrificial altar (129, 260,
etc.), a temple or dwelling-place (161, 130), ground (314) with a boundary
(*temenos* – 253), and most importantly a statue that can be embraced (115). At
one point the gaze of the statue is mentioned as the two disputing women both
claim the support of Thetis (246–7). In a theatre of masks, nothing need dis-

[41] The two major studies of the emblems by Vidal-Naquet in *MTAG* 273–300, and by Froma
Zeitlin, *Under the Sign of the Shield: semiotics and Aeschylus'* 'Seven Against Thebes' (Rome,
1982), both treat the play as a literary text and ignore the problem of what the spectators see
with their eyes.   [42] See above pp. 79–80.

tinguish a statue from an immobile living actor, and as in *Hippolytus* there is a strong sense that the goddess is present in her statue.

The sanctuary of Thetis plays an important part in the opening of the play when Andromache is tricked into leaving its protection by deceitful Spartans. In the play as a whole, the presence of the statue helps to focus a series of polar oppositions.

Inside/outside The outdoor shrine is a symbol of marriage (46), but Neoptolemus' marriage-bed which Andromache and Hermione never chose and now abandon is in the *skênê*. Thetis combines being married with having the freedom of the oceans, resolving a contradiction that the two mortal women cannot.

Young/old As a goddess, Thetis retains her youth, whilst her husband Peleus struggles against ageing and longs for rejuvenation.

Mother/whore Andromache seeks protection from Thetis as great-grand-mother to her son. Hermione is the legal wife, yet is childless, whilst Andromache has the son but cannot be married. Peleus attacks Hermione because Spartan women exercise naked, and Hermione later bares her breasts (830–5) and must still be under-dressed when her lover appears. The statue of the sea-nymph may simultaneously be a mother like Andromache, and erot-ically under-dressed like Hermione.

Exotic/Greek Menelaus attacks Andromache because she is Asiatic. Thetis is an exotic non-Grecian partner but of high social status because she is a goddess.

Animate/inanimate The immobility of the statue raises the question of whether gods are active in human affairs. The sanctuary and altar of Thetis provide a visual focus for the long description of the sanctuary and altar at Delphi where Neoptolemus is sacrilegiously murdered. As the grieving Peleus batters his head and appeals to the statue, the goddess appears floating through the ether, in other words on the crane, freely promising eternal life and marital bliss. The audience are entitled to wonder whether the inanimate sculpture can in fact signify and contain a deity of this improbable kind. The image of Thetis at the centre of the acting area draws together and reconciles contradictions which pull human beings apart and destroy their lives. Again we see that the statue is not a decorative addendum, but a crucial determinant of how the audience will respond.

In *Iphigeneia in Tauris* the statue at the centre of the action is not a fixed point but a portable object. It is interesting to note that the Taurian statue which Athene in the triumphant finale of the play destines for the Athenian temple at Halai was no longer in Attica when Euripides wrote. Pausanias believed that the authentic Taurian Artemis was the statue long possessed by the Spartans, whilst the statue at Halai formerly claimed by the Athenians was stolen by Xerxes. To support his theory, he expressed doubt that the Athenians could have been so careless as to abandon a truly precious icon. A wooden statue at Brauron was claimed in his day to be the true Taurian image.[43] This information greatly complicates our interpretation of the play's finale. The overtly patriotic celebration of the Iphigeneia cult in Attica may be a typical Euripidean irony, since the Athenians did not have the authentic statue, but the Spartans possibly did. Topographically the Taurian clifftop temple seems not so dissimilar to the temple at Brauron. The Athenians like the Taurian king had been robbed in the past, and their marginal sanctuaries were now once again vulnerable to attack.

We also have to consider what Euripides might have done to show that the skênê signified a temple. There is a blood-stained altar in the orchêstra (72–3), and hanging below the eaves of the temple Orestes and Pylades see spoils taken from the victims of blood sacrifice (74–5). We have examined the use of hanging objects in a Sicilian comic vase depicting a temple of Artemis (figure 10). An Attic vase of 390–380 depicts the scene of Euripides' play, with skulls, crowns and bands suspended above the shrine. A later south Italian vase shows captured weapons suspended from the temple, whilst another shows a human head and empty garment hanging beside the temple.[44] The device is so common in both comic and paratragic vase paintings that we must ask ourselves whether this convention was not also commonplace in fifth-century theatre.[45] If the dramatist wanted a theatrical sign that would turn the trompe l'oeil columns of his stage façade into a temple, then the display of some sheep skulls would have commanded instant recognition. Orestes could well have seen hanging objects on the skênê, permanent reminders of the threat of human sacrifice.

I argued in chapter 6 that in Oedipus at Colonus a statue of the eponymous hero of the deme of Colonus served as a sign of place, and that a visual opposition of tree and equestrian statue along the lateral axis served to organize the thematic oppositions of the play. Three tiny deictic pronouns stand as evidence for Sophocles' visual conception. We must ponder how common such a device was. At the start of Sophocles' Electra the pedagogue tells Orestes that they are in ancient Argos, the grove of Io. 'This,' he says, is the agora of Lycian Apollo,

---

[43] Pausanias iii.16.7–11; i.23.7; also viii.46.3, i.33.1. Strabo xii.2.3 confirms the Cappadocian image. We have documentary evidence of a wooden idol at Brauron around the time Euripides wrote: LIMC ii.i.620.   [44] LIMC 'Iphigeneia' 19, 24, 29.

[45] To cite only performance-related comic vases: the shrine of Ammon in HGRT fig. 283 has a drum and a weaving; that of Artemis in fig. 488 has wreaths; that of Hera in fig. 485, skulls and shields; that of Apollo in fig. 481, perhaps a diadem. The vines in fig. 521, ivy in fig. 534, and masks in fig. 538 indicate a sanctuary of Dionysus. There are more skulls in HGRT figs. 485, 486, 498, 507, 527, 531, and Taplin, Comic Angels pls.11, 14.

'here on the left' is the famous temple of Hera, and 'this' building is the palace of Mycenae (4–10). Since the Heraion is three miles south-east of Mycenae and five miles north-east of the *agora* of Lycian Apollo in Argos, we can only make sense of the text in relation to a schematic arrangement of the theatrical space. There is no single topographical point from which these sights could have been visible, and no obvious literary justification for the words.[46] A shrine of Lycian Apollo is used in the action later when Clytaemnestra places offerings before 'this' lord (635, 645) and prays to him on account of her dreams. Since the opening lines of the play encourage the actor to identify through gesture the stage emblem which will represent Lycian Apollo – presumably in the normal sacred location at the *thymelē*[47] – the opening reference to Hera must seem redundant in performance unless an image of Hera is also visible, serving (like the statue of Colonus) as an emblem of the place of which she is patron. If this inference is correct, then the statue must command the opposite *eisodos* to that used by Orestes, since he has not walked in past it. While Orestes' *eisodos* is associated both with Apollo's shrine at Delphi and with Agamemnon's tomb,[48] the opposite *eisodos* must be used for the entry of the female chorus.[49] A statue of Hera would thus define a lateral opposition of male and female, standing before the audience as a symbol of the matriarch of Argos. Its neglect would be conspicuous when Electra and Orestes concentrate their attention on male gods. At the climax of the play, when Orestes hurries in to kill his mother, he says that they 'must do obeisance first to the ancestral shrines of the gods, all these that stand before the gates' (1374–5). Electra in response prostrates herself before the statue of Lycian Apollo (1379–80), and no other god is mentioned. Sophocles' failure to clarify the moral issues surrounding the matricide has often been found problematic.[50] The irony that may or may not be present in the literary text becomes clear and purposeful in performance if we surmise that Orestes and Electra studiously ignore the image of the matriarch that stands silently by the gates and dedicate themselves selectively, like Hippolytus, to one statue alone.

---

46 On the lack of realism, see for example Kamerbeek in his commentary on the text (Leiden, 1974) 21.

47 The visual impact of the offerings on the centre line was made very clear in Deborah Warner's Royal Shakespeare Company production – Riverside Studios, London, 1991.

48 See Suzanne Saïd, 'Tragic Argos' in *Tragedy, Comedy and the Polis* ed. A. H. Sommerstein *et al.* (Bari, 1993) 167–89, pp. 178–80.

49 Compare Euripides' contemporaneous version, where the chorus enter with news of the Heraia.

50 On the critical dilemma, see R. P. Winnington-Ingram 'The *Electra* of Sophocles: prolegomena to an interpretation' in *Oxford Readings in Greek Tragedy* ed. E. Segal (Oxford, 1983) 210–16.

A tree next to the statue would be enough to signify the grove of Hera's victim Io. Trees are common emblems in comic vases, reflecting the prevalence of groves in Greek sanctuaries.[51] We have already examined the grove of Artemis on the Sicilian vase. On other comic vases, a laurel tree stands next to the courtyard altar of Zeus on which Priam is killed, perhaps emphasizing Apollo's link with the city;[52] a palm frond identifies the Libyan shrine of Zeus Ammon;[53] laurels and skulls show that a slave is stealing from a sanctuary;[54] and an actor holds a laurel branch beside a tripod to signify that the setting is Delphi.[55] In a more enigmatic vase, two actors with cloaks set as wings perform a ceremony around an altar on the trestle stage, whilst a laurel is set at ground level, protruding through the curtain at the base of the stage and signifying, I would suggest, that a sanctuary is being founded in the sky in a scene reminiscent of Aristophanes' *Birds*.[56] It appears from these examples that the comic stage used trees as iconographic signs in just the same way as paratragic vase paintings,[57] and we may reasonably infer that the tradition goes back to the fifth-century theatre.

In many paratragic vases, as in the comic example noted above, Apollo or his priest carry a laurel branch in order to mark their identity.[58] This iconographic convention is boldly exploited in Euripides' *Ion*. Laurel is integral to the cult of Apollo, being associated with Apollo's rape of Daphne in the vale of Tempe, and with his purification there after killing the Python.[59] In the play, the tree is also associated with his birthplace (919–22). Hermes at the end of the prologue exits to 'this laurelled hollow', and announces the entry of Ion bearing a laurel branch. Ion declares his intention of cleansing the precinct by sweeping with laurel, sprinkling spring water, and shooting the birds. As he sweeps, he sings a strophe addressed to his laurel branch and an antistrophe addressed to Apollo, both concluding with a paean (112ff.). The choreographic symmetry establishes the laurel branch as the icon of the god, and the one is addressed with the same actions as the other. When Ion sprinkles water, the

---

[51] See D. Birge, 'Trees in the landscape of Pausanias' *Periegesis*' in *Placing the Gods: sanctuaries and sacred space in ancient Greece* ed. S. E. Alcock and R. Osborne (Oxford, 1994) 231–46.

[52] Taplin, *Comic Angels* pl.19=*HGRT* fig. 493. For the laurel, compare Virgil's account in *Aeneid* ii.513. The altar is said to be 'god-built' at Euripides, *Hecuba* 23.   [53] *HGRT* fig. 483.

[54] *HGRT* fig. 527.

[55] A. D. Trendall, *Phlyax Vases* (*BICS* supplement 19, London, 1967) pl.1vb.

[56] Taplin, *Comic Angels* pl.11. For other interpretations of the tree, see 70 n.8 and 74 n.20.

[57] See for example C. Sourvinou-Inwood, 'Altars with palm-trees, palm-trees and *parthenoi*' BICS 32 (1985) 125–46.

[58] E.g. Taplin, *Comic Angels* pls.106, 109, 110; Moret, *Ilioupersis* pl.47/1. Compare also the 'Telephus' vase – Moret pl.52 – where Moret suspects a Euripidean influence. On Apollo Daphnephoros, see further *LIMC* II.i.214.

[59] C. Sourvinou-Inwood, *Reading Greek Culture* (Oxford, 1991) 194–5.

attendants may remove his laurel but more probably the branch remains at the altar. Ion threatens birds with his bow, and the bow as a familiar emblem of Apollo creates an iconographic link between him and the god who is his father. He declares that he will purify the precinct both with laurel saplings and with garlands (104), so it is also likely that he drapes laurel around the altar. Later, when his mother becomes a suppliant at the altar, she entwines herself in strands (*stemmasi* – 1310), and the reference helps to associate the altar with the *omphalos* which is also covered in strands (224). A laurel branch next to the altar would reinforce this association since a sacred laurel grew inside the Delphic temple.[60] There is probably enough laurel available in the *orchêstra* for Creusa to take some when instructed to circuit the altars with laurel shoots while her husband consults the oracle within (422–3). Her ambiguous exit line: 'what he decrees – he [it] is a god – I accept [receive]' makes theatrical sense if it accompanies the receiving of the young branch that *is* the god.

The insistent use of laurel in the play makes sense in relation to the finale when the decisive recognition token which identifies Ion's mother is a wreath of olive from the sacred tree at the site of her father Erechtheus' grave (1433–6). The wreath has not withered over the years because of its sacred properties. The Erechtheum was being built around the time of the play, and like Apollo's shrine at Delphi had a cleft, a serpent and a sacred tree in its interior.[61] Ion starts the play looking like an emblem of Apollo with his bow and laurel, but that familiar image is subverted when (as we must assume) Ion dons the crown of olive in order to define himself as Athenian – no longer Apollo but a rejuvenated Erechtheus (1465), his mother's son and not his father's. In the *Ion* Euripides claims for the Athenian Acropolis, the rock on which the audience sat, some of the magical properties associated with the sacred site of Apollo at Delphi. The manipulation of icons is the basis of his dramaturgical strategy.

Vegetation played an important part in Greek ritual practice, creating or enhancing a sense of sacred space. We can see the importance of olive branches in suppliant plays like Aeschylus' *Suppliants* or Euripides' *Children of Heracles*, or indeed Sophocles' *Oedipus the King*. Artemis' statue wears a crown from the virgin meadow in *Hippolytus*. Thyrsus and ivy appear in *The Bacchae*. Victors in the theatrical competition were crowned with ivy, as we see for example in the Pronomos vase, and it seems that many in the audience wore wreaths. We should expect vegetation, therefore, to be a widely used theatrical resource. I have suggested that olive branches were deployed in *Oedipus at Colonus* to define the symbolism of the left *eisodos*. A similar device could have been used

---

[60] See above p. 102 on the altar as *omphalos*.
[61] On the link between the two buildings see Roux, 'Trésors, temples, tholos' in *Temples et sanctuaires* ed. G. Roux (Lyons, 1981) 163.

in the *Hypsipyle*, where one *eisodos* leads to the sacred spring and the other to the grove and encamped army beyond. The chorus refer to Amphiaraus entering through the grove, and pray to Zeus 'to whom belongs this grove of Nemea' (99). It seems a reasonable guess that a tree was deployed to identify the *eisodos* associated with the grove.

And so we might continue. This chapter has necessarily involved much use of inference and circumstantial evidence, for we are dealing with visual information that we should not expect to be made explicit in the dialogue. Greek dramatists did not write down their stage directions. Their concern was to create meaning through the medium of performance, under their personal supervision. My concern has been with the techniques that were available, and with how these techniques could have shaped the meaning of the performance. In attempted reconstructions the important point is that we must not think pictorially but spatially. The key to creating a sense of place in fifth-century theatre was not the art of the scenographer but the deployment of objects and bodies in the three-dimensional space of the *orchêstra*. We must think not mimetically but iconographically, remembering that cult provided the Athenians with a rich visual vocabulary. The theatre had at its disposal a range of simple signifying objects which could, when used sparingly and in novel contexts and combinations, generate remarkably complex meanings.

CHAPTER 10

✌

Orchêstra and theatron

Perhaps the most difficult spatial polarity to extrapolate from dramatic dialogue is that of performers in the *orchêstra* and spectators in the *theatron*
(watching place). Rather than 'auditorium' (listening place) I shall revert to the
Greek term *theatron* in this chapter because of its visual emphasis. It is all too
easy to forget the *theatron* if one conceives Greek 'theatre' as art for art's sake,
and not as a social process. I shall end where I began by focussing on the pre-
misses of Oliver Taplin, which exemplify a widely held set of assumptions. In
a closely argued essay 'Fifth-century tragedy and comedy: a *synkrisis*',[1] Taplin
defines the actor/audience relationship in tragedy as being the inverse of the
relationship in comedy. His account is in part a response to post-structuralist
'metatheatrical' readings of tragedy such as Zeitlin's account of *Orestes* or Segal's
of *The Bacchae*.[2] He finds such readings, with their emphasis on self-referential textuality, both incompatible with his experience of performance and,
insofar as they have some validity, to be explorations of a genre at the point of
demise.

Taplin arrives at two main conclusions. First he argues for a form of passive,
individualized viewing. 'The intense concentration of tragedy calls for silence
– even your weeping should not disturb your neighbour!', and the 'helpless
emotion' of the chorus provides the audience with a model of how it should
respond. Second, he repeats the Aristotelian claim that tragedy should deal in
the universal, particularity serving to generate 'timeless truths'.[3] The idea that
the plague in *Oedipus the King* could relate in any direct way to the great
Athenian plague of 430–426 BC as Knox, for example, contends, is anathema
to him.[4] It will be clear from the argument of this book that I find these

---

[1] 'Fifth-century tragedy and comedy: a *synkrisis*' *JHS* 106 (1986) 163–74.
[2] See above p. 171.
[3] '*Synkrisis*' 172–3. The phrase 'timeless truths' is borrowed from Michael Silk.
[4] '*Synkrisis*' 167; B. M. W. Knox, 'The date of the *Oedipus Tyrannus* of Sophocles' in his *Word
and Action* (Baltimore, 1979) 112–24. See also V. Ehrenburg, *Sophocles and Pericles* (Oxford,
1954) 114–15.

conclusions unacceptable. Although in certain formal conventions, such as costume or reference to named living figures, Taplin is certainly right to argue that the two genres define each other by their differentness, the genres have a symbiotic relationship, for comedy draws life from deconstructing the world of tragedy. Comedy's perspective on tragedy is bound up with the process in which the audience was engaged, the process of judging a competitive skill. Aristophanes encourages the spectators to think about Euripides, Agathon and Aeschylus as men with specific philosophical assumptions, using specific staging techniques and linguistic idioms. The response of spell-bound emotion which Taplin attributes to the tragic spectator must in some way have cohabited with the critical response fostered by comedy. Critical awareness cannot have been a sudden afterthought. Tragedy is not 'essentially the emotional experience of its audience'[5] any more than comedy is essentially the cognitive experience of its audience, for thought and emotion are intertwined in the viewing of both. Taplin's Aristotelian thought/emotion dichotomy isolates the thinking/feeling spectator, and takes no account of social transactions in which the spectator is engaged. A more satisfactory theory of reception must take account of the context of viewing. Taplin's reference point is his own experience of viewing tragedy, and universalist assumptions seem to prevent him from considering how far reception in his own world is mediated by education, class, gender and other sub-categories of the fragmented post-modern self.

Taplin attempts to marginalize the issue of metatheatricality, and has particular difficulty with Euripides' parody of *The Libation Bearers* in the recognition scene of *Electra*, going so far as to question the authorship of the passage.[6] However, Euripidean 'metatheatricality' merely highlights the fact that every tragedy was a retelling, since tragedy relied upon a small corpus of myths. We should read Sophocles' *Oedipus the King* very differently if we possessed Aeschylus' *Oedipus* trilogy, for example. Saussure argues, in respect of language, that words create meaning through establishing differences with other words, and Gombrich applies much the same argument to the visual image.[7] For the Greek spectator the significance of the story must have lain not in the story *per*

[5] *GTA* 169.

[6] '*Synkrisis*' 171, seeking comfort in David Bain, '[Euripides], Electra 518–44' *BICS* 24 (1977) 104–116. Bain is a leading exponent of the thesis that tragedy avoids direct acknowledgement of the audience: see 'Audience address in Greek tragedy' *Classical Quarterly* 25 (1975) 13–25. Bain fights a rearguard action in 'Some reflections on the illusion in Greek tragedy' *BICS* 34 (1981) 1–14, admitting 'theatricality' as a category within 'illusion'. On the irrelevance of 'illusion' as a category, see most recently Christina Dedoussi 'Greek drama and its spectators: conventions and relationships' in *Stage Directions: essays in honour of E. W. Handley* ed. A. Griffiths (*BICS* Supplement 66, London, 1995) 123–32.   [7] See p. 4 above.

se but in the manner of its *re*telling, the way it differentiates itself from other tellings. The spectator's experience of the play in the present is indisseverable from his re-experiencing of plays (and dithyrambs and recitations) from his past. Derrida has popularized the notion that any pursuit of meaning is a pursuit of *différance* – differentiation subject to infinitely regressive deferral. Because of the way it isolates the work of art, Taplin's *Rezeptionsästhetik* seems to me to be a critical blind alley.[8]

Along with metatheatricality Taplin also rejects the concept of 'anachronism', having in mind for example, the apparently democratic nature of the assembly in *Orestes*.[9] The issue here is placed in a broader perspective by Vernant, who argued in a seminal essay that tragedy as a historical phenomenon is tied to the moment when Athenians could make sense of the world in terms both of heroic myth and of democratic politics.[10] Oedipus in *Oedipus the King* is thus simultaneously a hero of the Homeric ilk and a politician like Pericles, simultaneously a psychologically conceived character and a *daimôn*, simultaneously the embodiment of a divine force and a psychologically conceived character. Through the institutions of the festival, Vernant argues, the city 'turned itself into a theatre' and 'acted itself out'. Tragedy was 'born when myth started 'to be considered from the point of view of a citizen'.[11] It follows from Vernant's argument that the audience is looking at itself in relation to a different, pre-democratic world. The term 'anachronism' becomes irrelevant once we identify the audience as an integral part of the social process that is tragic performance. When Taplin claims: 'my responses as I sit in my seat are crucially different both internally and externally from those which would be provoked by similar events in reality',[12] Vernant's response would surely be that watching a play is part of 'reality', and is a lived democratic practice, the pursuit of politics by another means. In the frame of the festival there are different levels of participation: to eat the sacrificial beef, to dance in the procession, to dance in the dithyramb, to parade in armour, to dance in the tragic chorus, to sit enthroned as a priest, to display oneself as a member of the Council, to fund a chorus or sit as judge. There is no clear cut-off point at which one passes from the subject-position of spectator to the object-position of performer.

[8] See '*Synkrisis*' 164 n.8.

[9] '*Synkrisis*' 164, 171. See also *GTA* 165. Taplin gives qualified approval to P. E. Easterling, 'Anachronism in Greek tragedy' *JHS* 105 (1985) 1–10. Easterling comments on phenomena like money, reading and panhellenic games that do not belong to the world of epic. On 'anachronism' note also B. M. W. Knox's statement that the term is misleading because it is 'not the exception but the rule': *Oedipus at Thebes* (New Haven, 1957) 61.

[10] 'The historical moment of tragedy in Greece' *MTAG* 23–8 (first published in 1972).

[11] *MTAG* 33. See pp. 21–2 above.   [12] '*Synkrisis*' 165.

Taplin's phrase 'my responses as I sit in my seat' immediately defines a subject-position that is incompatible with Vernant's phrase 'from the point of view of a citizen'. Wooden planks did not provide individualized seats, and the spectator could not isolate himself 'in' them. In a densely packed *theatron*, body contact would have caused emotions (by which I also mean a form of understanding) to be transmitted by osmosis, and clearly the Greek audience was willing to weep publicly in a way that the modern western audience is not.[13] The influence of wine helped to liberate emotion, and there was an important role for 'rod-holders' in maintaining order.[14] Emotions in such an environment are infectious and the expression of a group as much as of an individual. I argued at length in chapter 2 against those who would draw a confrontational straight line between *orchêstra* and *theatron*, dividing the spectator as subject from the performance as object occupying the entirety of his gaze. In chapter 3 I argued against the assumption that the actors stood on a stage. Actors on this hypothetical stage would inhabit a heterotopia from which the audience was excluded, stage being isolated from *theatron* by the chasm of the *orchêstra* and by the intermediating responses of the chorus. Rather, the governing spatial paradigm, I have argued, was of a community gathered in a ritual circle around a surrogate altar. The spectator's gaze encompassed both the dramatic action and the assembled *polis*, and the response of the *polis* to the dramatic action was part of the individual spectator's experience as the performance unfolded in time. It was never the role of the chorus to dictate the audience's emotions. Rather, from the foot of the *theatron*, two competing subject-positions were offered to the spectator by the successful enthroned honorands of democracy and by the wooden statue of the god. The spectator had to negotiate the two subject-positions of citizen and *daimôn*[15] without recourse to an autonomous Cartesian ego, which is to say without any proprietorial claim to 'my responses'.

In the *Oresteia* Aeschylus established a middle path, neither placing the subject matter too close to the world of the audience as in Phrynicus' *Capture of Miletus*,[16] nor removing it altogether from the contemporary world of polit-

---

[13] Witness Ion's observation of an audience weeping – Plato, *Ion* 535e. Tears are also attested as normal in Xenophon, *Symposium* iii.11 and Isocrates, *Panegyric* 168. On overt responses of other kinds, see *DFA* 274. Iain Mackintosh, *Architecture, Actor and Audience* (London, 1993) 22 points out that in the modern theatre densities have changed since the Elizabethan period by a factor of 1:3 or 1:4.

[14] Philochorus records the continual wine drinking; Plato and Aristophanes the role of the rod-holder: *COAD* 301, 304–5.

[15] 'Demon', 'divine power' – a term set up by Vernant in opposition to *ethos* to account for human action in tragedy: *MTAG* 37.

[16] The audience wept because the play dealt with a recent communal trauma: Herodotus vi.21.

ical alliances, democratic reform, racial tension and scientific debate. When the action of the *Eumenides* shifted to Athens, the audience became incorporated in the play. The chorus moralize at a 'you' who can only be the Athenian spectator.[17] When Athene leads in her jury (566ff.), she has a herald sound his trumpet in order to gather the 'army'; she refers to 'this Council-chamber' (*bouleutêrion*) being full, and calls the 'whole city' to be silent. Her words make sense in relation to a *theatron* that contained armed youths and generals elected to lead the audience into war, the Council *en bloc*, and a potentially noisy crowd. Taplin denies that there is any crossing here of the actor/audience divide. When, for example, Athene addresses herself to the 'people of Attica' (681), for him this is merely an address to the jurors.[18] Yet Aeschylus' phrase is all-inclusive. The Theatre of Dionysus did not allow a sharp distinction to be made. In performance we must assume either that the jurors sat in front of Athene as Pickard-Cambridge imagines,[19] or else that, as in the productions of Peter Hall and Peter Stein, they sat behind her along the line of the *skênê*. In the first reconstruction, any gesture by Athene towards the jurors will also incorporate the honorands of the *polis*, and by extension the rest of the community above. In the second, which is theatrically more interesting because the audience can focus on the dilemma of the decision-makers, it is impossible acoustically for Athene to turn her back on the *theatron*, and words notionally intended for the jurors have to be addressed in the direction of the audience. The jurors within the play, like the jurors in the *theatron* who judged the *Oresteia*, have to be seen in their capacity as representatives of the *polis* at large.

It was clearly Aeschylus' strategy to blur the fact that the Areopagite jury at the time of performance belonged to a threatened and threatening aristocratic elite. Only when the jurors join her at the head of the closing procession does Athene refer in coded language to their lineage – 'children of Cranaus' (1011). They receive at this point as they head for the Areopagus their autonomous identity within the *polis*. I have argued that the schematic theatrical Athens of the trial scene, which fused into one Athene's temple, democratic law-courts in the Agora and the elite court of the Areopagus, was organized around the statue of Athene in the centre. As that statue is removed and incorporated in the procession (1024), the constructed space dissolves into the real space of the performance in Dionysus' sanctuary, a short walk from the Areopagus and the sacred cave beneath it. The final choral ode is sung by female escorts of the

---

[17] See A. Sommerstein's note on 526–8 in his edition (Cambridge, 1989). There is a useful account of the shifting actor/audience relationship in Peter Arnott, *Public and Performance in the Greek Theatre* (London, 1989) 18–21. [18] '*Synkrisis*' 166, repeating the argument in *SA* 394–5.

[19] *TDA* 46. Michael Ewans follows this staging in his annotated translation: *The Oresteia* (London, 1995) 208.

goddess and presumably also by the jurors.[20] The first strophic pair calls on the 'people of the land' (strophe) 'as a whole *dêmos*' (antistrophe) to be reverently silent, the second pair calls for ululation, and we must surmise that this was an invitation to the audience to break the tension and erupt with noise. The exit of the final procession is in one sense a rite of incorporation like the Panathenaia, and in another sense a rite of separation, for it includes an Olympian, chthonic goddesses dressed as foreigners, animals, Athenian aristocrats and Athenian women, everyone but the *dêmos* which sits in the *theatron*.[21] The democratic audience gathered around the statue of its own god, Dionysus, has its own separate identity. The world created in the *orchêstra* is always a heterotopia defined vis-à-vis the audience.

Though no other tragedy negotiates the actor/audience relationship quite so overtly, in every play the audience has to be positioned. The performers in a Greek theatre cannot look away from the audience, or over their heads, or into darkness and the dazzle of lights. The gestures and gaze of the performers necessarily embraced the *theatron*, and by this means incorporated the audience in the spatial field of the performance. English renaissance drama, as the 'new historicists' have shown, was preoccupied with constructing the individual as a subject.[22] Athenian drama was preoccupied, rather, with constructing the Athenian citizen (*politês*) as a subject. The Greek theatre had no compartmentalized boxes and no obvious vertical tiering, unlike the Elizabethan theatre, so the spectator viewed and was viewed by the performers as part of a homogeneous citizen body.[23] Many Greek tragedies are set in the city of Thebes which, perhaps because of its political antagonism to Athens and close relationship to the cult of Dionysus is, as Zeitlin has argued, often used as 'the negative model to Athens' manifest image of itself'. Zeitlin describes Thebes as the doomed 'other', an ideological construct which defines the opposite identity of Athens.[24] Viewing as Thebans seems to have proved a much more complex and fertile subject-position than viewing as Athenians.

[20] As Taplin believes in *SA* 411, though he does not note the corollary that there must be a direct address to the audience here. I do not understand why Sommerstein (note on 1032–47) feels that the *chôritai* (countrymen) of 1035 cannot be the audience. He recognizes (note on 1047) that the final line invites audience response.

[21] See Sommerstein's analysis of the procession in his note to 1021–47.

[22] For drama, the most important new historicist study is probably Catherine Belsey, *The Subject of Tragedy: identity and difference in renaissance drama* (London, 1985).

[23] There is no evidence for a lower *diazôma* or lateral gangway in the Theatre of Dionysus: see M. Korres, *Archaiologikon Deltion* 35 (1980) 'Chronika' 10 and fig. 1. Nor, therefore, is there any basis for reconstructing such a gangway at Megalopolis. Whether the theatre at Epidauros was planned in two tiers is still disputed.

[24] 'Thebes: theater of self and society in Athenian drama' *NTDWD* 130–67, p. 131.

Seven Against Thebes opens with Eteocles' words: 'Citizens of Cadmus, he who helms the ship of state must speak when the moment comes'. The obvious inference that Eteocles must address the audience is rejected by Taplin, as we saw in chapter 5. In pleading for a 'crowd' of three to twelve extras to avoid the embarrassment of direct audience address, he offers the analogy of the Elizabethan stage where three or four could represent a crowd.[25] The Elizabethan comparison is worth pursuing because it is clear that when Mark Antony speaks to his 'friends, Romans and countrymen', the dynamics of the Globe Theatre, with spectators standing on three sides of the stage, made it possible and inevitable that the actor should embrace the audience around him as fellow Romans. By leaning against the columns, the four actors who played Roman plebeians could appear to merge with the audience and speak as from the crowd.[26] The spectator in a proscenium theatre is deprived of any comparable sense of involvement.

Eteocles calls on the citizens young and old to don their armour and man the walls of the city that reared them. A gaze sweeping across the audience would serve to define the *theatron* as the walls of the city, enclosing the sacred core of the city represented by the *orchêstra*. The audience as surrogate Thebans are encouraged to share the sense of threat from an external enemy and view the assault on Thebes as if it were an assault on Athens. The audience are constructed as male warriors, and distanced from the insubordinate women who form the chorus. At the beginning of the play the chorus cannot possibly be said to mediate the audience's response. The audience may in a sense become fellow mourners later, but they remain onlookers, leaving to women the active ritual task of keening. The 'otherness' of the citizens of Cadmus for purposes of the play is not the genetic condition of being 'Theban' but the otherness of being a citizen ruled by a destructive and imploding royal family. Peter Arnott suggests that the audience in Aeschylus' play may also represent the encircling enemy,[27] but this does not accord with the centripetal development of the action, or with the exits which require the champions to move away from the audience to another space occupied by the enemy.[28] The case is very different in Euripides' *Phoenician Women* where the major scenes of the play could not possibly take place in front of a Theban assembly: the negotiations between Jocasta and her son who has secretly entered the city, and Teiresias'

---

[25] *SA* 130 n.1. Bain, 'Illusion' 4 attempts to fend off a defence of direct address by H. Y. McCulloch and H. D. Cameron in '*Septem* 12–13 and the Athenian *ephêbeia*' *Illinois Classical Studies* 5 (1980) 1–15, p. 5.

[26] *Julius Caesar* III.ii.73. Workshops in the reconstructed Globe Theatre have already served to clarify this point.   [27] *Public and Performance* 21.

[28] On the exits see p. 199 above.

confidential advice to Creon that Creon's son must be sacrificed. When Antigone surveys the Argive army, as I showed in chapter 6, her gaze swings across the *theatron* from west to east, assimilating the enemy Argives with the audience. There is no sense as in Aeschylus that the orchestral area stands metonymically for the city as a whole, and the Euripidean Eteocles can even say: 'Going to the seven-gated *polis* I will arrange the champions at the gates' (748–9) as though he inhabits a private space that is somehow separate from the *polis*. Only with the lifting of the siege, the arrival of the corpses, and the focus on the *skênê* as the house of Oedipus is there some suggestion in Euripides' play that the action is located at the core of the city. At the very end when leaving for Athens Oedipus appeals to the audience as an assembly, and his words could as well be addressed to Athens as to Thebes: 'O citizens of a famous fatherland, this is Oedipus' (1758). Euripides effects an easy transformation to the final speech in our manuscripts, which is a direct appeal by the chorus for victory in the dramatic competition.

It is a common convention that the audience are interpellated as an assembly, whether Thebans, Taurians, or Persians; they can even become an Athenian army gathered at the Callichoron well where the Eleusinian procession terminated.[29] The similar spatial dispositions of theatre and Pnyx made the convention obvious and natural. In *Phoenician Women* we see the orchestral area starting to become a private rather than a public space, a change which finds its most obvious expression in *Orestes*, where the democratic assembly is explicitly elsewhere. It is a house rather than a city that hostile forces besiege (762). Only when the protagonists have retreated within the *skênê* can Menelaus apostrophize the spectators as though they were citizens of Argos (1621–4). The emergence of a private space poses obvious difficulties for sustaining the convention of the chorus.

Unlike *Seven Against Thebes*, *Oedipus the King* plainly does begin with a crowd of visible extras, boys at the altar with branches of olive who are 'chosen' representatives.[30] The play starts in the private space before Oedipus' house, whilst the remaining Theban host is said to be at the *agora(s)*, and at shrines of Apollo and Athene which topographically lie outside the gates. The priest speaks of old men in the plural (17), but there is no evidence of others beside himself so perhaps priests in the front row are implicated by his gesture. The children are dismissed when Oedipus summons the 'people of Cadmus' to

---

[29] See *Bacchae* 1201–3 and *Heracles* 1389; *Iphigenia in Tauris* 1422; *Persians* 258–9; Euripides, *Suppliants* 584ff., noting the deictic at 392 and assimilation with the *polis* at 394.

[30] W. M. Calder in 'The prologue of *Oedipus Tyrannus*' *Phoenix* 13 (1959) 121–9 wants the audience to be the 'children'. He does not consider the problem of the branches. See also Rush Rehm, *Greek Tragic Theatre* (London, 1992) 157 n.2.

assemble (144). As the chorus arrive, the appearance of the altar is changed by the removal of boughs, and the sense of place changes also. In strophe A of the *parodos* the chorus pray to Apollo, implicitly identifying the altar before Oedipus' house as Apollo's. In antistrophe A′ they pray to Athene, to Artemis whose throne is encircled by the Agora, and to Apollo. The public space of Thebes that was initially defined as separate from the *orchêstra* is now present, and the audience starts to become the Theban assembly. In B the chorus sing of women congregating and of dead children's spirits flying away, and in B′ they end with a prayer to Athene. Their gestures must have reached up towards Athene's temple on the Acropolis, making a link between the plight of mythic Thebes and the plight of the Athenians, who were also coping with plague and with refugees. In C the chorus associate the plague with Ares the war-god, which makes sense in the context of war-ridden Athens, and in C′ they turn from Lycian Apollo at the altar to Dionysus their ultimate helper, and here the statue of Dionysus in the theatre must replace the Parthenon as the focus of the tableau. The fusion of the Athenian audience with the male population of Thebes is now complete, making it easy for Oedipus in the speech which follows to address himself to 'all Cadmeans'. The subject-position of the audience is the assembled *dêmos*, belonging at once to mythic Thebes and to contemporary Athens.

I argued in chapter 8 that in the later stages of *Oedipus the King* the *theatron* is associated with Cithaeron, the mountain of Dionysus. The performance interpellates the slope of the Acropolis as much as the citizen body seated on it. On Philoctetes' lonely island of Lemnos, where there can be no public assembly, Mount Oeta across the sea seems in the same way to be associated with the slope of the *theatron*. Philoctetes gazes across the sea at the community from which he has been severed, and Heracles gazes at the site of his apotheosis.[31] Ajax as he prepares to die addresses the audience while the chorus are absent (815ff.), and the conventions which Sophocles adopts for a soliloquy in *Ajax* are worth observing. Ajax describes for the audience in precise terms the tableau on the *eccyclêma*, and then prays to a series of gods located in the sky above or earth beneath: Zeus, Chthonic Hermes, the watching Erinyes, Helios on his sun-chariot, and Thanatos below. In the climax of his speech he passes from the sunlight to his home in Salamis and to famous Athens.[32] Earlier in the play the chorus established the importance of Salamis (596ff.), contrasting their island across the sea (in front) with Ajax inside the *skênê*

---

[31] Note in particular 719–29 where the chorus sing of Oeta while Philoctetes stands transfixed. On Oeta in the play see Charles Segal, *Tragedy and Civilization* (Cambridge, Mass., 1981) 347–8.   [32] On this speech, see pp. 164–5 above.

(behind), and they must have signalled a link between the Athenian audience and the Athenian island of Salamis. The audience are positioned when Ajax dies not as members of a feckless Greek army at Troy but as democratic Athenians for whom Ajax was a cultic hero. There can be no possible pretence in a Sophoclean soliloquy that the audience lies behind an invisible fourth wall.

Sophocles' manipulation of space is most obviously characterized by geometrical precision in respect of the four cardinal points. Euripides' hallmark is the definition of a centripetal movement from the margins or exterior of the *polis* to the centre. In the festival, the parading of the statue from the Academy to the theatre replicated the journey of the god from Eleutherae on the margins of Attica. This movement from the margins to the centre provides a ritual paradigm for many of Euripides' plays. The progressive structure of the *Oresteia*, moving from monarchical Argos to the centre of democratic Athens was clearly a powerful influence. In many Euripidean plays the protagonist departs for Athens at the end: Oedipus, Ion, Heracles, Medea and Iphigeneia. An Attic sanctuary may be established, like the tombs of Iphigeneia at Brauron, of Capaneus at Eleusis and of Eurystheus at Pallene. We shall look closely at one example of this centripetal strategy: the *Hippolytus*.

Troezen was the scene of Hippolytus' death, and the location of a major cult, but Euripides was probably being innovative when he set his extant version of the play in that town. W. S. Barrett comments that the setting in Troezen 'has no dramatic advantage, and is indeed a source of some inconvenience, and is unlikely to have had any motive other than that of variation'. He finds the excuse for Theseus' residence in Troezen biographically inappropriate, the constitutional position confused and Hippolytus' journey to the Eleusinian Mysteries irrelevant. However, 'all this is peripheral to the main action, and in the theatre will pass unnoticed; but in the study we notice'.[33] The theatre, I would suggest, was not so deficient a medium. The Greek theatre audience was trained to listen as the modern audience is not.[34] The difficulties which Barrett experienced when editing the text in his study stem from his perception of the play as a timeless work of art.

To Athenians in 428 BC, Theseus' temporary sojourn in Troezen across the Saronic Gulf must have appeared to be a metaphor for the temporary nature of Athens' possession of Troezen, which it annexed soon after it took Aegina in 458 and reluctantly returned to Sparta's sphere of influence in 446. Troezen was raided in 430 as Athens compensated for its loss of control over its own hinterland, and Athens' territorial claims were not forgotten when Cleon tried to

---

[33] *Euripides: Hippolytos* (Oxford, 1964) 15, 33–4.   [34] Knox, *Word and Action* 71–2.

negotiate the return of Troezen in 425.[35] In the prologue Aphrodite refers to her temple on the Athenian Acropolis and to its future link with Hippolytus (30–3). Her temple, she says, looks across at Troezen. A hundred metres to the east of the temple spectators at the top of the *theatron* would have been in a position to look at this same view across the gulf. We do not know when the cult of Hippolytus was established in Athens, but it is a fair inference that when Athens annexed Troezen it classified a convenient Mycenaean tomb as the tomb of Hippolytus, making a symbolic link between the Acropolis and the *polis* which it now ruled.[36] In Pausanias' day the people of Troezen also claimed to have the authentic tomb, but kept its location secret.[37] Euripides' play was thus bound up with the politics of cult, and with Athenian imperial ambitions.

In the first part of the play there is a strong sense of topography, with the meadows, mountains and salt-marsh of Troezen. Phaedra addresses the chorus as Peloponnesians (374) and sees Athens as an elsewhere from which her sons may be excluded (422–3). There is some acknowledgement of the god of the theatre when the chorus conclude an ode devoted to Aphrodite by picturing her as responsible for the birth of Dionysus (555ff.). With the arrival of Theseus, the setting seems to melt from Troezen into the real space of the performance, Athens, very much as the setting melted from Marathon to Athens in *Children of Heracles*. Theseus addresses the *polis* when he proclaims the rape (884), and also, according to one of the two manuscript traditions, when Phaedra's body is revealed to the public on the *eccyclêma* (817).[38] A rhetorical contest follows between Theseus and Hippolytus, and the chorus of washerwomen of Troezen seems an unlikely audience for the two orations. The audience must inevitably sense that, as on the Pnyx, it is they the *dêmos* whom the speakers are trying to persuade. Banishing Hippolytus from Athens and the

---

[35] D. M. Lewis *et al.* (eds.) *Cambridge Ancient History*, Vol. v (Cambridge, 1992) 116, 137; Thucydides ii.56.5, iv.21.3.

[36] Pausanias i.22.1 states that the sanctuary is behind the Asclepion. This sanctuary of Aphrodite must not be confused with the sanctuary of Aphrodite Pandemos further to the west. The temple of 'Aphrodite over (*epi*) Hippolytus' may be the one which Pausanias attributed to Themis. For the documentary and archaeological evidence and the site of the nearby tomb, see Luigi Beschi, 'Contributi di topografia ateniese' *Annuario della Scuola Archeologica di Atene* 29/30 (1967/8) 512–17. Diodorus iv.62 gives the official aetiology, stating that the Athenians carried Hippolytus' bones to Athens after Theseus' death. On the politics of tombs see A. J. Festugière, 'Tragédie et tombes sacrées' *Revue de l'histoire des religions* 184 (1973) 3–24.

[37] Pausanias i.22.2; ii.32.1.

[38] The reading '*polis*', accepted by Murray in the Oxford Classical Text, is dismissed by Barrett, p. 320, as the work of an actor because this should be a moment of 'purely personal grief', another instance of Barrett's depoliticizing of the play. Barrett realized belatedly (*Addenda* pp. 435–6) that the unambiguous address to the *polis* at 884 required him to bring on a crowd of extras to constitute a crowd.

lands which it has conquered, Theseus concludes by referring to his triumphs at two sites on the coastal road that leads round the gulf from Athens to Troezen (973–80). In the context of 428 BC these words must have been understood in relation to Athens' attempts to control the gulf, and Theseus' error in the play must relate to the errors of Athens.

Theseus speaks as a regular politician. He starts with general propositions about human nature that his listeners must accept, and then addresses the audience in the second person: 'look at this man!' (943). When he makes Hippolytus look at him and addresses him as 'you', he speaks always for the benefit of his listeners: 'such men are to be avoided, I declare to everyone' (955–6). Bandying words with Hippolytus, he concludes, is irrelevant in view of the evidence, and as evidence he offers the audience the corpse. Hippolytus responds in the language of an oligarch, reluctant to speak before the *ochlos* (mob – 986)[39] because he can speak more intelligently with the *oligoi* (987). He is happy to excel in panhellenic games, but wants to take second place in the *polis* and consort with his friends the *aristoi* (1016–18). In accordance with this stance Hippolytus seems to ignore the audience. He swears his oath to Theseus, not to an assembly that might judge him. The audience's opinion of the two speakers must have been affected by the very different ways in which it was addressed. The emotional response of the *theatron* to the two men was necessarily a political evaluation, for the *theatron* put the *polis* on display.

Hippolytus acknowledges the city when he makes his farewells, but his farewell to the '*polis* and land of Erechtheus' (1094–5) is couched distantly in the third person,[40] whereas his farewells to Artemis, the land (*pedon*) of Troezen and his young companions are in second-person address. The messenger who brings news of the accident maintains no such distance from the *theatron*, addressing himself to Theseus 'and the citizens who live in Athens and the boundary of Troezen' (1158–9). Theseus responds with anxiety on behalf of the two 'neighbouring cities', and the status of Troezen as a marginal but integral part of Attica is emphasized. Theseus at the end pronounces Hippolytus' death a loss to 'the boundaries of Athens and Pallas' (1459) and the chorus sing of a loss to 'every citizen' (1462). Given the emphasis of the text upon Athens' possession of Troezen and the knowledge of the audience that Athens did not possess Troezen, we must ponder how the audience reacted when Artemis, as a reward for Hippolytus' sufferings, grants him 'the honour of a cult in the *polis*

---

[39] For the oligarchic connotations, compare Pseudo-Xenophon, *Constitution of Athens* 2.10, Theophrastus, *Characters* 26.3, Menander, *The Sicyonian* 150. On Hippolytus as an aristocrat, see, for example, Knox, *Word and Action* 220.

[40] Perhaps recalling his third-person dismissal of Aphrodite: compare 'alla chairetô polis' (1094) with 'tên sên de Kuprin poll' egô chairein legô' (113).

of Troezen' (1424). Troezen becomes indisseverable from its cult hero. Hippolytus, as the illegitimate son of a non-Athenian mother, has no more claim to be Athenian than the city of Troezen does, and he is scarcely presented in the play as a figure whom democratic Athenians would choose to honour as a cult hero. The cult established by Artemis in Troezen is a cult of female mourning, and the Athenians no doubt caused women of Troezen to mourn when they raided from the sea. In its Athenian manifestation, Diodorus presents the Hippolytus cult as a cult of Athenian penance for Theseus' crime.[41] Recognition of what Troezen meant to Athens in 428 BC does not provide us with any simple message or key to the play, but it does move us closer to the complex 'point of view of a citizen'.

To isolate the audience from the spatial field of the performance, as Barrett, Taplin, Bain and others strive to do, is to deprive the play of a subtle but powerful instrument for the production of meaning. The meaning of a performance cannot be dissociated from the space in which it is sited. If we forget that the Acropolis looked out over the Saronic Gulf, then we neglect part of what gave Euripides' play meaning in the fifth century. The meaning of a play is not immanent in its written text but depends upon a specific spatial and temporal context. When Peter Stein presented the *Eumenides* performed by Russian actors in 1994, the audience knew that the actors had recently received the power to vote, and that that freedom was in jeopardy from forces that belonged to the past. The meaning of the two choruses turned upon a precise geographical and historical context. The fifth-century context, I have argued, is in certain respects recoverable. To understand the play as a physical construct in space helps us towards an understanding of what the play once meant to its intended recipients.

It is a common-place to assert that the massacre at Melos defines the context for *Trojan Women*.[42] Lattimore in the preface to his translation declares: 'I can hardly understand how the Athenians let him present this play.'[43] It becomes easier to understand when we conceive the play not as a mirror image of social reality held up to shock the audience but as a negotiation of the actor/audience relationship. Poseidon addresses his prologue to the audience: 'Now farewell, once fortunate city, polished bastion. Had Pallas daughter of Zeus not destroyed you, you would still stand on your foundations' (45–7). He at once compliments the audience, associated with the invincible power of Pallas Athene, and yet at the same time draws them and their Acropolis into the play

[41] Diodorus iv.62.
[42] There is a good discussion in N. T. Croally, *Euripidean Polemic* (Cambridge, 1994) 232–4.
[43] D. Grene and R. Lattimore (eds.) *Complete Greek Tragedies: Euripides III* (Chicago, 1958) 123n.

as the fallen city of Troy.[44] The situation is promptly inverted when Athene declares that she will punish those whom she has protected, making the position of the audience even more equivocal. The chorus both compliment Athens and include her among their oppressors when they hope to be enslaved by her rather than Sparta (207–13, 18–19). Later when the chorus address the king of Salamis on his island facing Athene's shore (799–803), the *theatron* becomes Athens insofar as Salamis is an Attic deme and symbolizes Athenian victory against barbarians, yet since the *theatron*, located as Salamis, faces the *orchêstra*, the *orchêstra* also becomes Athens. In the finale I have suggested that the *theatron* is taken to be the burning city of Troy.[45] The audience is for ever in a double relationship to the action, identified as both conqueror and victim. The encircling *theatron* places the audience not as remote and objective judges of a criminal war but as participants in an enactment that they have helped to create. The play can be seen as an exercise in disorientation.

Sophocles' last play seems an appropriate example with which to conclude. Although it was performed posthumously after the Peloponnesian War was over, we must consider it in the context for which it was intended. As I argued in chapter 6, *Oedipus at Colonus* did not in any sense offer the audience a pictorial image of Colonus, but synthesized elements from that topographical area and arranged them schematically. Colonus is constructed as a liminal space where life meets death (along the axis which leads into the dark *skênê*), and Athens meets her enemies (along the lateral axis which incorporated the barbaric Odeon). From one point of view the *theatron* is Athens, in other words the audience is itself, for Antigone gazes at the walls of Athens (14), and Oedipus after receiving a localized description of Colonus addresses himself to the city at large (108). Yet from another point of view Athens is an elsewhere located beyond the right *eisodos*. The icon of the horseman symbolizes the totality of Athens because it is located on the right-hand, Athenian side, but is also just one term in a nature/culture, tree/horse, goddess/Poseidon dialectic that defines the totality of Athens. Sophocles' Colonus is not a nostalgic utopia defining Athens' past, as Knox would have it,[46] but a complex heterotopia defining Athens in the present.

Many of the audience, a few days before the performance, would have accompanied the statue of Dionysus to the theatre from the area where the play is set and where Oedipus' mythic journey terminates. Both festival and play are concerned with the relationship between the centre, i.e. the place of the

---

[44] Croally, *Euripidean Polemic* 242–3 notes that the scholiast on lines 36–8 had no doubts about direct address in the prologue. See also Croally 188 on the representation of Athens as 'other' in tragedy.   [45] See above pp. 119–20.
[46] B. M. W. Knox, *The Heroic Temper* (Berkeley, 1964) 154–6.

theatrical performance, and a liminal space beyond the walls that defines by its otherness the nature of the centre. The festival celebrates a Theban god who belongs to Athens and not Thebes, whilst the play claims Attica and not Thebes as the burial place of Oedipus. Cult cannot be separated from political discourse, and the play must not be separated from its festive context. Colonus is both a theatrical construct and a real location known intimately to the audience and laden with associations. It was the deme of Sophocles,[47] so the setting must have been construed by the audience as some kind of testament containing Sophocles' own ideals. It was the area to which the Theban cavalry were driven back by Athenian cavalry in 408 BC in a desperate counter-offensive celebrated by a victory trophy. Also, it was in the sanctuary of Poseidon the Horseman in 411 that 400 men determined on overthrowing democracy. In *The Frogs*, written very soon after, Aristophanes is unambiguous in his plea that all those 400 oligarchs must be forgiven in time of crisis.[48] Sophocles' play, in privileging the figure of the horseman through its iconography, its narrative and its lyrics, is scarcely less unequivocal in his concern that the *dêmos* must not reject the elite. Athene has her place in Sophocles' Colonus, so does the god of the theatre (668–80), but Sophocles makes it clear that Poseidon too is part of what constitutes the identity of Athens, his audience. The play redefines the relationship between the sanctuary of Poseidon and the overtly democratic sanctuary of Dionysus. The performance conceived by Sophocles was both a political intervention and a religious ritual, for in the fifth-century Theatre of Dionysus there was no distinction. Although perhaps, when the play was first performed in 401 as the work of a dead master, it was already on the way to becoming part of Athens' theatrical heritage, to be fixed for ever on papyrus and in stone.

[47] There is inscriptional evidence: Mary Lefkowitz, *The Lives of the Greek Poets* (London, 1981) 76.

[48] D. M. MacDowell, *Aristophanes and Athens* (Oxford, 1995) 286. There is no epigraphic evidence for the date when Sophocles wrote, but the posthumous date of production supports anecdotal evidence that the play was written not long before his death in 405.

Select bibliography

Major contributions to the discussion in this book

Greek conceptions of space

Ballabriga, A. *Le Soleil et le Tartare* (Paris, 1986).

Gombrich, Ernst *Art and Illusion* (London, 1977).

Lefebvre, Henri *The Production of Space*, tr. D. Nicholson-Smith (Oxford, 1991).

Lloyd, G. E. R. 'Right and left in Greek philosophy' *Journal of Hellenic Studies* 82 (1962) 56–66.

Murray, O. and S. Price (eds.) *The Greek City from Homer to Alexander* (Oxford, 1990).

Padel, Ruth *In and Out of the Mind* (Princeton, 1992).

Polignac, F. de *La Naissance de la cité grecque* (Paris, 1984).

Segal, Charles *Tragedy and Civilization* (Cambridge, Mass., 1981).

Vernant, J.-P. *Myth and Thought among the Greeks* (London, 1983) (= *Mythe et pensée chez les grecs* (Paris, 1990)).

The Theatre of Dionysus

Dinsmoor, William 'The Athenian theater of the fifth century' in *Studies Presented to David Moore Robinson* ed. G. E. Mylonas (Saint Louis, 1951) 309–30.

Dörpfeld, W. and E. Reisch *Das griechische Theater* (Athens, 1896).

Gebhard, Elizabeth 'The form of the orchestra in the early Greek theatre' *Hesperia* 43 (1974) 428–40.

Hammond, N. G. L. 'The conditions of dramatic production to the death of Aeschylus' *Greek, Roman and Byzantine Studies* 13 (1972) 387–450.

Kolb, Frank *Agora und Theater* (Berlin, 1981).

Korres, M. 'Ergasies sta mnêmeia: Dionysiako theatro' *Archaiologikon Deltion* 35 (1980 [1988]) 'Chronika' 9–18.

Pickard-Cambridge, A. W. *The Theatre of Dionysus in Athens* (Oxford, 1946).

Scullion, John Scott 'The Athenian stage and scene-setting in early tragedy' (Ph.D. thesis, Harvard, 1990).

Shankland, R. S. 'Acoustics of Greek theatres' *Physics Today* (Oct. 1973) 30–5.

Travlos, John *Pictorial Dictionary of Ancient Athens* (New York, 1971).

Wurster, W. W. 'Die Architektur des griechischen Theaters' *Antike Welt* 24 (1993) 20–42.

Other theatres: reference and bibliography

Rossetto, P. C. and G. P. Sartorio (eds.) *Teatri greci e romani* (Turin, 1994) – Greek contributions by H. P. Isler.

The festival of Dionysus

Pickard-Cambridge, A. W. *The Dramatic Festivals of Athens* revised by John Gould and
D. M. Lewis (Oxford, 1968). Appendix added in the 1988 edition.
Seaford, Richard *Reciprocity and Ritual* (Oxford, 1994).
Winkler, John J. and Froma I. Zeitlin (eds.) *Nothing To Do With Dionysos? Athenian
drama in its social context* (Princeton, 1992).

Stagecraft

Dale, A. M. *Collected Papers* (Cambridge, 1969).
Dioniso 59 (1989) – special issue on theatrical space.
Hourmouziades, Nicolaos C. *Production and Imagination in Euripides: form and function of the scenic space* (Athens, 1965).
Ley, Graham and Michael Ewans 'The orchestra as acting area in Greek tragedy' *Ramus*
14 (1985) 75–84.
Rehm, Rush 'The staging of Suppliant plays' *Greek, Roman and Byzantine Studies* 29
(1988) 263–308.
Taplin, Oliver *The Stagecraft of Aeschylus: the dramatic use of entrances and exits in Greek
tragedy* (Oxford, 1977).
    'Sophocles in his theatre' in *Sophocle* ed. J. de Romilly (Entretiens Hardt 29, Geneva,
1983) 155–83.

Choreography

Arion 3 (1995) – special issue on the chorus.
Aylen, Leo *The Greek Theater* (Cranbury, N.J., 1985).
Calame, Claude *Les Choeurs de jeunes filles en Grèce archaïque* (Rome, 1977).
Georgiades, Thrasybulos *Greek Music, Verse and Dance*, tr. E. Benedikt and M. L.
Martinez (New York, 1973).
Kernodle, George R. 'Symbolic action in the Greek choral odes?' *Classical Journal* 53
(1957/8) 1–6.
Kitto, H. D. F. 'The dance in Greek tragedy' *Journal of Hellenic Studies* 75 (1955) 36–41.
Lonsdale, Stephen H. *Dance and Ritual Play in Greek Religion* (Baltimore, 1993).

Iconography

Green, J. R. 'On seeing and depicting the theatre in classical Athens' *Greek, Roman and
Byzantine Studies* 32 (1991) 15–50.
Moret, J. M. *L'Ilioupersis dans la céramique italiote* (Geneva, 1975).
Sourvinou-Inwood, Christiane *Reading Greek Culture: texts and images, rituals and
myths* (Oxford, 1991).
Taplin, Oliver *Comic Angels* (Oxford, 1993).

Index